# VISITOR'S GU
## Country Tr

G000088309

---

## How To Use This Guide

This MPC Visitor's Guide has been designed to be as easy to use as possible. Each chapter covers a region or itinerary in a natural progression which gives all the background information to help you enjoy your visit. MPC's distinctive margin symbols, the important places printed in bold, and a comprehensive index enable the reader to find the most interesting places to visit with ease.

At the end of each chapter an Additional Information section gives specific details such as addresses and opening times, making this guide a complete sightseeing companion.

At the back of the guide the Fact File, arranged in alphabetical order, gives practical information and useful tips to help you plan your holiday — before you go and while you are there.

The maps of each region show the main towns, villages, roads and places of interest, but are not designed as route maps and motorists should always use a good recommended road atlas.

Jökulsá Canyon National Park

# VISITOR'S GUIDE

# ICELAND

## & GREENLAND

## Don Philpott

## MPC
### HUNTER

Published by:
Moorland Publishing Co Ltd
Moor Farm Road West, Ashbourne, Derbyshire DE6 1HD England
Published in the USA by:
Hunter Publishing Inc,
300 Raritan Center Parkway,CN 94, Edison, NJ 08818

ISBN 0 86190 297 1

British Library Cataloguing in Publication Data:
A catalogue record for this book is available from the British Library

Colour origination by: P&W Graphics Pte. Ltd, Singapore

Printed in Hong Kong by: The Wing King Tong Co Ltd

Front cover photograph: *Dettifoss* (MPC Picture Collection).
Back cover: *Eskifjördur* (MPC Picture Collection).
Page 3: (MPC Picture Collection).

Illustrations have been supplied as follows: C. Lewer: pp 10, 94, 182 (top), 183 (top),
183 (lower); BSI Travel: pp 70, 79, 106, 151; H. Race: pp 95; C. Stacey: pp 182 (lower);
Danish Tourist Office: pp 198, 199, 202, 203, 206, 207, 210, 211, 214;
All other illustrations have been supplied by the MPC Picture Library.

**MPC Production Team:** *Editor:* Tonya Monk, *Designer:* Dan Clarke, *Cartographer:*
Alastair Morrison *Typesetting:* Christine Haines

### Acknowledgements
The author and publisher wish to acknowledge the assistance given
by YHA Adventure Shops and Icelandair in the preparation of this book.
Also Nicky Barber and Ursula McDonald for additional information

### About the Author
Don Philpott is the author of *Visitor's Guide to Norway* (World Traveller Series)
which was voted Guide Book of the Year by the UK Outdoor Writers Guild.

# CONTENTS

## Key to Symbols Used in Text Margin and on Maps

| | | | |
|---|---|---|---|
| ♠ | Church/Ecclesiastical site | 🚶 | Recommended walk |
| 🎿 | Winter Sports | ⊞ | Building of interest |
| Π | Archaeological site | ♣ | Parkland |
| 🌲 | Beautiful view/Scenery, Natural phenomenon | 🦌 | Nature reserve/Animal interest |
| 🏛 | Museum/Art gallery | 🦆 | Birdlife |
| ☀ | Other place of interest | ✳ | Garden |

## KEY TO MAPS

| | | | |
|---|---|---|---|
| ⬠ | City | 〜 | River/Lake |
| ◯ | Town | ⋯⋯ | National Park Boundary |
| ● | Village/Hamlet | ▬▬ | Ring Road |
| ■ | House/Hut | ▬▬ | Main Road |
| ✈ | Airport | ▬▬ | Track |
| △ | Mountain/Peak | ------ | Mountain Track |
| | Glacier | | |

## STREET PLANS

| | | | |
|---|---|---|---|
| | Road | | Garden/Park |
| | River/Lake | | Built up Region |

# FORWARD

Icelanders everywhere are fiercely proud of their homeland, and when they live abroad do their utmost to act as ambassadors for their country. So I am particularly pleased to have been asked to write the foreword to this new edition of the highly popular *Visitor's Guide to Iceland*.

Iceland is not cold and forbidding as the name might suggest, but a warm and friendly country, where the heat of the summer sun is only matched by the warmth of the people.

Iceland has so much to offer the traveller that it is surprising that not more people have discovered for themselves the charms of this lovely island — a land of constant contrast and change.

Don Philpott, although not an Icelander, has managed to capture the essence of this beautiful land of surprises, and his knowledge of the country portrayed in the book will be invaluable to any traveller.

If you fly in during the summer you can see the contrasts that make Iceland so exciting, the glaciers and the lava fields, the bustling fishing ports and fjords, the crystal clear rivers and lush green valleys.

Whatever the weather, there is no doubt that the climate is healthy and the country made for those people who want to get out and enjoy themselves.

While Reykjavík boasts many fine hotels, restaurants and shops, the real spirit of Iceland is best captured by getting out and discovering the constantly changing countryside. This guide helps you do exactly that.

Whether you want to walk or climb, birdwatch or swim, play golf or fish, pony trek or just laze, *The Visitior's Guide to Iceland* tells you where best to go and how to get there.

Iceland is a small country with a big heart and an enormous future. Once you have visited this fascinating land I am sure you will not be able to stay away.

Magnus Magnusson

# PREFACE

Iceland is a land of constant contrast and change. There are glaciers and ice-caps, volcanoes and hot springs, rushing streams and lush valleys. It is a large country with a small population and vast empty spaces that take your breath away with their beauty. It is home to spectacular waterfalls and the bubbling, spitting Geysir which gave its name to all the others.

As you fly into the international airport you can see why the Vikings called the country the Land of Ice. The largest glacier in Europe, Vatnajökull, dominates the island as you fly in. It is 8,400sq km (3,240sq miles) in extent and in some places the ice is more than 1,000m (3,280ft) thick. You fly in over the Vestmannaeyjar (Westman Islands) to the south, and steaming fissures which erupt periodically with uncontrolled ferocity can still be seen. In the north there are thermal springs and beautiful green valleys teeming with birds. During the summer there is permanent daylight and there is no pollution to filter the rays of the sun.

Iceland has still to be discovered as a tourist island although each year the number of visitors grows. Many tourists come here to walk over snow capped mountains, pony trek across lava deserts, play golf or simply relax beside a hotel pool somewhere different. There is something to do for everyone: sailing, fishing, climbing, birdwatching or just relaxing. The people of the Land of Ice are some of the most friendly on earth and a warm welcome is assured.

# 1

# AN INTRODUCTION TO ICELAND

## History

Iceland gets its name from the first Vikings who arrived there in the ninth century, although Irish monks had been living there as hermits for some years previously. Possibly the first mention of Iceland was made by a Greek seafarer in 330BC. He talked of a land called *Ultima Thule*, six days sailing north of Britain. Certainly by the late ninth century there were several hundred monks living on the southern coast in the area of Kirkjubaer, and they fell easy prey to the bands of pirates that frequently raided. The first Viking settler is reputed to have been Ingólfur Arnarson who came from Norway in AD874. He established his home by the lake which is now surrounded by the capital, Reykjavík.

Over the next 60 years, until AD930, the Viking colonisation continued, mostly along the coast. As the Norsemen extended their control, the Irish monks were forced to leave. Iceland was, therefore, the last European country to be settled. The period between AD870 and AD930 was a time of a great colonisation. By AD930 the island's population was certainly 20,000 and could have been double this. The Viking fleet sailed from Norway and entered and attacked many countries, including Britain and Ireland. Other vessels braved the Atlantic and stormed the Labrador coast while others penetrated the Mediterranean. The Viking longboats, up to 30m (98ft) in length, were used for raids, while smaller vessels were used for trading.

It was also a time of great conflict in Norway and there were many wars between rival war chiefs. Those defeated were forced to leave, and many sailed for Iceland to found a new kingdom. Their route took them first to Britain and Ireland, and many of the ships landed in Iceland carrying Irish slaves who had been rounded up to labour on the new farmsteads. Many of the Irish later earned their freedom and moved to the islands off the south-west coast where they farmed and fished — the islands being named after these men from the west — the Westman Islands (Vestmannaeyjar).

At the beginning of the tenth century the country was ruled by a number of chieftains and in AD920 Ulfljót, one of the wisest and most learned, was chosen to travel to Norway to study its laws and system of administration so that a similar code could be introduced for Iceland. In AD930 the various chieftains gathered and formed the Althing, the country's first parliament, in the magnificent natural setting of Thingvellir, in a valley about 50km (31 miles) north-east of the capital. The Althing, or General Assembly, was a form of Icelandic Commonwealth made up of thirty-eight independent chieftains. A constitutional law code and a judicial system was introduced, with a Supreme Court held annually at Thingvellir. This form of republican government lasted until 1262 when Iceland became subject to Norway, and later to Denmark. Because Iceland was colonised so late, and perhaps because of the influence of the learned Irish monks, and later the Viking scholars, almost all the history of the island has been recorded. This documentation is found in the *Book of Settlements* and in the *Book of the Icelanders*, which were written in the twelfth and thirteenth centuries.

Christianity was introduced to the island in AD1000 from Norway, and over the next two centuries the pagan gods were gradually replaced by the Roman Catholic religion. The first bishopric was established in 1056 in the south of Iceland at Skálholt, and a second at Hólar in the north 50 years

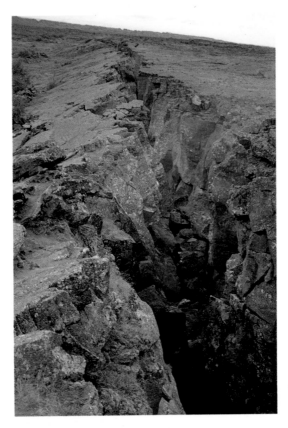

*Fissures resulting from volcanic activity are a common sight in Iceland*

later. At both sites monasteries and schools were established, and they became the country's main centres of learning. The establishment of the monasteries saw the start of the period during which many of the Sagas were written.

In the late tenth century, Icelanders discovered and colonised Greenland, led by Erík the Red. He had fled to Iceland after being banished from Norway, and his constant feuding earned him a further 3 years' banishment from the island. It was while he was in exile that he discovered Greenland. When he was allowed to return to Iceland he recruited settlers and together they sailed for Greenland where two colonies were established and survived until the fifteenth century, when the weather deteriorated and it became much colder.

At the turn of the millennium Icelanders sailed the North Atlantic to discover North America under the leadership of Leif Eiriksson, one of the three famous nautical sons of Erík the Red. Despite this incredible achievement in AD999, some 500 years before Christopher Columbus 'discovered' the New World, their attempts to settle there failed.

Towards the middle of the thirteenth century the fortunes of Iceland began to sink fast. The weather had turned much colder, crops failed and the fishing grounds were being 'robbed' by foreigners. The Commonwealth-style government collapsed and civil war broke out. In 1262 Iceland came under Norwegian rule and a new monarchial code was introduced in 1271, the Agreement of Union which had been concluded between the Althing and the king. It was to start 500 years of oppression

*Geothermal activity at Námaskard. The hill on the left is Námafjall.*

under foreign rule. Just over a century later, in 1380, all the Scandinavian countries swore allegiance to Denmark and the King of the Danes reigned supreme.

In 1349 the Black Death struck the country wiping out at least a third of the population. The Plague struck again in 1402 and for 2 years ravaged the country killing again, at least a third of the inhabitants, and wiping out entire communities. It was in the first part of the fifteenth century that English traders started to visit Iceland regularly. They wanted to buy dried fish which until then had not been exported to any large scale — the main income being derived from the export of cloth spun from the wool of the island's hardy sheep. The English traders bought huge quantities of cod and this sparked off a change in the island's economy, and a dependence on fishing that still exists today.

Traders from many parts of the world visited Iceland, but less welcome was a band of pirates from Algeria who, in 1627, overran the island of Heimaey, slaughtering most of the islanders and carrying off the rest as slaves.

Under Danish rule the people of Iceland were forced to convert to Lutheranism, and both bishoprics were occupied by foreigners in the fourteenth and early fifteenth centuries. Between 1540 and 1550 all Church property was confiscated and handed over to the king. The Danes also imposed their own trading regime on the island which drained money out of the country and into the coffers of Denmark; in 1602 the Royal Trade monopoly was established.

Absolute monarchy was imposed in 1662 and all governing power was transferred to Copenhagen. For the next century the fortunes of the island continued to decline because of the repressive trading methods and the progressive cooling of the climate. The eighteenth century brought smallpox, sheep diseases, two disastrous famines and the eruption of Lakagígar in 1783, volcanic activity from which lasted for 2 years. At least 9,000 people starved to death during the famines and thousands of farm animals were killed. By the end of the seventeenth century, the weather suddenly turned much harsher with winters so cold in 1695 and 1696 that even the sea froze. A census taken in 1703, the first ever undertaken, showed a population of about 50,000 of whom a fifth were beggars or dependants. By 1709 the population had been ravaged by smallpox and had fallen to 35,000. There was a brief recovery which was short-lived; there were famines in 1752-7 and 1783-5 and natural disasters, which caused poverty so acute that by 1787 the harsh trading rules were lifted and all subjects of the Danish king were given the right to trade in Iceland. The position was not helped by the blockade imposed by the English navy during the Napoleonic Wars.

In 1800 the Althing was dissolved but the independence movement in Europe was growing and in 1809 a Dane, Jörgen Jörgensen, backed by a London merchant, seized power in Iceland. His reign was short-lived, however, and he was quickly ousted following the arrival of a British warship. The struggle for freedom continued, and was led in Iceland by Jón Sigurdsson who lived from 1811 to 1879 and is now the country's national hero. In 1843 the Althing was allowed to meet again as an assembly and in 1854 all trade restrictions were lifted.

In 1874 the country celebrated the thousandth anniversary of the founding of the first settlement with a new constitution from the King of Denmark, King Christian IX, and the power to control its own finances. Effectively it brought about an end of the absolute rule and paved the way for home rule which was granted on 9 April 1904. The island's first co-operative had been launched in 1882 and the National Bank was founded in 1885.

At the end of World War I Iceland's sovereignty was accepted by Denmark, although it remained united with Denmark through the king. The millenary of the Althing was celebrated in 1930. The final ties with Denmark were severed during World War II. In May 1940 British troops occupied Iceland to protect North Atlantic sea lanes and prevent an invasion by Germany from Scandinavia. On 8 July 1941 the United States took over the defence of Iceland following agreement between the two governments. Later Iceland joined the United Nations as an independent state. On 25 February 1944 the Althing announced it was ending the Act of Union and this was supported by 97 per cent of the voters in the hastily convened plebiscite. On 17 June of that year, more than 20,000 gathered at Thingvellir to hear Jón Sigurdsson, the President of the Althing, declare Iceland a Republic.

The early 1970s were dogged by the 'Cod Wars' with Britain which resulted in Iceland declaring a 200-mile limit round her coast and excluding UK trawlers. The 200-mile zones have now been adopted by almost every maritime nation. Diplomatic relations with Britain were severed for a short time but the 'Cod Wars' ended in 1976. In 1974 the 1,100th anniversary of the first settlement was celebrated by the opening of the road over the widest glacial rivers south of the Vatnajökull glacier, thus completing the circular road around the island.

## Geography and Climate

Iceland is situated in the North Atlantic Ocean almost equidistant from New York and Moscow. It lies between 63° 24' and 66° 33'N, and between longitude 13° 30' and 24° 32'W, and is the second-largest island in Europe after Britain. It is close to the Arctic Circle yet only one of its northerly islands actually lies inside it. The country has a total area of 103,000sq km (39,756sq miles) and a coastline of about 6,600km (3,700 miles). The island is 300km (190 miles) wide north to south, and 500km (300 miles) across from west to east, and there are scores of islands off the coast, although many of them are uninhabited. Four-fifths of the island is above 200m (658ft).

Geographically, Iceland is considered as part of Europe yet there is nowhere else on the continent with a similar climate. The north-east coast is affected by the bitterly cold waters coming down from the Arctic Ocean while the rest of the island is warmed by the Gulf Stream. Greenland is 285km (180 miles) away and closest to Iceland; Norway is 1,000km (625 miles) distant, and Scotland 798km (almost 500 miles). Iceland lies over a submarine ridge which joins Scotland and Greenland, and which prevents the cold water from the lower depths of the Norwegian Sea, which lies to the north and east of Iceland, penetrating southwards. The temperatures at the seabed are much higher to the south and west than to the north and east of Iceland, as one branch of the Gulf Stream reaches up to the south coast and flows west and north around the island.

The Polar current reaches Iceland's north-east coast, resulting in considerably colder temperatures. The mean sea temperature in the coldest month is about 5-6°C (41-3°F) off the south and west coasts, but only 1-2°C (34-6°F) off the north and east coasts. The respective summer temperatures for these areas are 10-11°C (50-2°F) and 7-9°C (45-8°F) again being the lowest off the north-east coast.

With the exception of some narrow fjords containing large amounts of fresh water, ice is very rare in Iceland's navigational waters. However, the Polar current carries large quantities of ice and icebergs southwards along the east coast of Greenland. Wind and current can sometimes force this ice over into the Gulf Stream, which then carries it eastwards along the north coast of Iceland, where it can block the north and east coasts and produce Arctic conditions. During the present century, however, it has seldom been seen near Iceland.

Because Iceland is situated on the boundary between the temperate and the Arctic zones, winters are mild, but stormy and humid. The Reykjavík mean January temperature is about the same as in Copenhagen. Periods of severe frost are rare owing to the warming influence of the sea in winter. Summers are, however, quite cool although the temperature for the warmest months averages between 9°C (48°F) and 12°C (53°F). Warm days with temperatures of 20°C (68°F) or over are rare near the coast, though they occur more frequently in the sheltered valleys away from the wind where, however, night frosts occur more often. The highest temperature recorded in Iceland is just over 30°C (86°F) while the lowest recorded in Reykjavík in the last thirty years is below -15°C (5°F). Rainfall is high during all the seasons, with snow over the high grounds and in the north in winter. The southern slopes of the glaciers get most rainfall, while the least falls on the plateau north of Vatnajökull. The snow lies at a height of 1,000 to 1,500m (3,280-4,920ft) and above, being highest north of Vatnajökull. The valleys of the north receive only about half the rainfall of the southern areas.

Gales are frequent and change direction rapidly with the passing of the depressions coming from the west. However, the air is usually clear and pure and even distant mountains appear quite near.

The Icelandic climate is characterised by alternating calms and gales, thaws and snow, good and bad weather. As a general rule if it is fine in the south, the weather will be bad in the north, and vice versa. There is also an Icelandic saying which goes, 'If you don't like the weather just wait a minute'.

So it can be seen that Iceland is not, in fact, a particularly cold place. Of course, in the winter proper clothing is necessary to keep out the cold, but it is often possible to walk around the town even in late autumn with only a jacket for protection. If you travel north into the lush green valleys beneath Akureyri, the summer temperatures can be very warm.

Whatever the weather, there is no doubt that the climate is healthy. The winters are not as severe as in many parts of mainland Europe and it is not unusual for Reykjavík to have no snow throughout the winter.

In midsummer along the lowland plains the afternoon temperatures may get up to 15°C (59°F) which is just the right temperature for backpackers, walkers and campers. As the very clean air increases visibility, and the intensity of the sun's rays, it is very easy to get a beautiful tan after only a few days. In fact, the weather often feels much warmer than it actually is. The increased visibility can also be deceptive. It is possible on a good day to see the snow-capped tip of the glacier Snæfellsjökull from Reykjavík, even though it is almost 120km (75 miles) away.

A great advantage of being so far north is that during the summer, the sun is almost perpetually above the horizon so it never gets dark. The midnight sun is a sight worth seeing, especially in the north of the island.

The cool climate has another advantage in that it deters many of the insects and reptiles that can prove a nuisance in hotter climates. There are no snakes in Iceland, but for a couple of weeks in late July or August the midges can be a pest.

The special climate has helped to form the massive glaciers which occupy more than 11 per cent of the total area of Iceland. The essential requirement for glacier formation is that more snow should fall each year than can melt. Gradually the snow depth increases and it is compressed, and becomes ice. Vatnajökull is Iceland's (and Europe's) largest glacier covering 8,400sq km (3,240sq miles) and in places the ice is more than 1,000m (3,280ft) thick. By measuring the snow layer it has been found that on some of the glaciers in southern Iceland annual precipitation must amount to between 5,000 and 6,000mm (200 and 240in) or as much as 500mm (22in) a month. That compares with the monthly precipitation at Sandur on the north coast of only 30mm (1.2in).

## Geology

One of the most exciting things about Iceland is that in geological terms it is a new country, literally being shaped as we walk around it. One day in 1984 in Reykjavík there was an earthquake which registered 3.7 on the

Richter scale, while on the other side of the country Krafla erupted, as it had done every year for the previous 9 years. A 9km (5½ mile) fissure opened up and lava, smoke and dust was hurled hundreds of feet into the sky. Although the earth's crust is normally about 30km (18½miles) thick, in Iceland it is only 10km (16 miles) deep and scored with deep cracks and fissures.

The enormous forces which still push and pull the island are caused by the movement of tectonic plates which meet beneath the country. These plates split and separated to form the continental land masses, and where they touch, areas of immense activity will usually be found. Iceland is one of most active volcanic countries in the world and there are about two hundred volcanoes, at least thirty of which have erupted since the country was first settled. On average an eruption still takes place every 5 years. Nearly every form of volcanic activity takes place somewhere in Iceland which is why it is so attractive to geologists. In 1783 the world's largest fissure eruption took place when Lakagígar erupted along its 32km (20 miles) of craters spilling lava over 565sq km (218sq miles). The gases and ashes from this eruption devastated farming, polluted the meadows and led to one of the greatest famines in the country with the loss of thousands of lives. The fumes and gases from this eruption are said to have killed three-quarters of all the sheep and horses on the island, and half the country's cattle.

Iceland is built up of volcanic material. The eastern and western parts of the country consist of tertiary basalt, comprising roughly half the total area, whereas the central parts consist of volcanic material from the Ice Age mixed with water, glacial and air deposits, the so-called Palagonite formation. Approximately 10 per cent of the total area is covered with post-glacial lava. There is now no volcanic activity in the basalt areas. The highest volcanoes are cone-shaped (Öraefajökull [2,118m or 6,950ft], Eyjafjalljökull [1,665m, or 5,464ft]), always having an ice cap on the top, while others are shield-shaped (Skjaldbreid) and rift-shaped volcanoes are common.

Some rifts are quite open while others are more or less closed, and when eruptions take place rows of lava and volcanic ash craters are formed. Laki, for instance, is a 25km (15½ mile) long row of 100 craters and the eruption in 1783 lasted for more than 6 months.

Hekla is an elongated mountain ridge superimposed on a short range of craters. It produces both lava and ash. The last major eruption, in March 1947, threw a column of debris and smoke 36,000m (100,000ft) into the air and the lava covered 64sq km (25sq miles). It is Iceland's most famous volcano and has erupted fifteen times. Throughout the Middle Ages it was feared throughout the Roman Catholic world as the Abode of the Damned. The 1947 eruption lasted for 13 months and in May 1970 a number of small craters on the mountain erupted throwing out lava for 2 months. The last eruption occurred in 1990.

Katla is a fissure covered by the Myrdalsjökull. The glacier melts during

*Sulphur, hot springs and mud pools at Námaskard*

eruptions causing huge floods, explosions that rock the country and it rains ash that turns day into night. The production of lava is usually insignificant. Katla last erupted in 1918 but has erupted at least thirteen times since the first settlement of Iceland. It is said that when Katla erupts the flood water exceeds the volume of water carried by the Amazon river. Askja in the north-eastern highlands last erupted in 1961, but its eruption in 1875 was the last to cause great damage.

The most dramatic eruption of recent times occurred in 1973 and started in Heimaey, the only inhabited island of the Vestmannaeyjar (Westman Islands), on 23 January. The entire population of about 5,300 were evacuated to the mainland in a matter of hours without loss of life. The eruption lasted for almost 5 months and half the town was buried in the lava flow; the rest was covered in a thick layer of ashes. The island was the centre of the fishing industry, and the harbour and all its installations were saved by the quick action of scientists who poured cold sea water on to the lava which succeeded in halting the flow. Heimaey is one of the wonders of Iceland. The lava wall still hovers over the town and houses can be seen projecting underneath it. The greatest miracle was that the lava wall, more than 7m (20ft) high, came to a halt only feet from the hospital, and so it too was saved. Since the eruption most of the islanders have returned and it is once again a thriving fishing community. It is a staggering fact that almost 30 per cent of all the lava that has flowed on earth over the past century has been on Iceland.

Two types of lava are to be found in Iceland. *Apalhraun* corresponds to the Hawaiian *a-a-lava*, and has a rough, slaggy surface, while *helluhraun*, is similar to the *pahoe-hoe* lava, which is smooth and often has a rope-like surface.

Iceland consists mostly of mountains and high plateaux and its average height is 500m (1,525ft) above sea level. The highest point is Hvannadalshnjúkur in the Öraefajökull glacier in south-east Iceland at 2,119m (6,950ft). Post-glacial lava covers about 10,000sq km (3,861sq miles) and the largest lavafield is Ódádahraun, covering about 4,662sq km (1,800sq miles).

There are frequent submarine eruptions around Iceland and the most famous occurred on 14 November 1963 when three islands were thrust up from the ocean bed south of the Vestmannaeyjar. Two of the islands later collapsed, but the third remained and is called Surtsey. It has an area of almost 4sq km (1½ sq miles). The eruption continued for more than 2 years and the island is now closely guarded so that scientists can monitor the attraction and development of vegetation and animal life. It is possible to fly over the island but permission to land is rarely given.

Earthquakes, too, are common in Iceland although recently there have not been any as ferocious as those recorded in the eighteenth and nineteenth centuries. The most damaging occurred in the southern lowlands in 1784; in 1896 another destroyed many farms. The village of Dalvík in Eyjafjördur in the north was partly destroyed by an earthquake in 1934.

Earthquakes have also been recorded around Krafla after its eruptions which have taken place every year since 1975. Unfortunately the volcanic and earthquake activity started shortly after work began on the country's first geothermal power station designed to trap the natural heat deep under the surface. Although completed for some years, the power station is now only working at maximum capacity of 30 megawatts because of the subterranean activity.

The last serious earthquake occurred in 1976 in the north-east when a number of tremors caused damage in the fishing village of Kópasker.

Iceland is also known for its geysers and hot springs. There are two types of hot spring, the *hver* which is a water or steam spring up to 100°C (212°F), and a *laug* where the water is only warm or lukewarm. Hot springs are very common in the volcanic areas although the *laug* also occurs in basalt formations. The Deildartunguhver in Borgarfjördur yields 250 litres (55 gallons) of boiling water every second and is probably the world's largest hot spring.

The Great, or Old, Geysir is the best known geyser, but in recent years it has spouted only seldom and irregularly. It used to be 'persuaded' to perform, however, by the warden of the area who threw large bars of soap down into its mouth although this has now been discouraged. The surface of the water starts to bubble more and more violently; the water shoots upwards suddenly and then, with a sound of rushing wind, the geyser sends its jet 15-18m (50-60ft) into the air. It has been known to hurl its waterspout 55m (180ft) into the air. It was this geyser which gave its name to all the others around the world.

Iceland is richer in hot springs, mud pools and steam holes than any other country on earth and it is a strange feeling to cross a glacier, with ice metres thick, only to encounter a near-boiling hot spring.

The main high temperature areas are Torfajökull, east of Hekla, and Grimsvötn, in the Vatnajökull glacier; and to a lesser extent Hengill, near Reykjavík, and Kerlingarfjöll, Námafjall, Kverkfjöll, and Krísuvík, south of the capital.

There are approximately 250 geothermal areas in Iceland with nearly 800 hot springs, with an average water temperature of 75°C (167°F). Only a tiny percentage of the springs and their geothermal energy has been tapped by the population but the total power available from the biggest area alone is said to be equivalent to 1,500 megawatts.

The Icelandic word for a glacier is *jökull*. They cover about 11½ per cent of the land, about 11,000sq km (4,228sq ft). Vatnajökull is the biggest glacier in the world, outside Greenland and Antarctica. South of it are massive sand and gravel plains, where the rivers formed by melting ice spread out in all directions, and are constantly changing course. Conditions here are identical with those prevailing in Jutland and North Germany during the last Ice Age. In the last few years the climate has become warmer; many of the glaciers are now retreating and some of the smaller ones have virtually disappeared. This warming marks the end of the last mini-Ice Age which lasted from about 1600-1900. Almost all types of glaciers can be found in Iceland, from the small cirque glaciers to extensive glacier caps.

There are other sizeable glaciers in the central highlands, such as Langjökull, 1,025sq km (395sq miles). On a good day one of the smaller glaciers, Snaefellsjökull, across the bay from Reykjavík can be seen.

Although it is possible to cross the glaciers great care needs to be taken because there are many crevices and avalanches which can be a real danger.

Iceland is criss-crossed by rivers which fall into two categories, glacial and clear water. The glacial rivers rushing down from the high ground are blue-grey in colour, carrying with them minerals and debris from the ice. The clear water rivers are red from lakes or rainfall and are sparkling clean. The water is safe to drink almost everywhere on the island. The longest river is the Thjórsá, in the south, which runs for 230km (143 miles). The second is in the north-east, the Jökulsá á Fjöllum, 206km (128 miles). Due to the constant upheaval of the land, there are many spectacular waterfalls; the most spectacular are Gullfoss, with a drop of 32m (105ft), Dettifoss 44m (144ft) and Skógarfoss 70m (200ft). Needless to say, the Icelandic word for waterfall is *foss*.

About 7 per cent of the total usable hydro-electric power in Iceland has been utilised; it has been estimated that if it were all to be harnessed it would provide up to 4,000 megawatts.

There are also many beautiful lakes in Iceland, the most famous of which, Myvatn, is also an internationally famous bird reserve. Many of the lakes are formed by subsidence, or by volcanic craters filling up, while others are created when lava flows dam rivers. Iceland's five biggest lakes are: Thingvallavatn, 83sq km (32sq miles); Thórisvatn, 68sq km (26sq miles); Lögurinn, 52sq km (20sq miles); Hóp, a lagoon lake covering 45sq km (17sq miles); and Myvatn, extending to 38sq km (14½sq miles).

## Vegetation and Animal Life

When the Vikings arrived in Iceland the country was wooded between mountain and shore, according to Ari the Learned. These woods probably contained low-growing birches and willow, traces of which can still be seen today. Most of the woods were felled for fuel, however, and the introduction of sheep and the onset of cold weather prevented their regrowth in the Middle Ages. Volcanic eruptions with their gases, and the advance of the glaciers during the latest 300-year-long mini-Ice Age from 1600 also destroyed large tracts of woodland. Experiments have shown that birch and a number of species of fir can survive, providing that sheep can be kept away. Thanks to extensive plantings and 'adopt a tree' schemes, there are sizeable areas of woodland again in many parts of Iceland.

The largest birch wood is to be found in East Iceland at Hallormsstadar-skógur and there is another in the north at Fnjóskárdalur. Small remains of old woodlands can be found in a number of other inaccessible places, especially along the rapid glacial rivers to the south of Vatnajökull. Large areas which were formerly covered with woods are now partially or completely devoid of vegetation, and consist mostly of stone or gravel. The soil has long since been blown away. Moss and grass are, however, more widespread in Iceland than in northern Scandinavia and Greenland.

Although large tracts of the highlands are quite bare of vegetation, fertile meadows are to be found in the lowlands between 500m and 700m (1,640-2,300ft) and even higher, and there are various plants and flowers on the slopes of the hills. Although there are about 740 species of vascular plants in Iceland, nearly 300 of these are dandelions and hawkweeds found in the highlands. Grasses and sedge are the commonest vascular plants, but beautifully flowered members of the pink, saxifrage, rose and daisy families are also common. The flora is of mixed but predominantly European origin.

Plants of special interest for Europeans are those found in Iceland but not in the British Isles or North Europe. The most common of these is the arctic fireweed or river beauty, a willowherb (*Epilobium latifolium*) with its purple flowers. It grows densely on gravelly riverbanks, in river gorges, or gravelly dried out river beds.

The broad-leaved willow (*Salix callicarpaea*) is to be found growing all over the country, as well in the lowlands as in the central highlands. The northern green orchid (*Limnorchis hyperborea*) has sweetly scented flowers, and is to be found on grassy slopes in the lowlands. Lyngbyes sedge (*Carex lyngbyei*) is a tall and beautiful sedge, often growing very densely and forming a broad zone of vegetation out from the shores of small lakes.

Another species of special interest is the marsh felwort (*Lomatogonium rotatum*) with fine blue flowers. It grows in bogs, especially near the coast; it is common in the northern part of Iceland and is also found in Arctic Russia.

In Northern Iceland there are some Arctic species not found elsewhere on the island, for instance alpine whitlow-grass (*Draba alpina*), the foliose saxifrage (*Saxifraga foliosa*), the mountain heath (*Phyllodoce coerulea*), the upright primrose (*Primula stricta*), and the arctic harebell (*Campanula uniflora*). One of the most interesting species in Iceland is the sword moss (*Bryoxiphium norvegicum*) which in spite of its name, is not from Norway. It is typically found at the Lake Kleifarvatn in Krísuvík, in south-west Iceland, only 25km (15½ miles) south of Reykjavík. It has a curious geographical distribution, it is found in north-east Greenland, in some regions of North America and also in Mexico and the Far East.

About 450 species of lichen and about 550 species of moss are found in Iceland. With very few exceptions the Icelandic lichen flora is of a Scandinavian character. One species, *Neuropogon sulphureus*, which is common in the Icelandic mountains about 600m (1,970ft) is only found on the islands in the Arctic Ocean, yet in the southern hemisphere it can be found on the Antarctic continent, and in some parts of the high Andes.

The largest area of woodlands is at Hallormsstadur, consisting mainly of birch and the tallest trees extending to about 10m (33ft) high. The rowan, aspen and tea-leaf willow can be found but these species are not widespread. In a few places the tree line reaches up to 600m (2,000ft), but it is generally between 300m and 400m (1,000 and 1,300ft).

The central highlands and the mountains are almost bare of vegetation above the 700m (2,300ft) level. Only scattered species of very hardy Arctic-alpine plants can survive here. In the lowlands too, there are large areas devoid of vegetation, mostly because of lava flows. It is interesting to study the flora taking a foothold in the crumbling lava of the older flows as it turns to soil. First moss establishes itself and this mixes with the lava sand to provide a base for dwarf shrubs and later for birch.

The best examples of this lava flow vegetation can be found in the Búdahraun and the Myvatn area. In these lava flows there are always ravines and in this sheltered environment an even more luxurious vegetation of ferns, herbs and grasses develops. The warm soil around the hot springs also provides favourable conditions for plants, and some species can only be found in such places in Iceland.

Iceland is at the crossroads of several migration routes, so in addition to its resident bird population, it gets visitors from all points of the compass. It is the westernmost outpost of a number of Old World species and the easternmost of some New World ones. In all some 240 species of birds have been seen in Iceland at one time or another, and of these eighty nest in the country. There are seven common passage migrants or winter visitors and a number of regular drift visitors; the remainder are accidentals brought in by freak weather. A great attraction for bird watchers is the tameness of the birds. One reason for this is the small size of the human population compared to the size of the country, some 240,000 people in a 103,600sq km (40,000sq mile) area. Iceland's most famous bird is the Iceland falcon which is now fully protected. It is still widely distributed in the rocky and mountainous parts of the country and is a wonder to watch as it swoops through the air. The white-tailed eagle, once common, is now rare and there are serious fears about its chances of survival. There are only about ten breeding pairs left, mostly in the Breidafjördur area in the west and the mountainous north-west peninsula. The small merlin is the third bird of prey to be found in Iceland.

Two species of owl can be found, the magnificent snowy owl, which is very rare and restricted to certain wild parts of the central highlands, and the short-eared owl, found in low-lying moorland and valleys. The short-eared owl is one of nine species which have settled and bred in the country during the gradual warming of the climate in the last few decades. This owl feeds on mice and small birds, while the snowy owl, like the falcon, usually preys on the ptarmigan, which is the country's most important game bird. There are only nine nesting passerines, mostly because of lack

## CODE FOR VISITORS

1 Please respect the signs of the Nature Conservation Council and the Public Roads Administration traffic and other signs.
2 Driving off roads and tracks is prohibited.
3 It is forbidden to damage or destroy vegetation.
4 Gathering firewood and lighting fires on or near vegetation is prohibited.
5 Where there is no vegetation, fires may be lighted, care being taken not to cause any danger and to leave no marks.
6 Those who travel in the open countryside shall take care not to leave behind refuse. All refuse should be deposited in proper refuse containers.
7 It is prohibited to make marks on natural features.
8 It is prohibited to spoil hot springs and pools, eg by throwing rocks or other objects into them or by damaging the sinter surrounding the springs.
9 Export of birds, eggs, egg shells and nests is unlawful.
10 In protected areas there are special rules. Only the Nature Conservation Council can allow exemptions from these rules:
Activities which alter the landscape or living nature are prohibited.
Collection of natural objects such as animals, plants and rocks is forbidden.
Camping is limited to designated campsites in or close to inhabited areas and is excluded in National Parks and areas of Scientific Interest.

of suitable habitats, especially the absence of real woods, and to the scarcity of insect life.

Iceland has an international reputation as one of the major breeding grounds for waterfowl in Europe, and Myvatn is the home in the summer for tens of thousands of birds. This shallow lake supports Europe's and perhaps the world's, largest concentration of breeding duck. On the lake and surrounding rivers all seventeen species of duck which nest in Iceland can be found; sometimes more than 150,000 duck are assembled on the waters and lake shore.

Two American representatives of the duck tribe, the Barrow's goldeneye and the harlequin, nest here. The Barrow's goldeneye only nests at Myvatn while the harlequin breeds throughout the island. The scaup is the lake's most abundant duck but other species to be found are the tufted duck, common scoter, and long-tailed duck. The common pochard is a new immigrant and still rare.

There are two nesting species of geese in Iceland and passage migrants. The greylag goose inhabits the low-lying district, while the pink-footed goose inhabits the central highlands. The white-fronted goose, brent goose and barnacle goose are visitors. The eider is the island's most common duck and there are more than 200 breeding colonies.

The whooper swan is a common breeding bird, and Iceland is one of the few places in Europe where this is so. It is most numerous on the lakes of the central highlands.

There are still huge colonies of breeding sea birds around Iceland, and the most common species are the common guillemot, Brünnich's guillemot, the puffin, the razor-bill, the kittiwake and the fulmar. The puffin

*Plants take root despite the seemingly inhospitable terrain*

*Flowers proliferate among the rocky outcrops: this was taken at Hafragilsfoss*

does not only breed on the cliffs; huge colonies can be found on low-lying grassy islands. It is one of the commonest Icelandic birds with a population running into millions. Both the birds and eggs are eaten by the people living on the Vestmannaeyjar.

The taking of birds and eggs is a centuries-old tradition and used to be a valuable source of food. In the middle of the last century, records show that tens of thousands of fledglings were taken from the nests each year. By the turn of the century more than 50,000 fledglings were being taken annually from the huge fulmar colonies on Grímsey. The meat was eaten then, or salted or dried for the winter, the feathers were used for bedding and the rest was melted down for oil for the lamps.

Iceland is one of the few places where the ranges of the common and Brünnich's guillemot overlap, and the two species nest in mixed colonies. Two other members of the auk family are the black guillemot, which nests in small colonies among boulders on rocky coasts and islands, and the little auk, a high Arctic species which is now practically extinct.

The Westman Islands (Vestmannaeyjar) are an excellent place to study birds; three species of the petrel family can be found there; the Manx shearwater, Leach's petrel and the storm petrel, which are not found anywhere else in Iceland. There are also gannet colonies on four of the outlying islands, although the largest is on Eldey, off the south-west coast. There are about 15,000 pairs of gannets nesting in this isolated rock. The cormorant and the shag are both common and most abundant in the bays of the west coast, Faxaflói and the Breidafjördur.

Despite its name the Iceland gull does not nest in Iceland but in west Greenland although it is a common winter visitor. The arctic tern is the only tern to be found and it is abundant; and the skuas are represented by the arctic skua and the great skua. The former is common while the latter inhabits the glacial outwash plains in the south-eastern and southern parts of the country. Only the arctic or blue fox is native to Iceland. Mice and rats came ashore with the settlers, and reindeers now live wild in the western highlands. There are no reptiles or amphibians in Iceland.

There are strict laws governing the photographing and visiting of sites of rare birds, especially eagles, falcons, snowy owls and little auks. Permits are only issued by the Ministry of Education following a recommendation from the Bird Protection Committee, and there are heavy fines for breaking these laws.

The farmers mostly raise sheep, which was until 1914 the main occupation. For most of the summer the sheep are grazed on the extensive meadow and heathland pastures, often far up into the mountains. The flocks are rounded up for slaughter in the autumn before the first of the heavy snows. The breeding ewes are kept indoors throughout the winter as are cattle. The breeds of sheep, cattle and horses are all indigenous, derived from Nordic origin. Dairy and sheep farming are the most important enterprises in all parts of the country and beef production is of relatively little importance. Wool is an important by-product of sheep farming. There are about three-quarters of a million sheep on the island and about 60,000 cattle.

Modern farming techniques, machinery and drainage equipment is allowing more arable land to be created. Four hundred years ago cereals were grown, but the onset of much colder weather put an end to this. Today the main crop is still hay to feed the animals during the long winter months, but more land is constantly being recovered for cropping.

## Government

Iceland has been a democratic republic since 1944 with a president elected by a majority vote every four years. There have been four Presidents to date, Sveinn Björnsson (1944-52), Asgeir Asgeirsson (1952-68), Kristjan Eldjarn (1968-80) and the current head of state Vigdis Finnbogadottir, who also holds the honour of having been the first woman ever to be elected President of a democratic country.

Legislative power is in the hands of the President and Parliament, the Althing, whose sixty-three members are elected every four years from the island's six political parties. The Prime Minister appoints Ministers who automatically receive a seat in the Althing. The Althing is divided into a lower and upper house with equal constitutional power. Ordinary bills are discussed three times in each chamber and if the chambers cannot agree, the bill is put before the united Althing where it must receive at least two thirds of the vote to be passed. Iceland is divided into sixteen administrative districts each with its own council and drawing members from every parish within its area.

## The People and Industry

The people of Iceland are mainly of a mixed Scandinavian and Celtic stock. The first settlers were Norwegian, and the language and culture have always been Scandinavian, although there are Celtic influences brought in by the Irish colonists.

The Sagas are one of the world's richest literary collections. They were written down mostly in the thirteenth century and were a detailed account of the settlement of Iceland and its subsequent history. They give a graphic account of life, customs, superstitions, and are an essential read if you really want to understand the nature of the Icelandic people.

The Icelanders are so proud of their heritage, and so anxious to preserve it, that they have passed a law which stipulates that it is illegal to give a child a non-Icelandic name.

Less than 20 per cent of the population now live in rural areas, and a third of the people live in and around Reykjavík. For 800 years almost all the population lived in the countryside, but at the turn of this century, the migration to the towns began, helped largely by the dawning of industrialisation.The rural inhabitants live mostly on the 5,000 or so farms.

Living on the farms used to be a hard life. The summers were short and filled with hard work although food was plentiful. The winters were long and dark, times for the family to be together, times of shortages. Much of the land is unproductive and so farming is not a major economic factor. Although the roots of the country lie in the rural areas (it was on the farms and in the country monasteries that the Sagas were written), the emphasis has now switched to the towns. In 1880 there were only three towns in Iceland where 5 per cent of the population lived; but now there are nineteen towns and thirty-eight villages where 86.9 per cent of the population live. Iceland is the most sparsely populated country in Europe, with an average of two inhabitants per square kilometre.

Greenhouses heated with hot water and steam from deep in the earth provide salad crops and fruit, even bananas. The first greenhouse to be heated in this way opened in 1924 and there is now a large complex of glass, east of Reykjavík.

The major industry, however, is fishing, accounting for 70 per cent of the country's exports. Although it occupies only 5 per cent of the population, it provides more than 10,000 jobs in canning and associated industries. Cod and haddock are the most important species, although prawns and lobsters are a lucrative catch. Fish farming is becoming important and there is still some whaling for scientific research and sealing although the former is likely to be phased out, and the island's only whaling station, to the north of Reykjavík is probably going to stay open as a tourist attraction preserved as a museum to the industry. There has been much concern due to overfishing, culminating in the 'Cod Wars' of the 1970s, when restrictions where increased to 200 miles.

Industry is a relatively new development in Iceland although there have always been cottage and farmhouse industries producing the famous Icelandic knitwear, and other crafts. Industry now, however, employs more people than farming and fishing together although their basic product is still fish and agricultural produce. The largest industrial plant is at Straumsvík, to the east of Reykjavík; a Swiss-owned aluminium reduction factory which imports ore from Australia. The huge red and white smelter towers are visible for miles. The island has its own cement and nitrogen fertilizer plants and the machine and building industries are growing in importance. There is a diatromite plant near Myvatn which produces filtering agents for the brewing and chemical industries from the processed skeletons of minute creatures that form a thick layer on the bottom of the lake.

Iceland is fortunate in having virtually unlimited supplies of energy and electricity simply by tapping into geothermal wells, or building hydro-electric stations on the cascading rivers and waterfalls.

Iceland is now rapidly developing a reputation as a conference venue and facilities are available in Reykjavík to hold international meetings. The country has recently played host to two such meetings which focused world attention on them. It was the venue of the world chess champion-ships in the 1970s, and more recently, and more momentously was the venue for the Reagan-Gorbachev summit.

## Travel Information

Icelandair flies regularly to the international airport at Keflavík from a number of European and North American cities. Scandinavian Airlines (SAS) flies from Copenhagen to Iceland, and there are also flights from Oslo and Stockholm operated on a pooled basis with Icelandair. Connect-ing flights are available from a number of major cities. In addition to normal one-way and return fares a number of other excursion and family fares are available, and there are also special group rates.

One of the best ways of travelling to Iceland and seeing the country is to go on an arranged package holiday and several of these are now available. Flying in to the international airport at Keflavík can be one of the highlights of the trip if the weather is fine. As you begin your descent the flight path normally takes you over the Westman Islands and you should be able to see mountains and glaciers running down to the southern coast. Keflavík, with its new terminal buildings, is unique in Europe in that you can enter the duty free shop and purchase alcohol on arrival as well as departure.

There is a bank at the airport which will change foreign currency and travellers cheques, and a tourist information desk. Cars can be hired at the airport, although it speeds things up if these have been booked in ad-vance, and there are taxis and buses to take you into Reykjavík. The buses normally drop passengers at the Loftleidir Hotel in Reykjavík. The 48km (30 mile) journey takes about 40-50 minutes depending on the time of day.

Passengers must re-confirm their return flights at least 24 hours before departure. Buses leave the Loftleidir Hotel to give you plenty of time to check in and bus tickets can be bought from the desk in the hotel foyer.

Because of the distances involved, and the state of the roads, flying is the most popular way of internal travel. Almost every community has its own small airstrip, although it is difficult when looking at some of them to see just how the aircraft land there. There are three main air operators — Icelandair (Flugleidir), and its two subsidiaries Flugfélag Nordurlands, which operates out of Akureyri, and Flugfélag Austurlands, operating from Egilsstadir. These airlines operate throughout the year and are heavily relied on during the winter when many of the roads are impass-able. Because the weather can change so quickly, it is always advisable to check in advance that a scheduled flight is running, and you must be prepared to face delays on occasions.

There are scheduled services from Reykjavík to Akureyri (6-7 flights daily), Bakkaförddur, Bildudalur, Borgarfjördur, Breiddalsvik, Egilsstadir, Fáskrúdsfjördur, Flateyri, Grímsey, Hornafjördur, Húsavik, Ingjaldssandur, Isafjördur, Nordfjördur, Ólafsfjördur, Patreksfjördur, Raufarhöhn, Keykjanes, Saudárkrókur, Siglufjördur, Sudureyri, Thingeyri, Thórshofn, Vestmannaeyjar and Vopnafjördur.

From Isafjördur there are flights to Bildudalur, Flateyri, Ingjaldssandur, Patreksfjördur, Reykjanes, Sudureyri and Thingeyri.

From Akureyri there are flights to Egilsstadir, Grímsey, Húsavik, Isafjördur, Kópasker, Ólafsfjördur, Raufarhöfn, Siglufjördur, Thórshöfn and Vopnafjördur.

From Egilsstadir there are flights to Bakkafjördur, Borgarfjördur, Breiddalsvik, Fáskrúdsfjördur, Hornasfjördur, Nordfjördur, Reykjavik and Vopnafjördur. There are also flights from Breiddalsvik, Fáskrúdsfjördur and Nordfjördur to Reykjavik.

Apart from the normal fares there is a number of special packages including family fares – only one adult pays the normal fare, the other adult and children aged between 12 and 20, are entitled to a 50 per cent discount, and children aged between 2 and 11 pay half the regular children's fares.

Standby fares are available on a number of flights affording big savings, and groups, senior citizens and students are also entitled to discounts. Many of these flights are met by bus services so that you can continue your journey, and a number of airports have taxis, or facilities to call them. If you have a long journey to make on arrival, it is a good idea to book your taxi in advance.

There is a weekly passenger and car ferry service via the Faroes, but these can be affected by the weather. The route by ferry to Iceland is from Aberdeen on the east coast of Scotland to Tórshavn in the Faroe Islands, and then from Tórshavn to Seydisfjördur on the eastern coast of Iceland. You no longer have to go to Lerwick in the Shetland Isles. There are also links by ferry with the towns of Bergen in Norway and Hantsholm in Denmark.

The ferry lands at Seydisfjördur, one of the prettiest settlements on the east coast, and you then have a spectacular car journey to make over the mountains to Egilsstadir, the main town of the region. Buses also meet the ferry to take passengers to Egilsstadir.

For drivers arriving in Iceland for the first time, the road out of the port and up the hairpin bends is a good introduction to island driving. Stop somewhere safe as you climb out of the valley and take in the spectacular views of the port nestling in its fjord, and the plunging cliffs with scores of waterfalls as the backdrop.

The Iceland Steamship Company maintains a regular freighter service from many ports in Northern Europe and the USA to Iceland, and special passenger rates can be arranged.

Car ferries ply between Reykjavik and Akranes, sailing across Faxaflöi and there is a larger ferry sailing from Thorlákshöfn on the south coast to the Westman Islands. In the west a ferry operates between Stykkishólmur carrying both cars and passengers to Brjánslaekur, via the Breidafjördur Islands, while another sails between a number of ports along the Ísafjardardjúp. There are regular sailings from Akureyri to the island of Grímsey. There is also a ferry service to the island of Hrísey in Eyjafjördur.

It can be quite exciting driving in Iceland because the roads vary from good in the south to almost impassable inland. It is worth remembering that it is little more than 15 years since the road around the island was completed. In 1974, to commemorate the 1,000th anniversary of the first settlement, the final stretch of the coastal ring road was completed when the section below the Vatnajökull glacier was opened. This elevated roadway was a remarkable piece of engineering, because year after year, flood waters from the thawing snow came down from the mountains and glaciers, sweeping away the roads and bridges in their path. The completion of that road means that it is now possible to travel completely around the island and it can be a rewarding, if somewhat bumpy experience.

One must keep to roads that are marked on the maps. There are plenty of tracks to follow but many of these are made by farmers or people who know the area thoroughly and the stranger straying onto these is likely to get lost. Sandstorms and fog often cause unexpected problems, with reduced visibility, and caution should always be exercised when crossing fords. The water is very clear and therefore may be deceptively deep. Glacial rivers are also very dangerous to cross even in four-wheel drive vehicles. The currents are usually very strong and large boulders can easily be swept along by them.

Because there are large stretches of uninhabited countryside, there are rescue huts for passengers in emergencies. They are not meant to accommodate the ordinary traveller, and provisions and first aid equipment should never be touched unless urgently needed. Traffic in Iceland gives way to the left. International signs are used and there is adequate signposting on most of the main roads.

One of the best ways to see the island, and one of the cheapest, is to travel by coach. There are frequent excursions and tours leaving from Reykjavík, Akureyri and other towns, as well as a remarkable island bus service. It is possible, over a few days, to do the round trip using scheduled coach services staying on campsites, hostels or cheap hotels overnight. It is also a very good way of meeting the people of Iceland, because their natural friendliness will almost always lead to conversation. The coaches normally leave early in the morning and can be on the road for up to 12 hours, but they stop regularly for comfort and refreshment breaks. In both Reykjavík and Akureyri there are also inter-town bus services.

Iceland buses are like no others, and when you see the roads they have to travel over, you can understand why. Most of the buses are specially built, with higher than usual clearance, because of boulders and pot holes, four-wheel drive and two way radios so that the driver can keep in touch with base.

BSI, the Icelandic Bus Routes Union, operates most of the scheduled services although it and a number of small companies also run tours. During the summer months, the buses run into the interior, and this is one of the best ways to explore, letting the driver do the hard work while you enjoy the scenery.

If you plan to use the buses to travel around the island, there are a number of special discount tickets available. An Omnibus Passport can last from 1 to 4 weeks and allows you to use all the scheduled routes, apart from the interior ones. You can get off where you like, spend some days walking or exploring before continuing the journey. There is also the Full-Circle Passport which allows you to travel the ring road, but once you have decided which way you are going, you must continue your trip in that direction. You are still allowed to break your journey when and as often as you like.

If you plan to travel the island by bus, get hold of a copy of the BSI time-table. Although only available in Icelandic, it is understandable and will allow you to work out a route using the forty or so scheduled services which cover almost 4,000km (2,480 miles) of roads.

Car hire is expensive, especially if you want a four-wheel drive vehicle, but an all-terrain vehicle is absolutely essential if you plan to get off the main routes and use mountain roads. It is a good idea to have an international driving licence, but it is not essential.

When you pick up your hire vehicle, check it out carefully. Make sure the tyres are in good condition, that the spare tyre is usable, and that you know where the jack and tools are. Often the vehicles come without any English manuals so make sure you know the basics before you set out. If you are planning to go into the remote areas, make sure you have a good tool kit and spares, and if you plan to drive along some of the more dangerous mountain roads, go in convoy with at least one other vehicle.

Icelandair Hertz Car Rental will provide a map showing all the garages around the island which will help out if you have a problem, but all these are located on or near the ring road. Once you head into the interior, you are very much on your own, although there may be isolated farms where you can get help or fuel. All types of cars can be rented for use, either on a daily or weekly basis. The rate is normally calculated on a daily hire charge plus mileage. Fuel and 25 per cent sales tax are not included.

The Iceland Tourist Board issues a number of useful leaflets for visiting drivers. It would be a good idea if 'How to Travel in the Interior of Iceland', and 'Some Things You Must Know', were automatically handed over to vehicle hirers.

It is essential when travelling to have good maps and there are large scale charts available of most areas. There is also a very good road atlas published by Landmaelingar Islands, which is ideal for motorists and planning routes.

Don't get confused by road signs. Often when you are moving off a main road, the signpost will not indicate the number of the road you are

*Many Icelandic roads, including many major roads, are not surfaced. This is part of the main circular route around Iceland leading to Grímsstadir, close to Mödrudalur farm, the highest in Iceland.*

about to drive on, but the road it connects with. Some stretches of roads in built up areas have paved surfaces and there are even occasional stretches of dual carriageway, but these are not really needed. There are traffic jams in the cities during the rush hours, but generally the roads are quiet.

The major roads in the south, especially those from the international airport at Keflavík leading into Reykjavík, and those to the other towns in the south-east and south have asphalt surfaces. Most other roads are of graded gravel and while in the summer all roads are open, great care should be taken before venturing too far off the beaten track. To do any serious travelling in the hinterland, a four-wheel drive vehicle is necessary, and it is much safer to travel in pairs so that one vehicle can be on hand to pull the other out of trouble if necessary.

There were no roads in Iceland before 1900 and when the tracks were created they were primarily for pack horses. In fact, until quite recently horses were used as the main method of carrying goods, provisions and materials inland. There have never been any railways on the island.

There are now about 11,000km (6,800 miles) of roads, although more than 20 per cent of these are country roads linking farms and rural settlements. There has also been an intensive bridge building programme and now all the main rivers are crossable by bridge rather than having to find a suitable fording place as used to be the case some years ago.

There are a number of rules which have to be followed if you are planning to go off inland by yourself. Never drive on vegetation off the road. There is little enough of it about in Iceland and it takes a long time to recover. It could also lead to soil erosion. The mountain roads and tracks are only passable using four-wheel drive vehicles.

For touring in summer, lightweight woollens are necessary, a sweater or cardigan for the evening, as well as waterproofs and sturdy footwear. Swimming gear is essential whenever you are travelling because there are numerous hot pools, warm springs and heated swimming pools.

The best hotels are in Reykjavík but there are many first-class establishments to be found elsewhere in Iceland, especially in the north. The top hotels are of international standard, although there are many others to suit all budgets. In the summer, many of the schools in the country have 3 months' holiday and these buildings are converted into 'summer hotels' for travellers. The basic facilities of bed, washrooms and kitchens are provided, and you have the choice of eating a prepared meal or catering for yourself. There are also guesthouses available in most towns, and many private houses offer bed and breakfast accommodation, especially in Reykjavík. It is also now possible to stay on farms in Iceland and terms include both room only and full board. There is no tipping in Icelandic hotels, breakfast is not always included in the price of the room, although most hotels have their own restaurants offering a full meals service.

There are many camping sites in Iceland. There is a large site in Reykjavík near the main bus terminal, and another in the city centre, next to the magnificent swimming pool. Some sites are well appointed with showers and toilets, although in some of the remoter areas naturally there are fewer facilities. Most communities have a municipal camping site just outside the town, and camping is generally permitted anywhere in Iceland, unless there are signs specifically forbidding it. Camping is not allowed inside the country's three national parks, nor in areas of special scientific interest, although notices are not generally on display. One can normally camp near farms or fenced land, but one should obtain prior permission from the farmer.

There are many youth hostels in Iceland. Many country hotels also offer special reduced priced accommodation for travellers who provide their own sleeping bags. In the hinterland, there are a number of huts owned by the Icelandic Touring Club. It is normally best to check if these are available as they are frequently used by large groups. In these huts one must provide one's own sleeping bag and food. Groups travelling with the club always have priority.

There has been quite an upsurge in catering standards in Iceland in the last few years, although the top hotels have always offered an international cuisine of a high standard. In Reykjavík there are now many small establishments offering excellent varied food, such as salmon, raw shark, sheep's head and Icelandic blue cheese. Needless to say, the fish restaurants are excellent but there are also now American burger bars and a host of other foreign cuisines. It must be said that eating out is not cheap, although standards are high. Because breakfast is not always included in the hotel's overnight charge, it is often better to eat out and there are many restaurants and cafés offering budget breakfasts.

Most hotels and restaurants have licences to serve spirits and wines but until recently strong beer was almost unobtainable — a remnant of the prohibition laws. The only beer generally available was low-alcohol or non-alcoholic beer. The Government has now decided that normal strength beer can be sold and many bars have sprung up in Reykjavík. Most offer food and entertainment and stay open until the early hours. There are, however, some restaurants which are 'dry' and only soft drinks are available.

It is worth mentioning that Iceland is one of the few countries in the world where you can buy your duty free drinks as you go into the country. Tourists can bring into Iceland, tax free, one litre of wine or other drinks (up to 21 per cent alcohol), or twelve bottles of beer, as well as one litre of spirits, and 200 cigarettes or equivalent of other tobacco products.

There are discos in both Reykjavík and Akureyri, and the Broadway, in the capital, claims to be the largest disco in Europe. Friday and Saturday are the most popular nights. Icelanders are very fond of dancing, and most communities organise their own dances to which tourists are made welcome. These may not be held regularly but they are always well advertised.

All musical tastes are catered for in Reykjavík and apart from ballroom dances at some of the hotels, and the discos, there are classical concerts, jazz clubs and folk clubs. There are nine cinemas in Reykjavík alone, and all towns of any size have their own cinema. Films are normally shown in their original language with Icelandic subtitles, and releases tend to be up to date. Normally only a main feature is shown.

During the summer months in Reykjavík there is a presentation of traditional Icelandic folklore, with songs, dances and Saga readings. Performances are held several times a week between early July and the end of August. The performances are normally in English. The Icelandic Opera also presents a series of musical evenings in July and August, although the National Theatre and Municipal Theatre are closed in the summer.

The Society of Icelandic Solo Singers gives recitals of Icelandic poetry and songs every week in July and August and Icelandic documentary films are screened daily during the summer in Reykjavík.

Shops are open weekdays from 9am to 6pm and on Saturdays from 9am or 10am to noon, although many close for the whole weekend. Offices are open 9am to 5pm weekdays only, and few work on Saturdays. Shops offer the normal range of goods and there are many gift and souvenir shops. Favourite souvenirs are sheepskins, woollen goods, jewellery, and lava pottery. Icelandic wool is especially soft yet strong, and much of the knitwear is handmade.

Almost every sort of sporting facility can be found. Swimming is the most popular activity and there are heated pools in all large towns.

*Bare rock accounts for approximately 10 per cent of Iceland's landscape*

Because the water is heated from geothermal wells, swimming is an all-year-round activity, even if the air temperature is at freezing point or below. Most of the swimming pools also have 'hot pots'. These are pools which tap straight into the hot water reservoirs underground and their temperatures vary from very hot to scalding. Saunas and sulphur pools are also common throughout the island.

There are a number of good golf courses around the country and golf is now a very popular pastime with the Icelanders. For the last few years a very successful international tournament — the Arctic Open — has been held at the Akureyri Golf Club. The tournament is always played in mid-summer on what is proudly claimed to be the most northerly 18-hole course in the world.

The national religion is Lutheran but there is complete freedom of worship. About 2 per cent of the population is Roman Catholic, and Reykjavík has a Roman Catholic cathedral.

## Fishing in Iceland

There are no fish diseases in Icelandso all fishing gear brought into the country must be sterilised. Apart from trout and salmon, there is fishing for char, and fishing lodges providing excellent holidays are now being established. Skiing is available in many areas, especially in the north. Iceland has some of the best and cheapest salmon and trout fishing in the world. It has one of the few capital cities (possibly the only one), where salmon can be caught in the town; and in places, especially off the north coast, fishing is free.

While Iceland has always been popular with fishermen because of the good sport, attempts are now being made to increase facilities. Fishing lodges are being built alongside the best stretches of water, and an excellent one has now been built to the north of Reykjavík on the Laxá (Stóra Laxá) river.

Iceland has three species of sports fish generally distributed — the salmon, brown trout and char. In addition there is the stickleback and the common eel. Two other species of trout can also be caught, but both are 'imports'. Rainbow trout were originally introduced from Denmark and are now bred on fish farms for stocking lakes and rivers. They are also farmed commercially. A few pink salmon have also been caught, and these are believed to be descendants from North Russian stock which have migrated. Both of the last two species have been fished for the last 25 years.

Salmon always return to the river in which they were born to spawn, so salmon found in Iceland are truly Icelandic fish. The salmon's huge areas of travel have led to serious problems of conservation in the last few years. Overfishing in one area can lead to serious depletion of stock returning to spawn in another. International agreements have now been signed which should help reduce overall salmon catches and help the species increase again. In 1984, however, 23,582 salmon were caught by use of a rod or line.

In Iceland, almost all the salmon is caught inland, in rivers and lakes. In most cases fishing for salmon at sea is banned by law, even though many other countries permit this. Because the salmon is caught inshore, it is classified as freshwater fish, as are the brown trout and char. Often the trout and char go to the sea to feed, and sea trout and sea char provide excellent fishing as they grow bigger and faster.

Iceland has at least sixty rivers with salmon, and many more with trout. The salmon can be found anywhere along the river's length from a few kilometres to more than 100km (60 miles) inland. The island's best salmon fishing is to be found in the south-west, in the rivers around Reykjavík, and two-thirds of the catch is taken in this region. The best rivers are the Ölfusá-Hvítá complex, Sog, Brúará and Stóra Laxá in Arnesysla. In the Borgarfjördur valley there is another Hvítá river system with its main tributaries of Grímsá, Thverá and Nordurá.

The river Ellidaár runs through Reykjavík, and this is probably the country's most famous salmon river, with one of the highest yields. Another good stretch of water is to be found north of Reykjavík on the river Laxá in Kjós.

In the north-west of the country there are many good stretches of river around the Dalasysla district. The Húnavatnssyla area also has many good waters including Midfjardará, the Laxá, Blandá and Vatnsdalsá. The best salmon river in the north-east is the Laxá which flows majestically, with many deep pools and islands, from the town of Húsavík. Other good waters are to be found in the Thistilfjördur and Vopnafjördur districts.

There is not much salmon fishing in the south-east, although there have been catches. Most of the rivers are glacial, and therefore short, although they do contain sea trout. Sea trout weighing up to 20lb are not uncommon in the Skaftá to the west of the Vatnajökull glacier.

Trout can be fished almost anywhere on the island's coastal plains, but the best areas are in the south-east and south-west. Sea char is most common in the north-west, north-east and south-west, and is the main fish of the short, fast flowing rivers of the north-west peninsula.

There is also good lake fishing and offshore fishing. Lake trout of up to 26lb are not unusual, but lake char is the commonest fish. In the south-west there are about twenty first class fishing lakes, of which Thingvallavatn is the largest. It is about 40km (25 miles) east of the capital. Other good lakes are Apavatn, east of Thingvallavatn; Hlídarvatn and Kleifarvatn, south of Reykjavík; and Hvalvatn, Reydarvatn, Langavatn, Hítarvatn and Oddastadavatn.

The Húnavatnssyla district, in the north-west, also has many fine fishing lakes. Hóp is the country's fourth largest lake, and there are also the lakes of Vesturhópsavtn, Svínavatn, and Laxárvatn.

Lake Myvatn dominates the fishing in the north-east. It is the country's fifth largest lake, and being able to hire a boat, and row out into the middle of this beautiful lake, is a wonderful experience, even if you don't catch anything. The views make it worthwhile.

The south-west, because of its glacial, heavily mineralised waters, has a number of lakes which cannot support fish life. The country's second largest lake, Thórisvatn, is to be found here, but it has no fish. Some brown trout can be found to the south in the group of lakes known as Veidivötn.

The Icelandic salmon varies between 4lb and 12lb and between 55cm and 85cm (21in and 33in) in length. Every year, fish approaching 30lb are caught, and the record is a 49lb fish (after bleeding) which was caught in a cod net off the island of Grímsey in 1957. It was 132cm (52in) long. The largest rod-caught salmon was taken in 1946 at Ida in the Hvítá river in Árnessysla. It weighed 38½lb.

Sea trout can weight up to 20lb, though most weigh between 1lb and 4lb. Sea char are usually smaller, weighing in at between 1lb and 2lb, although some of 12lb have been taken.

The lake brown trout usually grow up to 4lb, although a giant one weighing 26lb was caught at Thingvallavatn. Lake char is the commonest species in the lakes and can vary enormously in size, from anything from 3 or 4oz to 12lb. The average weight is between ½lb and 2lb.

In Thingvallavatn, a special variety of char can be found. It grows to about 20cm (8in) in length and weighs about 4oz.

Salmon may only be fished for 4 months of the year, from 20 May to 20 September. Net fishing starts on 20 May, but generally rod fishing is not allowed until June, and the date varies according to the area. In the north, because the rivers are colder, the fish do not travel up the rivers until July and this is generally considered the best fishing month. August is usually good, and in some years exceptional, while in September, the sport is beginning to decline.

The sea trout season opens on 1 April and closes on 20 September. The best early fishing is in the south as the trout make their way to sea. The main fishing season, however, is in July and August as the fish return to the rivers to spawn. Fishing in the lakes is allowed from 1 February to 26 September, except at Thingvallavatn, where the season closes on 31 August. The best fishing is from late May until the middle of July.

The traditional methods of winter fishing through the ice are still practised in some areas, although this is a very chilly way of catching your supper. Fishing rights are held by the landowner. Many owners have formed themselves into associations to control the fishing. The fishing is often rented out on a yearly basis to clubs or individuals, who allocate rights. The right to fish is usually granted from 1 to 3 days, and because of the excellence of the fishing the finest stretches are booked up months, sometimes years ahead. Fishing is controlled to protect the stock, and limits are imposed on the numbers of rods allowed on each stretch. This means that a fisherman can be given a stretch of river several hundred metres, or even kilometres long, so there is no shortage of places to cast from.

Fishing is allowed for 12 hours a day, from 7am to 10pm with a 2 or 3 hour break for lunch. The fisherman is usually allowed to keep all his catch. Trout fishing permits can normally be obtained on the day by applying direct to the farmer, or through his agent, who is usually to be found in the nearest town or hotel.

Most Icelanders prefer to use a rod for fishing, and although netting is allowed in some areas it is becoming less popular. Fly rods of 2.7 to 4.2m (9 to 14ft), and casting rods of about 2.7m (9ft) are preferred for salmon using bait of earthworm, artificial fly, spinner or lure. The most popular artificial flies are: Black Doctor, Blue Charm, Crossfield, Silver Doctor, Silver Wilkinson and Silver Grey. Similar baits are used for trout.

The larger fishing lodges provide food and bedding, although self-catering is available in some. The smaller lodges have basic facilities and fishermen must fend for themselves. Many hotels now offer fishing package holidays, if there are good waters nearby.

For health reasons the use of fishing equipment, including waders and rubber boots, which have been used while angling abroad is prohibited, unless it has been disinfected according to the rules.

## Horse Riding in Iceland

For hundreds of years the Icelandic horse (for horse it is despite its small size), has been the most useful animal on the island. It has been the pack horse, and until recently, the only means of transport in many parts of the

*Cod's heads drying in the sun. These are exported to such places as Nigeria as they are a valuable source of protein.*

country. It is still used by farmers each year to round up the tens of thousands of sheep grazing on the lowland plains.

In common with horses in many other parts of the world, the animal has generally fallen into disuse as a working beast, and is now kept mainly for sport, which takes a number of forms, from trekking to racing. Horses are kept for fun and weekend recreation, but breeding establishments have been developed, and the best animals are now being sold abroad, where they command high prices.

The horses were introduced almost 1,000 years ago with the first Viking settlers. For most of this time, the stock has remained pure with no imports allowed to adulterate the strain. The animal is small, but muscular, with long, flowing mane, wide back and proud head. Unlike most horses, if it is reined in the Icelandic horse will begin to gallop, which it does remarkably well considering both its size and the toughness of the terrain. The average size of the Icelandic horse is about 13 hands. Consequently, one's feet are relatively near to the ground, which can be a problem. The sure-footed beasts pick their way through the rock-strewn countryside and it is often necessary to lift one's legs quickly out of the way of sharp rocks.

Although the Icelandic horse is one of the purest strains of any in the world, it comes in a wide range of colours. Over the centuries, only the strongest have survived the harsh weather and tough winters, and the breed today is tough, reliable, and generally amiable. It has five distinct gaits — the walk, trot and gallop, in common with other breeds, and the pace and *tölt*. These are Icelandic specialities, which allow long distances to be travelled without too much discomfort. Both are delightful to watch when the horse is being ridden by an expert. A good Icelandic horse will carry a rider day after day, as it has done for centuries.

For those interested in trekking, lack of experience is not a barrier. The horse is a perfect solution to the problem of seeing large tracts of the countryside without resorting to four-wheel drive trucks.

The idea of undertaking a long cross-country trek, spanning several days, and sleeping out or in one of the mountain huts, is a very appealing one. Riding has many advantages over walking. It is different, it allows more ground to be covered more quickly than on foot, and above all, it is fun. It is also like riding back into history because for a thousand years the horse was the only way to travel, and many of the roads and paths have been trodden by these sure-footed animals for centuries.

There is now a wide range of rides and treks to choose from, and there is something to suit all tastes. It is possible to hire a horse on the outskirts of Reykjavík and spend some time sightseeing around the edges of the city, or to sign on for a tough trek into the heartland of the country, spending many nights out.

The Icelanders take their riding seriously, and indeed, almost everyone does ride. There is no need for expensive clothes. Jeans and wellington boots are fine, together with a thick jumper, reliable waterproof and windproof jacket, and gloves. A hard hat is sensible, especially in the countryside because the ground is very rocky, but generally the animals at the trekking stables are so sure of where they are going, and so docile, that there is little fear of falling.

Equally there is very little instruction, because almost none is necessary. It takes about 3 minutes to demonstrate how to hold the reins, how to persuade the animal to turn right and left, how to stop and how to walk on.

The other marvellous thing about riding in Iceland is that it is one of the last open countries in Europe. There are no miles of barbed wire, or fences with 'keep out' notices. People respect the rules of the countryside, and the landowners allow them access to it. On a trekking trip, obviously the group stays together but individuals are actually free to go almost anywhere they want. It is a freedom that is all too rare. Iceland on horseback is an unforgettable experience.

## Climbing and Skiing

There is no other area in Europe superior to Iceland for the diversity of terrain it offers to walkers, climbers and skiers. There is year-round skiing in the north, some excellent winter skiing, and of course, climbing to suit all tastes; rock climbing, full-scale mountain assaults or ice-climbing.

The interior of the country is a vast outdoor activity centre where you can learn new skills, or put old ones to the test. There are not many places where, as in Iceland, it is possible to walk day after day over glaciers and snowfields. Most of the other areas of the world offering such facilities tend to be very remote, and a visit involves major expenditure and planning.

It does not take long to fly to Iceland and one can be on the glaciers in an equally short time. Once there, a kingdom of wonder and mystery, one where several days can pass without seeing another person, is open to the visitor. Iceland is Europe's outback.

The entire centre of the country, however, does not consist of ice and snow, although it is mountainous and rugged. In the summer months, coaches travel through the heart of the mountains taking passengers to the northern coast, and there are many tracks accessible to four-wheel drive vehicles. It is even possible to cycle across Iceland, although it is necessary to carry the bicycle across the snow.

In many ways Iceland seems to be made up of many different sceneries, each stolen from a different country, but collectively like no other country on earth. In parts of the interior, the mountains and deeply carved glacial valleys are reminiscent of the Scottish Highlands, and the walking is about the same, even though the altitudes are higher. In other parts, the snow-capped peaks and glaciers are more reminiscent of the High Alps, or parts of the Himalayas.

There are many mountains to climb, and many mountain chains to ski down. It is possible to take a single day trip from Reykjavík to explore the mountains, and there are several of these climbs to choose from, such as Esja, at 909m (2,982ft), or Hengill, at 803m (2,634ft). From the top of Esja, there are the most spectacular views of Reykjavík and beyond. It is said that on a good day you can sometimes see Greenland off to the west, but it is frequently cloudy. The climb to the top is a favourite walk of the people of Reykjavík and it is said that on a summer's day, even 80-year-old women can be seen making their way to the top.

The interior of Iceland is made up of mountains and high plateaux, an uninhabited and treeless area. It rises to an average height of 500m (1,640ft) above sea level, with the highest point being in the south-east of the country.

Where the ground is not covered with glacier, there is lava sand, gravel and lava rock, which is sharp, awkwardly shaped and difficult to walk on. At this altitude, the precipitation falls as snow but all the water is drinkable, unless it is direct melt from the glacier. The rule to remember is that if the water is clear, it is safe to drink; if it is blue or cloudy, it has come from the glacier. It can be boiled and drunk but there is usually a supply of clear water to be found.

There are maps of some of the interior, especially Skáftafell, but basic mountain crafts are needed before setting out on an expedition. The most important of these are compass reading and survival training. It is very easy for mists suddenly to swell up, or for snowstorms to take place on the very high ground. Visibility can be reduced to almost nothing and then the environment can become hostile. It is essential to be fully prepared, with full camping gear and rations at the outset of the expedition. Often the only thing to do in bad weather conditions is to pitch a tent and stay put. There are a number of mountain huts scattered about, but even for the experienced guide they are almost impossible to find in such conditions. The weather is too unpredictable and the terrain too rough to take any chances.

The best way of touring inland is to go on an arranged trip or to employ a guide. There are expeditions planned by many companies and the Iceland Travel Association also runs trips which last from a weekend to several days. Just reaching the starting point of an expedition can be an adventure. The round-the-island road system is now more than adequate, but off the beaten track, things can get a little bumpy. The Icelanders know how to drive their four-wheel vehicles, and they hurtle along seemingly unmarked trails, and splash through raging boulder-strewn rivers. More often than not, the vehicles travel in pairs, so there is usually one either to tow or push the other out of trouble. After a journey of crashing and bumping over these tracks for a few hours, it is quite a relief to get out and start walking. All the vehicles also carry two-way radios which is a reassurance.

There is a lot of skiing to be enjoyed in Iceland, mostly in the hills around the coast. Here there are increasing facilities for both alpine and cross-country skiing with ski lodges and lifts. Skiing inland is very dangerous, and best left to the most proficient. Here there are no facilities, and the terrain is generally too difficult for all but the best skiers. There is the added problem that as there are no facilities everything — tent, food, stove and so on — must be carried.

In the north, it is possible to ski in the Akureyri area all the year round, and there is the advantage of almost permanent summer daylight.

The two recommended areas for exploration and short expeditions are Kerlingarfjöll (Ogress Mountain), about 200km (125 miles) from Reykjavík, and the mountains lying behind Akureyri in the north.

The Kerlingarfjöll is a huge area in southern central Iceland and is best reached by using a rough road, Kjalvegur, which connects the north and south of the country. It is easily accessible in summer by four-wheel drive vehicles and it takes up to 8 hours to reach it from Reykjavík. On the way the route passes the Great Geysir, the glaciers of Langjökull and Hofsjökull, and close by the hot spring area of Hveravellir. The Kerlingarfjöll covers an area of almost 150sq km (58sq miles) and the mountains are cut in two by a deep gorge. The region is said to be the most varied as far as scenery and geology are concerned of any in Iceland. The mountains are reminiscent of the Alps, although they are smaller, rising (generally between 800m (2,624ft) and 1,500m (4,921ft). The mountains are particularly famous because of their striking colours, especially when the sun is shining on them. Composed mostly of tuff, basalt and liparite of varying colours, they make a marvellous subject for photography.

In the region there are also hot mud springs and steam springs where it is possible to take a bath surrounded by snow, and in places the heat has carved out strange caves and tunnels where it has broken through the snow crust.

The only road off the Kjalvegur goes to Árskard (732m, 2,400ft), which is an ideal base because there is plenty of water. It is also popular with many young Icelanders in the summer for skiing, because there is both sun and snow on the slopes of Snækollur (1,478m, 4,850ft). Courses are run here weekly for both beginners and experienced skiers. There is a hut run by the Iceland Travel Association, and in the summer it is advisable to book well in advance, because this valley is so popular.

If it is not possible to get into the hut, which is well equipped, there is camping along the rivers, where some of the most perfect pitches are to be found. The vegetation in the valley is lush, especially when compared to the starkness of the surrounding snow and ice. There are trees for shade, crystal clear water to drink, and usually a lot of warmth as the sun gets trapped in the valley.

There are many climbs within reach of the hut, and ascents of Snækollur and Árskardsfjall (919m, 3,015ft) give magnificent views into the heartland. The Hofsjökull glacier is also close but it is advisable only to venture out on to the ice with experienced guides. In places the ice is so deeply crevassed that it is necessary to walk hundreds of yards along a narrow

*Horse-trekking is an exciting way to enjoy the spectacular scenery around Iceland*

*Exploration of the glaciers should only be attempted under the supervision of experienced guides*

ridge to find a point narrow enough to jump across, and then repeat the whole thing again. It is a wonderful experience, and one that should be undertaken if at all possible.

While this region is remote, the mountains around Akureyri could not be more accessible. They are easily reached by road within minutes from the town and they afford marvellous climbing, skiing and hiking. There is now a ski hotel within 10 minutes' drive from Akureyri (also within walking distance), which accommodates skiers during the late winter/early spring, and hikers during the summer. It is 500m (1,640ft) above sea level and the surrounding countryside is regarded as the best area for winter sports in Iceland. The best skiing is from mid-March to May, but the intrepid can ski all the year round by going higher.

In the summer there are a number of walks based around the ski hotel, and the staff will give you details. From here there are many interesting places to explore including the nearby Glerá Valley which is famous for its unusual flora.

The average height of the mountains around Akureyri is 1,200m (4,000ft) and they are formed of basalt and some liparite. They are craggy, but climbable with care. The highest mountain in northern Iceland is Kerling, but others worth climbing are Stryta, Súlur and Kaldbakur on the other side of the fjord. The glaciers of Glerárdalsjökull and Vind-heimajökull, which literally means 'Home of the Winds', can be visited. There is also some difficult rock climbing around Hraundrangar, in the Öxnadalur valley, although transport will be needed to get there. Almost anywhere in Iceland affords good climbing, but other areas recommended by the Iceland Travel Association include Snaefellsnes peninsula in the west, the Vestfirdir, Austfirdir and Myvatn.

The ITA, or the Iceland Mountaineering Club, have huts which can be used in emergencies. The areas below all have one of these huts. Thórsmörk Valley, 153km (95 miles) from Reykjavík, surrounded by glaciers and towering mountains, enjoys its own sunny micro-climate in the summer which attracts plants and birds. Landmannalaugar (185km, 115 miles, from Reykjavík), is an area famous for its hot springs, and to get there the route passes close to Hekla. It is possible to climb Hekla because although the ascent is long, it is not too difficult. Hagavatn (149km, 92½ miles from Reykjavík) is a lake at the foot of the 'Long Glacier', called Langjökull. Hvítárnes (171km, 106 miles, from Reykjavík) is spectacular. It is another lake on the other side of the Long Glacier. The glacier actually plunges down into the water and huge chunks break away to float off as icebergs. It is possible to climb up on to the glacier behind the lake, but the waters are too cold to swim in. Rumour has it that the ITA hut here is haunted. Tindafjallajökull mountains are close to Thórsmörk but a long, hard climb is needed to reach the hut at 874m (2,867ft). On the higher slopes, up to 1,462m (4,796ft), there is permanent snow suitable for all-year-round skiing. Fimmvörduháls (180km, 112 miles from Reykjavík) is a ridge at 1,000m (3,281ft) which connects the Myrdalsjökull (1,493m,

4,898ft) and Eyjafjallajökull (1,666m, 5,466ft) glaciers. It is a good area for climbing, skiing and walking, but it is very exposed and often subject to severe weather. The Katla volcano erupted through the Myrdalsjökull in 1918.

It is essential, before spending any time out of doors in Iceland, to have the best camping and climbing gear, and it must be well proven. It can be very windy on the exposed slopes and extra guys will be needed for tents. The ground is extremely hard and special tent pegs will be needed. Lightweight, cheap pegs will simply buckle and be useless. It can get very cold on the mountains so a three-season bag is necessary, or even a four-season bag if you are out in early spring. A reliable tent is a must, and one that has proved it can stand up to gale force winds and heavy falls of snow. For the sake of a little extra weight, a survival bag, especially a Gore-Tex type, is a good idea.

Climbers will need crampons, snow axe and ropes; these are advisable even if you are just crossing snow or glaciers. Other essential pieces of equipment are a whistle, and a first aid kit. Clothing must be warm, windproof and waterproof. Temperature fluctuations can be enormous between the hot sun in the valleys, and the bitterly cold winds on an exposed snow face. Thick trousers or breeches are advisable, together with warm shirt, jumper and anorak. Waterproof jacket and overtrousers are necessary, and gaiters are useful to keep out the wet snow and small stones. A warm hat and gloves will help keep in the heat, and a pair of sturdy shoes, mountain boots or 'bog trotters' completes the kit.

Many Icelanders wear wellington boots because they are ideal for wading across the many streams. If the water is too deep, it is also quite easy to remove these boots and wade over. There are now quite a lot of combination boots available, mostly of Scandinavian origin, which combine the sole of a mountain boot with the upper of a wellington. This gives greater waterproofing together with grip. Do not just wade across and hope your boots will dry out. It is a recipe for blisters or worse as the water can be very cold and boots just do not dry. Take boots and socks off and stow them in your rucksack. Some people carry a spare pair of socks to slip on when fording a stream so that they do not slip on the submerged rocks. Obviously, if you are out on the trail for some days, a spare set of clothing is essential as well as food and fuel.

Iceland is a country that has a great deal to offer outdoor enthusiasts, and the rules to follow are the rules any sensible climber or walker would stick to. Be prepared; do not attempt to do too much; let someone know where you are going and how long you expect to be away; and do not be afraid to ask for advice. The Iceland Travel Association, Iceland Mountaineering Club or various travel companies are only too willing to help you.

## Walking and Hiking

Almost everything that has been said about climbing in Iceland can be applied to walking and hiking, except that there is much more room to do it in; the central highlands, the mountains and glaciers, along the fjords on

*This remote valley is at Námaskard*

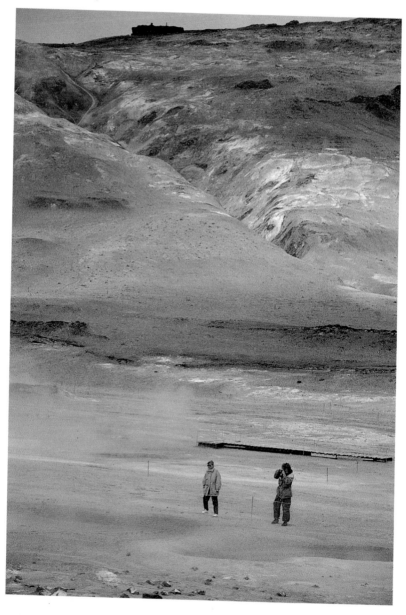

the east and west coasts; the beautiful countryside around Lake Myvatn are all ideal walking areas.

The major difference between walking or backpacking in Iceland as opposed to the Scottish Highlands, or the Alps, is simply the remoteness of the place. It is quite possible to be several days away from the nearest farm so there are problems with logistics. Everything must be carried, and it is necessary to be self-reliant and competent. It is a daunting thought

*The Öxnadalur Valley, west of Akureyri*

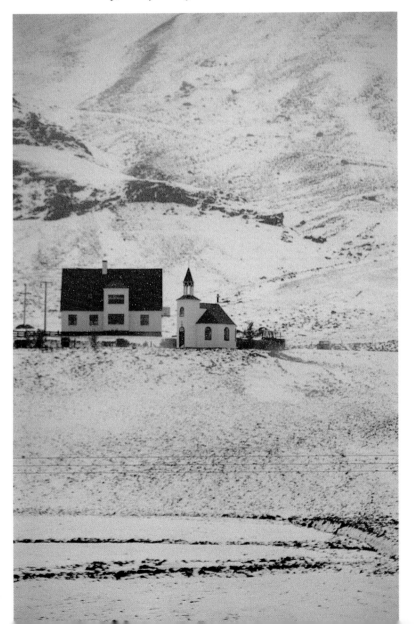

that the nearest telephone might be 2 or 3 days' hard walking away.

The remoteness of Iceland and its northerly position also means that the weather can be much more inhospitable than that of countries further south. It is quite possible that in the mountains the weather can turn nasty; it can quickly close in, or snow, and ferocious Atlantic gales frequently come rushing in. It is this very remoteness, however, which forms a great part of Iceland's attraction.

In planning any expedition into the mountains on foot, it is necessary to discover first what current conditions are like from either the Iceland Travel Association, Iceland Mountaineering Club, local hotel or even local farmer. Always err on the side of caution when packing, and take more than necessary rather than less. Have enough spare clothes, extra rations, and fuel to last, and an adequate supply of waterproof matches. There are not many trees in Iceland and it is a crime to chop them down for firewood, so fuel must be carried to heat food or water. There are suppliers of gas cylinders in all main centres, and most garages also stock them. It is also possible to get paraffin at a number of garages and obviously petroleum.

In many places you will have to camp on rock or very hard ground, so take suitable tent pegs — ones that will not buckle as they are being banged into the ground, and which can be retrieved when packing up. The weather can turn very quickly and gales can rush in from the sea, so extra guys are a good idea. The wind can also play havoc with attempts to cook. Unless you can get good shelter you will not get maximum use from your fuel if the wind is constantly blowing the flames about. A ridge tent or dome with an awning or extension is ideal for both storage and cooking.

If driving and camping weight is no problem, you can keep a lot of food in the vehicle. If you are backpacking you must always have emergency supplies to cover you for a couple of days, and stock up whenever you have the opportunity. There is a 10kg (22lb) limit on imported food (and some products are banned), but as food is expensive, it is sensible to bring in the staple and dearest items. Things like milk, cheese and bread are readily available and the bread lasts for days very well.

Most people prefer to use their own tried and tested equipment, but if you want to cut your weight down while travelling to and from Iceland, there are a number of camping suppliers.

It may be easier to participate in an organised walking holiday. In these, before the group arrives, advance food depots have been set up which not only means less to carry but also a more varied diet along the way. Groups must still be fit, however, and loads of 20kg (44lb) are normal.

The weather still catches many people unawares, especially the glare of the summer sun reflected off snow. Sunglasses are advisable as well as suntan cream and lip salve. In various parts of the country, especially around Lake Myvatn in August and early September, mosquito repellent is a good idea.

It is a good idea too to join the Youth Hostel Association and carry an International Card, if you are planning a walking holiday in Iceland. There are youth hostels to stay in, or mountain huts to make a change from canvas, and such a night indoors can be a welcome relief.

There are maps of the interior but they tend to be rather lacking in detail and too much reliance should not be placed on them. Efforts are now being made to produce accurate large scale maps of the most popular areas, and there are good map shops in all the towns. Being able to read a map is an important asset, and everyone should be able to use a compass. Often when the clouds close in, and visibility is nil, it is still possible to continue using the compass bearing. Remember, however, that compass variations will be greater in Iceland then countries further south. Almost every community has a campsite nearby, usually with toilet and water laid on, but not always. The campsites near large communities can usually be recognised by the toilet which is housed in a tall, steep-sided wooden hut, all roof and no walls. Some campsites are free, but a small charge is made at others and it is wise to enquire just in case.

Iceland is a magnificent country to explore. It is a harsh, rugged countryside which is at times daunting, but almost always magnificent. There can be few finer holidays than a week or two in Iceland with a rucksack and the freedom to go where you please. The only other essential item is a camera, and plenty of film. It is advisable to take as much film as you will require into Iceland with you because it is very expensive to buy locally. Further information on travelling in Iceland, sports and pastimes is available in the Fact File at the back of this guide book.

# 2
# REYKJAVÍK AND THE SOUTH-WEST

The first introduction to Iceland is **Keflavík**, important as the site of the international airport, as a trading centre, and for its closeness to the United States air base, which is part of NATO's North Atlantic command. In fact, until the new airport terminal was opened, one's first impression of the island was misleading, with American-style cinemas, social clubs and American spellings until the route to Reykjavík headed out into the typical Icelandic landscape. The thermal activity around Keflavík is evident as clouds of smoke and steam burst from fissures in the ground, and the smell of sulphur can be strong in the air.

Keflavík has been an important trading centre for at least 500 years. There are records that German traders landed on the coast here as early as 1500. Originally Keflavík was a series of farms owned by the Bishop of Skálholt and the name is recorded as far back as 1300. These church estates eventually passed to the Danish Crown. An early English record of 1540 reports that a merchant from Ipswich in England traded there from 1513, and the presence of the German traders is reflected in some of the Germanic names in the area. Keflavík received its first official trading licence in 1566 which was awarded to a German merchant from Hamburg called Jochim Thim, but trading powers reverted to Danish merchants after the Monopoly was introduced by the Danish king in 1602.

Keflavík achieved town status in 1949 and is currently enjoying a boom. It has become the second largest export port in Iceland, there is a flourishing fishing industry and many other industries. It has a population of well over 6,000 and there is an enormous amount of building going on, as there is in all the towns and villages in the south-west peninsula.

Keflavík has a hospital, a swimming pool, a sports ground, three hotels, cinema and many garages, shops and restaurants and an indoor sports hall. There is an interesting craft museum, the Vatnsnes, which shows the tools and equipment used by tradesmen and craftsmen of the area in the past.

For the 50km (30 mile) drive into Reykjavík, the road follows the southern shore of Hafnarfjördur along the northern shore of the

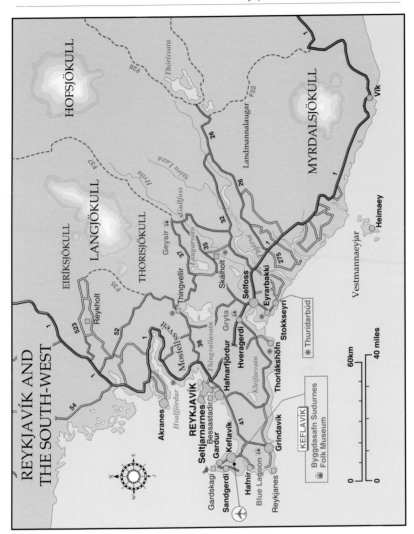

Reykjanes peninsula. This stretch of road is dual carriageway, a luxury in Iceland. On the landward side there is a huge grey gravelly lava desert, with huge piles of clinker-type rocks thrown up into strange shapes. Occasionally, there are mosses and lichens, but this is a treeless landscape looking very much like the aftermath of some massive open mining project. The landscape, however, shows just how new the country is, the rocks lie piled as they were heaved up from the ground, and the vegetation still has not had time to take a hold, although it becomes lusher as one nears Reykjavík.

One has still to remember that this is still an earthquake area — a continuation of the mid-Atlantic fault — and many of the lava domes and craters have huge cracks and fissures. There are a few scattered houses along the shores of the fjord, and it is a barren landscape inland — green and brown mosses and lichens and black lava. Occasionally there are patches of tufted rough grass, and for a few brief weeks, the scenery is brightened by clusters of wild purple lupins.

You can also spot some way from the road, wooden trellises which are used to dry the fish. Huge quantities of cod heads are still exported to Africa, and these can be spotted suspended from the wooden frames.

It is perhaps worth stopping off at the **Blue Lagoon**, just off the road from Keflavík to Reykjavík. There is no mistaking it, because on the other side of the natural lake, there is a power plant which harnesses all the free heat. A small hotel has now been built by the lagoon and there is a pathway down to the water. The water is a strange, almost cloudy blue, thick with all the chemicals coming up from below the ground with the rising water. It is not a good place to swim if you have open cuts, although the waters are said to be very beneficial for people with skin diseases. You can have a dip at the pool, and then take a shower before continuing your journey, or you could book into the hotel for a night to give you more time to explore this fascinating geological area.

The popularity of the Blue Lagoon is increasing and a growing number of people suffering from skin problems now fly to Iceland for treatment there. Facilities for the bathers, with changing rooms and showers, are constantly being improved, and a little sandy beach has now been created on the hotel side of the lagoon.

If you continue along Route 41 towards Reykjavík you can spot away to the right, one of the most recognisable features in southern Iceland, the cone of **Keilir**, which rises to almost 380m (1,246ft) beyond the stark lavafield of Strandarheidi.

Ahead and in the distance, are the huge red and white striped towers of the Straumsvík aluminium works, and beyond the first glimpses of Reykjavík across the water. The landscape starts to improve, there is more greenery, and horses, cattle and sheep graze. The road then skirts the fast growing town and port of Hafnarfjördur. You can turn off left here to visit Álftanes, the peninsula which houses the president's official residence at Bessastadir. Just before Hafnarfjördur, you can turn right on Route 42 which takes you south through the lava deserts and mountains into a very active geothermal area.

You can get out of your vehicle at Krísuvík, and walk around the jets of steam gushing from the ground, and the scalding hot, bubbling mud pools. There are signs warning you that the area is dangerous, and you must keep to the path. It is an exciting introduction to a country that is still shaping itself under your feet.

One of the first things you have to learn when travelling around in Iceland is that the atmosphere is so unpolluted, and the sunlight so intense, that even in bad weather, things always look much closer than they really are. It is quite possible to see 40 or 50km (25 or 30 miles) in good visibility, so when you start to see the multi-coloured roofs of Reykjavík, it still is a fair distance away. There has been a tremendous amount of building going on in the south-west, and all the major settlements around  Reykjavík are expanding fast.

**Reykjavík**, the smokeless city, is the most northerly capital in the world, lying north of the 64th parallel. It was the home of Iceland's first settler; when Ingólfur Arnarson landed on the southern shores of Faxa Bay in south-west Iceland in AD874 he made his way inland until he found a large lake and it was by this that he built his homestead. According to the Sagas when Ingólfur Arnarson first sighted land, he threw the religious 'pillars' overboard and swore that he would settle where they came ashore. Thus he came to the lake named Tjörnin (which literally means 'The Pond'). He must have been impressed by the geysers and hot steam pouring from the ground, and maybe it was because of this that he called the place Reykjavík, which means 'Smoky Bay'. Like many other things, the name conjures up a completely false impression. Iceland is not a land of ice, and Reykjavík is not smoky. In fact, because all heating and hot water is supplied naturally from deep in the ground, there is no need to burn fossil fuels, so Reykjavík is one of the most smoke-free cities in the world. The lake near which he settled is still in the centre of the city which now houses a third of the island's population.

The first sight of Reykjavík comes when approached from the international airport at Keflavík 30 miles away. Suddenly in the distance, across the bay, the multi-coloured roofs of Reykjavík can be seen. Corrugated iron is still the favourite roofing material in the town and residents paint them a host of colours which adds to the capital's charm.

Reykjavík is the heart of the country because within its boundaries and the surrounding towns, more than half the population of the country is to be found. The city houses the commercial, governmental and cultural life of the country and contains all the official government ministries, as well as the libraries and museums recording the country's heritage.

Reykjavík is a modern capital with skyscrapers, international standard hotels and restaurants, but it also has a remarkable old world charm and there are many old buildings which add to this character. It is a city full of contrast, from the bustling harbour and fishing port with its evocative smells and excellent fish restaurants, to the bustle of the modern shopping centre a short walk away.

The old centre has been carefully preserved, and many old buildings have been uprooted and rebuilt in the Folk Museum, in Arbaer, one of the  eastern suburbs. There is a surprising number of trees in Reykjavík, as well as ponds and lakes teeming with tame birdlife, many of the species considered rare in the British Isles, and gardens with neatly cut lawns and borders of brilliantly coloured flowers. The city sprawls leisurely around the bay, and despite the fact that it is the country's capital, there is an air of relaxation. The people of Reykjavík work hard and play hard. Many will visit one of the open-air swimming pools before breakfast, and it is not unusual to see elderly men and women in their 70s and 80s walking

*The Blue Lagoon*

around the pool in their swimming costumes even though the air temperature is only a few degrees above freezing. Many office workers go for a swim before going in to work and housewives will often call in to do a few lengths before going home to make breakfast for their families.

There are many lovely old buildings to see in Reykjavík including the Parliament House, built in 1881, and the old Government Building which dates from the mid-eighteenth century. Both are in the old centre of Reykjavík between the harbour and the lake. Nearby are the National Library and the National Theatre which are next to each other and close to the statue of Ingólfur Arnarson. Other sites worth visiting are the University, National Museum and Nordic House, which was designed by the world famous Finnish architect Alvar Aalto. There are many churches, including the old cathedral near to the Parliament House, and the towering new Hallgrímskirkja, the city's most recently built church. Reykjavík is also very proud of its Town Hall which is actually built on the lake.

The traditional buildings of Reykjavík are to be found in the Folk Museum at Árbaer. The open-air collection houses several old buildings as well as a fine old church and farmhouse, both turf-roofed, which date back to the beginning of this century.

Most of the older houses are built with wood, but cement is now being used widely in construction, especially for the large estates of flats which are now springing up. Iceland has a policy of promoting house-ownership, and very cheap loans are made available for families wishing to own their own property.

The best way to see Reykjavík is still on foot, although taxis and a regular bus service are available for the less mobile, or those wishing to go further afield. Taxis are plentiful and cheap and can be hailed in the street or ordered by telephone. All the top hotels have direct lines to the taxi companies. The cabs can be identified either because they have the word 'taxi' displayed, or they have a sign bearing the letter 'L' on a yellow background.

The main bus station is at Hlemmur, at the junction of Laugavegur, Hverfisgata and Raudarárstígur. There are frequent services both in and around the city. If you plan to spend some time in Reykjavík, it is a good idea to buy tickets in advance because it is cheaper. Bus stops are marked with the letters 'SVR'. There is only one fare on all routes, and the drivers are not allowed to give change. Discount tickets are available from the drivers and at Laekjargata, Hlemmur, Grensás and Borgartún 35. If you need more than one bus to get to your destination, ask the driver for a transfer ticket (*skiptimidi* in Icelandic and pronounced *skiptimithi*) when entering the first bus.

Parking in the centre of Reykjavík, as with any large city, can be a problem although there are car parks and parking meters. It is best to park on the outskirts, or leave your car in the hotel car park, and either walk or use public transport.

The harbour, where fishing boats are unloaded, can be visited, followed by the National Museum or the Árni Magnusson Institute, which houses  the priceless Saga manuscripts. A visit to the hot water storage tanks above the city gives remarkable views across Reykjavík and the bay beyond, with the towering Mount Esja in the background. There is no better sight than to watch the fishing boats return late in the evening with the midnight sun lighting the sky.

The oldest part of the city is between the Tjörnin Lake and the harbour and includes two squares, Austurvóllur and Laekjartorg. Further east, away from the sea can be found the shopping areas of Laugavegur and Austurstraeti, cinemas and theatres but everywhere can be reached on foot without any difficulty.

The city's oldest building is in Adalstraeti at number 10, and dates back  to 1752, thirty-four years before Reykjavík was granted city status. It was built originally as a weaving shed, and is now a restaurant and bar called Fógetinn, which means 'The Sheriff'. It was named after Skúli Magnússon (1711-94), whose statue stands at the corner of the street. As High Sheriff of Iceland he encouraged the development of craft industries, and almost all were centred on Adalstraeti, Bishop Geir Vídalín lived at number 10 from 1807-23 and has the distinction of being the only bishop to be declared bankrupt.

Another of the oldest surviving houses is Stjórnarrádid, in Laekjargata, built between 1761 and 1771 as a jail. It is now Government House,  accommodating the State Offices of the President and Prime Minister. It is worth walking to the rear of the building to see its attractive walled garden. There are many attractive old timber buildings overlooking the lake. These include two that have been converted into fine restaurants, and the Grammar School built in 1844, which also housed the Althing until the present Parliament building was opened. The school used to be approached by a bridge, which explains how the nearby Skólabrú (School Bridge) street gets its name.

The grey Parliament Building on Austurvöllur Square was finished in 1881, and is dominated by the statue of Jón Sigurdsson (1811-1879), one of the leaders in the island's fight for national independence. The statue is entitled *The pride of Iceland, its sword and shield*. The square is on the site of Ingólfur Arnarson's original farmstead and during road works in the spring of 1992, the old freshwater well was unearthed.

By the lake and just round the corner is the corrugated-clad Idnó building, originally the headquarters of a craftsmen's guild, and the home of the Reykjavík City Theatre Company from 1897 until it moved into its new premises in 1987.

There are also many old houses in Hafnarstraeti and Vesturgata, which together form the fourth side of the Old City. Many of these buildings  were originally owned by Danish merchants and there are a number of beautifully restored timber buildings dating from the mid-nineteenth century. One of them, Fálkahúsid in Hafnarstraeti, now houses the Icelandic Handicrafts Centre. It used to be where Icelandic falcons, the gyrfalcon, were kept before being sent to the court of the King of Denmark. Today the roof bears two impressive carvings of falcons, on either side of a Viking longboat. Next door, at Vesturgata 2 is a woollens shop, which stands over the site of the City Gate through which everyone arriving at the harbour had to enter.

Hafnarstraeti (Harbour Street) used to be on the water's edge, but is now separated from it by Tryggvagta, which was built on land reclaimed from the sea by infilling. The large mosaic mural decorating the Tax Office was created by Gerdur Helgadóttir.

Anyone with a head for heights has to go to the top of the 75m (246ft) tall spire of Hallgrímskirkja on Skólavörduholt. There is a lift to the top of this imposing twentieth-century church and the panoramic views from the top on a clear day are breathtaking.

In front of the church stands the statue of Leifur Eríksson, the first European to set foot in the New World. The statue was a gift from the USA to celebrate the 1,000th anniversary of Iceland's Parliament. The newest observation post in Reykjavík is the huge glass dome of the Perlan (Pearl) which dominates the skyline. The revolving restaurant on Oskjuhlíd hill, an island formed only 10,000 years ago, stands on top of the tanks which hold hot water pumped from deep underground before it is piped around the city. Beside the restaurant there are exhibitions on the ground floor and a 'mechanical' geysir that erupts at regular intervals alongside the huge central staircase.

The City Hall opened in of 1992. It stands beside and extends into the lake, and apart from its administrative function, it also houses exhibitions. There is a café and excellent close-up views of the birds on the lake.

The Nordic House, on the edge of the university campus, has a library and permanent exhibition devoted to the Nordic way of life. It also stages concerts and film shows, and has a café. It was designed by Finnish architect Alvar Aalto in 1961.

Other places worth visiting are the Arbaer Folk Museum, a sprawling open-air museum on the city outskirts in which one can find many old buildings. Most come from Reykjavík but others have been brought from all over Iceland. They were carefully dismantled, transported and rebuilt

*The statue of Ingólfur Arnarson near Reykjavík harbour*

after restoration. There is an interesting turf-roofed wooden and stone church from the nearby town of Hafnarfjördur. In the summer the museum hosts a number of displays and exhibitions featuring traditional crafts and skills. Arnarhóll, which means Eagle's Mound, is near Laekjartorg, and has an imposing statue of Ingólfur Arnarson looking out to sea.

The Arni Magnússon Institute at Arnagardur, houses Iceland's Manuscript Institute, and is named after the eighteenth-century Secretary of the Danish Royal Archives. He spent ten years in Iceland (1702-12) collecting thousands of old manuscripts, most of which were destroyed when fire swept through the University in Copenhagen where they were stored. On 21 April 1971, the surviving manuscripts were returned by Denmark to Iceland and the Institute, specially built to house them.

The National Library, on Hverfisgata, was built between 1906 and 1908, and was the first Icelandic building made entirely by Icelandic craftsmen. It started out as a store for ice cut from the lake which was needed for fish processing. In the 1960s it was a nightclub but it burned down in 1971 and lay derelict for ten years, until being rebuilt by the Government to house the State art collection, formerly held in the National Museum.

The National Museum of Iceland was founded in 1863 originally as the Museum of Antiquities. The first exhibits to be registered were grave gods discovered in a richly furnished Viking grave discovered on a farm near Myvatn in 1860. A campaign was immediately launched for somewhere to house them and the idea of the National Museum was born. The museum moved to its present home on Hringbraut, in 1950. The museum is on two floors, the ground floor housing exhibits from around the world, and items from Iceland's nautical and agricultural past, as well as many models, while on the first floor there are exhibits from Iceland's Viking period and many religious relics. The most famous exhibit is the carved door from Valthjófsstadie which dates from around 1200. It is one of the finest examples of ancient North European wood carving and depicts a mounted warrior slaying a dragon. The door is thought to have been made for a nobleman's home, before being used as a church door. There is a guide in English available which is worth buying, as not all the exhibits are clearly explained in English.

The Asgrimur Jónsson Gallery is an exhibition of paintings by one of Iceland's greatest artists. Born in 1876 he showed so much promise that the Icelandic Government gave him a grant to study in Italy. He was Iceland's first major landscape painter but was increasingly influenced by the impressionists. The exhibition is in his house in Bergstadastraeti, which he left to the nation.

The Ásmundur Sveinsson sculptures are exhibited both inside and outside the artist's home which is now a museum. Sveinsson (1893-1983) started as a wood carver but after training in Copenhagen and Paris turned to sculptures with concrete as a favourite medium. It is impossible to miss the museum because it resembles a giant igloo and was designed by the artist. In later years he worked with metal and many of his mobiles are exhibited here as well. He was a prolific sculptor and many of his abstract sculptures in concrete adorn the city's parks. It is sometimes possible to visit the sculptor's studio. As opening times vary, consult the tourist office first. The sculptor's museum is not to be confused with Ásmundur Sveinsson House in Freyjugata, which was designed by the artist in the mid-1930s and caused quite a stir because of its unusual appearance. Today it does not even cause eyebrows to be raised and it is the home of the Association of Icelandic Architects who stage art exhibitions there.

The Einar Jónsson Museum also houses a large collection of sculptures in the original home of the artist. Regarded as Iceland's leading modern sculptor, he specialised in religious and political themes, and his most visible work is the statue of Jón Siigurdsson. The artist designed the cube-shaped building and a grant from the Government allowed him to build it and work there.

Also worth visiting is the only Catholic church in Iceland, and Dómkirkjan, the Lutheran cathedral. At the end of the eighteenth century, when the Danish king abolished the Catholic bishoprics in Iceland, he established a single Lutheran diocese centred on Reykjavík, and ordered the cathedral to be built. It has undergone considerable renovation in recent years, not all for the better.

The Maritime Museum housed an interesting exhibition of boat-building through the ages, there is an exhibition of textiles, many with religious themes, at the small Kirkjumunir museum in Kirkjustraeti, and the Kjarvalsstadir art gallery displaying the works of Jóhannes Kjarval, in the Miklatún Park, is worth a visit.

The Natural History Museum at Hlemmtorg is small but houses an interesting collection of Icelandic flora and fauna, including a specimen of the extinct Great Auk. The Botanical Gardens are also worth visiting if you are interested in plants. The gardens house around two-thirds of all the plants found growing naturally in the country.

Other things to see are the Numismatic Museum, a collection of coins, decorations and books in Einholt, and the Post and Telecommunications History Museum covering the history of telecommunications on the island. For a flavour of Iceland try to catch a summer performance of *Light Nights*, Iceland's longest running theatre production. The first performance was in 1970 and it is still going strong. It is a mixture of live theatre and audio visual presentations which tell of Iceland's history, music and folklore. The other highly recommended production is *The Volcano Show*, staged every summer in Hellesund. It is a 2½ hour long award-winning film about volcanoes and nature, and it features many of Iceland's recent eruptions, including the birth of Surtsey. The films are screened twice daily in English.

Reykjavík and area has a number of excellent swimming pools, the two most convenient are Sundlaug Vesturbaejar and Sundlaugrar Reykjavíkur. Both are heated with water from natural hot springs and have sauna and sunbathing facilities.

*Hotel Borg in Posthstræti, Reykjavík*

*Hateigskirkja, Reykjavík*

Public toilets are not common in Reykjavík but they are available at Bankastraeti, about forty yards or so from Laekjartorg Square, at Hlemmur bus station, in the pedestrian tunnel under Miklabraut at Lang-ahlíd, on the south-east corner of Miklatún, and in the Hljómskálagardur park, just to the south of Tjörnin.

The tourist information centre at Bankastraeti 2 is open from 8.30am to 6pm Monday to Fridays, from 8.30am to 2pm on Saturdays, and 10am to 2pm on Sundays during the summer. It has a large collection of videos about the island and its mini-cinema where you can view them. There is also a tourist information desk in City Hall. There is an English language monthly newspaper, *News from Iceland* which gives details of news and events, and you can even take out a subscription to have it delivered when you get home.

When driving or travelling around the country, look out for the 'i' for information sign, where you can get advice on local sights, campsites, accommodation and so on.

There are two professional theatres, an opera house, ten cinemas and a biennial art festival. There is also a film festival, and several fine galleries. For nature lovers there are many fine walks in and around the city which enable you to see the country's rich birdlife at close hand. Another source of surprise to visitors is that one of the best salmon rivers in Iceland runs through the centre of the city.

Reykjavík's top hotels are of the highest standards and you pay accordingly. Rooms are usually very spacious and well appointed but be wary of the well stocked mini-bars — a binge could seriously damage your wallet. A list of accommodation can be found in the additional information section at the end of this chapter and a full list of boarding houses and private houses offering accommodation can be obtained from the tourist office.

There are more than eighty fine restaurants in Reykjavík serving many of the country's speciality dishes. Some of the best fish in the world can be tried at the restaurants around the harbour.

The cuisine of Iceland tends to be international, especially in the bigger hotels but there are many local dishes which should be tried. The local salmon and trout are, of course, magnificent and can be served in a variety of ways. Herring, too, come in many preserves and flavours. Then there are shrimps and small lobsters which are caught off the south coast. You must try *graflax*, raw salmon pressed with special herbs, and quite delicious, and Iceland's cheap caviare.

It is not surprising that lamb and mutton figure largely in the diet because there are so many sheep on the island. One traditional dish is smoked mutton called *hangikjöt*, and another, *svid*, calls for a tougher constitution. It is a whole sheep's head which has been boiled, and it is usually presented complete on a plate. Although not a pretty sight, and quite a challenge to eat, it is worth the effort.

Ptarmigan, the island's most prolific game bird, is served in a rich sauce, and the dish is called *rjúpa*. *Thorramatur* on the menu usually means pickled meats, while dried fish is served as *hardfiskur*. Also worth trying, especially for breakfast is *skyr*, a sour yoghurt that is eaten with sugar and cream.

Two other specialities are raw shark, known as *hákarl*, and *hverabraud*, a ryebread baked in the ground in the heat of the thermal soil. There are many stories about how *hákarl* is prepared, and most are enough to put you off the dish, but it is a delicacy worth trying. Because the country lies in the path of the Gulf Stream many sharks can be found off the coast. When one is caught and killed, it is buried in the ground and the position marked. After a certain length of time, the fish is dug up and strips of the raw flesh eaten. It has a most unpleasant smell but does taste delicious, even though to some this may be an acquired taste.

Most restaurants and hotels will serve wine with the meal, and cocktails and spirits before and after. Strong beer is now available, although low alcohol or alcohol-free beer is more widely on sale. The island's home brew is a fiery spirit known as *brennivín*, which is also affectionately called Black Death. A measure of *brennivín* in the beer can be a wonderful pick-me-up, while two or three are likely to knock you down. Hotels and restaurants in the capital normally serve alcohol from noon to 2.30pm and from 7pm to closing time which is around midnight. The cocktail bars of the bigger hotels will stay open later. Pubs are becoming more popular, the first one opening in 1985. They are more like wine bars, but you can get food as well as beer, wine and spirits. They are good places to meet and many have live music. Most have dress codes and employ doormen to enforce them, and almost all stay open very late.

Leaving Reykjavík, other places of interest to visit in the south-west area of Iceland include **Bessastadir**, in Álftanes; this is the official residence of the President of Iceland. It once belonged to Snorri Sturluson, but the estate later became the property of the Crown and the residence of the Danish Governor. For a time it was the seat of higher education in the country but has been the presidential residence since Iceland became a republic in 1944. The magnificent white buildings are among the oldest in Iceland, some dating back to 1763, and the fine old church, also painted white, is well worth a visit.

**Heidmörk**, to the east of the capital, is a public park that actually belongs to Reykjavík. Although the capital has many trees and bushes, they are not so common outside urban areas, and the park is a popular place for people seeking a little peace. The grounds contain a large number of different species of bushes.

**Krísuvík** is 36km (21 miles) south of Reykjavík, and it is an interesting area of hot springs. A long time ago there used to be a sulphur mine there. It is now surrounded by lavafields which give the impression of a very lunar landscape.

**Hvalfjördur**, to the north of the capital, is the longest fjord in the south-west. It is very deep, and served as a naval base for the Allies during World War II, although the base has now been demolished. Iceland's only whaling station is situated in Hvalfjördur and the landing and cutting of whales has been a great attraction during the summer, with coachloads of visitors arriving from Reykjavík. The future of the station is now in doubt because Iceland, as a party to the international whaling agreement, has decided to stop whaling. The whaling station may be converted so that it can be used for other forms of fish processing, or it may be left as it is, as a museum to an industry which is fast disappearing.

**Akranes** is one of the largest fishing ports in the country and also has the only cement factory in Iceland. There is a daily ferry boat connection with Reykjavík, and the town has hotels, guest houses, restaurants and a camping site at Gardabraut. There is a tourist information centre, hospital, swimming pool, indoor sports stadium, a cinema and a folk museum. There is also a fine sandy beach and a golf course.

**Thingvellir**, 50km (31 miles) to the east of Reykjavík, is the national shrine of Iceland, its most historic site, and one of its most beautiful places. The oldest existing parliament in the world first met here in AD930. The Althing met here every year to enact laws, including the law passed in AD1000 to introduce Christianity into the island. It has always been the focal point for the country, and whenever a major event is to be celebrated, thousands of people come here. At the celebration of the 1,100th anniversary of the first settlement on Iceland in 1974, more than 60,000 people packed into Thingvellir.

Nearby Lögberg is the cliff overlooking the place where the Althing (assembly) met, and speakers stood to address the gatherings from this point. Nearby is Drekkingarhylur, the drowning pool, where mothers of illegitimate children were drowned. It is sited in the river in Almannagjá, a lava gorge, which with the Oxarárfoss waterfall, is an impressive sight.

Peningagjá is the Money Chasm, and people still throw coins into the clear waters. The coins give off strange reflections as they drop through the water, but it is said that if you can follow your coin all the way down until it comes to rest on the bottom, your wish will come true.

There is an old church at Thingvellir, and the pastor is also warden of the national park, which covers part of the area. Beside the church is the national burial ground.

**Thingvallavatn** is the largest lake in Iceland 83sq km (32sq miles) and 100m (328ft) deep, and nearby is Valhöll, a hotel and excellent restaurant that is open for the summer months only.

A few miles to the east of Thingvellir is **Laugarvatn**, an education centre beside a lovely lake of the same name. During the summer months, the schools become hotels and the area is a popular tourist resort. One of the main attractions is the natural hot water saunas. There is a small changing room, where for a few pence you can strip and shower before walking to the wooden sauna cubicles. There are very strict hygiene standards in Iceland and it is compulsory to shower before entering any swimming pool or sauna. The saunas stand side by side; one is hot and the other very hot. The most hardy prefer to have a sauna and then plunge into the very cold lake. However, it is as well to note that the saunas can be quite overpowering, if you are not used to them, be careful at first. The area has also become very popular as a centre for pony trekking, and you can ride to the attractions if you like.

**Gullfoss**, the 'Golden Waterfall' east of Laugarvatn, is the best-known waterfall in Iceland, and it is spectacular on a sunny day. It is 32m (100ft) high and the spray splashes up into the sky so that if the sun is shining, it produces a beautiful rainbow. Perhaps the only problem with Gullfoss is photographing. There is a small monument at the fall to Iceland's first conservationist, Sigrídur Tómasdóttir, a farmer's wife who successfully resisted attempts to have the watercourse altered. She looks out today at the falls she saved, and the foaming glacier river Huítá tumbling into the deep gorge below.

**Geysir**, 30km (18½ miles) south-east of Laugarvatn, at Haukadalur, gave the world the word geyser. It can send up columns of water 60m (200ft) high. For many years it was inactive, but as previously mentioned, the warden of the area has found a way of persuading it to come to life, by throwing bars of carbolic soap into the bubbling crater. It is an incredible sight. Gradually, as more soap is thrown in, the water in the mouth of the crater begins to bubble more vigorously, and a great deal of foam is created. The bubbles get bigger and bigger until they form spouts into the air, and then suddenly with a roaring rush, the geyser flings its water column upwards.

Close by is **Strokkur**, a much smaller but very active geyser, which constantly bubbles and spouts. A great achievement with Strokkur is to photograph it just before it spouts. The crater gradually fills with water

*(Opposite) Gullfoss is considered to be Iceland's finest waterfall*

*Gullfoss in winter*

until it is level with the top. Then the pressure from below forces the surface water upwards forming a bubble, and the trick is to photograph it just before the bubble bursts and the water is sent shooting upwards. There is a hotel near the geysers, as well as a garage and snack bar.

A good way of seeing all these sights, if you do not have your own transport, is to take a bus from Reykjavík. There are daily round trips, both guided and unguided, from the capital taking in both Gullfoss and Geysir; some trips visit Thingvellir as well.

**Skálholt**, to the south-east of Laugarvatn, is steeped in history. It was the greatest centre for learning in Old Iceland, and was the episcopal seat for southern Iceland from 1056 to 1796. All that remains of these times, however, is a tunnel that ran from the old church and farm to the school. There is now a new church on the site.

A detour up the Thjórsárdalur is rewarding. A farm from the times of the Sagas has been reconstructed based on the ruins of the nearby Stöng farmstead, which was destroyed when Mount Hekla erupted in 1100. Nearby is the Búrfell hydro-electric power station with good views of Mount Hekla.

Back at the coast, **Seltjarnarnes** lies alongside Reykjavík and attained municipal status in 1974. There is some industry (mostly fishing), but it is really a dormitory town for the capital. There is a large sports hall, swimming pool and community centre.

**Mosfellssveit** has developed a great deal in the last few years, as residents of Reykjavík have moved out to build larger houses and apartments. Again, it is mostly a dormitory town supplying the capital with workers, although there is some industry, notably the Álafoss factories which produce woollen goods.

**Kópavogur** has grown faster than any other town in Iceland. There were few buildings before the last war, but today there are buildings everywhere and it is a thriving community. A new civic centre is being built and there are cinemas, swimming pool and a disco.

Between Kópavogur and Hafnarfjördur is **Gardabaer**, most of whose residents work in the capital. The town does have a shipbuilding yard, as well as metal and chemical industries. The landscape of Gardabaer is very varied, and the old lava that once flowed from Búrfell to the sea has taken on strange forms.

**Hafnarfjördur**, a fishing port, is the home port of many trawlers. The fishing industry is the basis of its inhabitants' employment, although a number of other industries have sprung up. The town is located on a fjord which provides an excellent natural harbour. The volcano Búrfell, about 5km (3 miles) east of the fjord, erupted 7,000 years ago. The lava flowed along the northern side of the fjord forming a high, sheltering wall, Hamarinn, creating a natural harbour.

At the beginning of the fifteenth century, the English started to trade with Icelanders. Hafnarfjördur became an English trading port and remained so for about three-quarters of a century, as it had one of the best harbours in the south-west part of Iceland, and there were rich fishing banks just off the coast. German merchants then started to compete with the English for special rights and facilities in Hafnarfjördur, and there are accounts of a battle between the two groups in the town, which ended with a German victory. After this, the Germans were virtually in full control of Hafnarfjördur. They built houses, commercial buildings and a church.

At the beginning of the seventeenth century the Danish king issued a decree to the effect that only Danish subjects with special trade licences could trade with Iceland. The Danish trade monopoly was in force until the year 1787 — almost two centuries. Some enterprises founded then still existed in the town when it was given municipal rights in the year 1908, although by then, most had passed into the ownership of Icelanders. In the early nineteenth century Bjarni Sivertsen established a shipyard which prospered and he is regarded as the 'father' of Hafnarfjördur. His house, built in 1803, has been faithfully preserved and now forms part of the town museum.

Near Hafnarfjördur and towards the hot springs area in Krísuvík, there are three lavafields created by separate eruptions. First is the Hvaleyrar lavafield, whose exact age has not yet been determined. Next is a younger field of lava which flowed about 2,200 years ago, cooling off and solidifying before it managed to reach the sea, called Óbrynnishólabruni. Then a low mountain range called Undirhlídar comes into view. The road goes through a pass in the range, called Vatnaskard. On the hillsides are extinct craters from a volcanic eruption in the period following the settlement of the country, and the new lava flowed from there over the older lavafield, Óbrynnishólabruni, and all the way into the sea at Straumsvík on the coast south of Hafnarfjördur. There the lava-flow formed a wall, creating a sheltered natural harbour, in much the same way as the harbour at Hafnarfjördur was formed. This lavafield is called Kapelluhraun and derives its name from a chapel built there in Catholic times in honour of St Barbara. Past Vatnaskard is the Lake Kleifarvatn. Brooks from the surrounding hills empty into it, but no outlet is visible.

Close to Hafnarfjördur is the aluminium factory in **Straumsvík**, which is Swiss-owned and which imports its raw materials from Australia. The huge red and white striped towers of the plant can be seen from Reykjavík quite clearly on good days. There is also a factory producing electrical appliances, the only one of its kind in Iceland. Hafnarfjördur makes an interesting day out. The waterfront area with its old houses and the strange lava formations are worth visiting, together with the Hellisgerdi Park and ornamental gardens. There is a guesthouse and several restaurants and pubs.

**Vogar** is a small fishing town which, with surrounding **Vatnsleysus-trönd**, has a population of just a few hundred. South-east of Vogar is an ancient sheep shelter, one of the largest and most spectacular in Iceland.

**Njardvík**, is another town whose roots are firmly in the fishing industry. The town is divided into two parts Inner and Outer Njardvik. There is a very unusual church, triangular in shape, which was consecrated in Outer Njardvik in 1979. The church in Inner Njardvik is made of stone and was built in 1886. It has a good harbour and many fishing-related industries, as does **Gardur**, which also boasts one of the island's best golf courses. At **Gardskagi**, at the northern tip of the peninsula, there is a very varied birdlife, so it is a good place for ornithologists, while nearby **Sandgerdi** is another small fishing village. South of the village lies **Básendar**, Iceland's most important commercial harbour until it was destroyed in a great flood in 1799.

**Hafnir** is a small village standing on the banks of Ósbotnar, a small bay. It is especially well worth visiting, because it can trace its roots back for centuries. South of Hafnir are towering cliffs, home to tens of thousands of birds.

**Grindavík**, on the southern coast of the Reykjanes peninsula, is a bustling fishing port, and fishing accounts for most of its livelihood. There is a community centre, health care centre, and, of course, a swimming pool. It was granted municipal rights in 1974. The town is a good base to explore the area and coastline, with its rich birdlife, and the Reykjanes National Park. There is a campsite and guesthouse, and a café near the harbour where you can mingle with the fishermen. Nearby is a statue called *Hope*, which shows a fisherman's family looking out to sea awaiting his homecoming. Close to Grindavik is the Blue Lagoon, famous for its

*The Strokkur geyser (below and opposite) is the most active in the world*

mineral waters with healing powers. The waters are pumped from sources 1,646m (5,300ft) below ground.

**Thorlákshöfn** is a town whose population used to swell dramatically during the fishing season. For centuries, farmers would leave their homesteads during the summer, and move to Thorlákshöfn to fish. It was not unusual for people to have two jobs, and many fishermen have alternative employment to tide them over the periods when they cannot go to sea. Many fishing boats still use this port because it has one of the best harbours in the south.

North of here **Hveragerdi** is one of the country's largest and most famous hot springs areas, particularly useful as it is so close to Reykjavík. The geyser Gryta spouts every 2 hours without fail. Most employment in this area is based around horticulture and there are many greenhouses, which use the natural hot water for heating.

The town is popular with tourists and has a hotel, swimming pool and health resort. The national agricultural college is also sited here. The town can trace its origins back to the founding of a wool processing factory at Reykjafoss in Varmá. The first electric generator to be used east of Hellisheidi was installed at the water falls in 1906. The first greenhouses were erected in 1929 growing a wide range of crops, mostly salad vegetables, but even bananas have been grown. A visit to the Eden Garden Centre, a massive complex housing greenhouses, gift shops and cafés makes a pleasant excursion.

**Selfoss** is the largest town on the south coast, although in fact it is about 15km (9 miles) inland. It is an industrial and commercial centre, and the centre for one of the most fertile farming districts in the country: it has the largest dairy farm in Iceland. There are good sports facilities, with both an indoor and outdoor pool, a hotel, restaurant, cinema and museums.

The south coast's main harbour for many years was **Eyrarbakki**, and fishing is still the main occupation, although the population is decreasing. One of the country's oldest buildings can be found here, to the east of the church, Húsid built in 1765, is the former home of a Danish merchant. In the town are many old wooden buildings. The beach is noted for its beauty and surf, and it is a good area for bird watching. Another notable beach may be found at **Stokkseyri**, another fishing and agricultural centre. Close to the village there is an interesting folk museum, Rjómabúid.

## Tour of the South-West and South, by Car

Many places in the south and south-west can be visited within a day from Reykjavík if necessary, but there are enough hotels and hostels to allow frequent halts, if so desired.

Follow the main road out of the capital, to a fork as the road climbs up onto Hellisheidi. The road to the right leads down into Ölfus and to Thorlákshöfn. Just before the latter, there is a crossroads. A left turn follows Ölfus Way to rejoin the main road to Hveragerdi. A right turn

leads to Selvogur, a curious, sparsely populated area. Strandakirkja at ⌂
Engilsvík is worth a visit. From Selvogur there is a route back to Reykjavík
via the hot springs at Krísuvík and along the shores of Lake Kleifarvatn,
or you can continue along the coast to Grindavík.

From the crossroads at Ölfus, it is a straight road to Thorlákshöfn, a
fairly young fishing town, with a good harbour, and from where the daily
ferry sails to the Vestmannaeyjar (Westman Islands).

From the fork on the lower slopes of Hellisheidi, the main road branches
left up Hveradalir over the top of Hellisheidi (374m, 1,227ft) and down to
Kambar to Hveragerdi, with its hothouses heated by the thermal springs.
Reykir Horticultural College is situated above the river Varmá. There is a ✳
hotel, and the unique Eden Garden Centre. Here bananas and other
tropical fruits are grown under glass, as well as horticultural and salad
crops and flowers.

From Hveragerdi, continue along the main road, skirting the southern
slopes of Ingólfsfjall (551m, 1,808ft) and on to Selfoss. The bridge over
Ölfusá is quite new, because the original, built in 1891, was destroyed
when it collapsed under the weight of two lorries in 1944. **Selfoss** is a
market town and its first house, Tryggvaskáli, built in 1890, is still standing, just east of the bridge. The river Ölfusá with its rapids and deep pools
is the pride of the town. There are two filling stations, hospital, campsite,
museum and art gallery, swimming pool and supermarket, and two 🏛
hotels. The Hotel Selfoss has a very good restaurant, and a very noisy
Saturday night disco, although it must be said the local youth do not start
to party until midnight. It is a good base to explore the area of hot springs to
the north of the town, and as it is the last major settlement along the southern
coast before Höfn, it is a good idea to stock up with the essentials, especially
if you are planning to spend some time at Skaftafell National Park.

South of Selfoss are two fishing villages, Eyrarbakki, which has a well
preserved Danish merchant's house, dating back to 1765, and Stokkseyri
which has converted an old fisherman's hostel into a museum. 🏛

Back over the bridge at Selfoss, towards Reykjavík, a right turn leads
past Ingólfsfjall. A left turn at the bridge over Sog goes through
Grafningur and west of Lake Thingvallavatn to Thingvellir, via the hydro-electric station at Ljósifoss, and Steingrímsstöd then east of the lake.

**Thingvellir** is the most historically significant place in Iceland, also the ⚐
site of the lava gorge of Almannagjá, the waterfall Öxarárfoss, and the old
farm and the church, all within easy reach of Hotel Valhöll. In the distance
one can see a mountain range. Lake Thingvallavatn is the largest in the
country.

From Thingvellir routes lead across Mosfellsheidi to Reykjavík, or east
via Gjábakki to Laugarvatn, or north by a mountain road over Uxahryggir
to Lundarreykjadalur or through Kaldidalur between Ok and Langjökull
to Húsafell in Borgarfjördur in west Iceland. Along the Grímsnes road ⚐
from Selfoss is Kerid, which is well worth a visit; a lake in an extinct
explosion crater.

A left turn at Svínavatn leads to Laugarvatn with its boarding schools, used for summer hotels, and its natural sauna pools. From Laugarvatn either follow the summer road to Thingvellir via Gjábakki, or drive up Langárdalur, over the river Brúará and on to Gullfoss and Geysir, Iceland's two most celebrated tourist attractions.

Haukadalur, the site of an ancient school, is just north of Geysir. There is a mountain road from Gullfoss which leads north with the Lake Hvítárvatn on the left and Kerlingarfjöll mountain range on the right. There is a summer ski school at Ásgardur in Kerlingarfjöll. The Icelandic Touring Club has a hut there and at Hvítárnes. The road continues up Kjölur between two glaciers, Langjökull and Hofsjökull, to Hveravellir where there is a touring club hut, hot springs and a swimming pool.

Instead of taking the Laugarvatn turn-off, the Grímsnes road near the river Brúará goes to **Skálholt**, which was a bishop's seat from 1056 to 1784 and for centuries the site of an important school. Recent decades have seen some of its former functions re-established. There is now a church there, and a folk museum. Among the relics from former times is Bishop Páll Jónsson's tomb dating from 1211.

East from Skálholt, a road leads over the river Brúará to join the Skeid-Hreppar road. A little to the west of Skálholt there is the Biskupstungur road which also leads to Geysir and Gullfoss via Aratunga where there is a restaurant open during the summer. East from Selfoss and left on to the Skeid-Hreppar road leads to the Skálholt road, then to the route for Gnúpverjahreppur and Thjórsárdalur. A number of farms were buried in ash during the Hekla eruption of 1104 and one of them, Stöng, has been excavated. Further down the valley, one can see a reconstruction of the same historical farm, Skeljastadir, which was built in 1974, at the time of 1100th anniversary celebrations. The country's largest hydro-electric power station is in Thjórsárdalur at Búrfell (not to be confused with Búrfell near Hafnafjördur). It harnesses the Thjórsá river. There are several beautiful waterfalls in the valley; one of them, Háifoss, is 122m (400ft) high. The road continues up and out of Thjórsárdalur across a fairly new bridge at Sandafell. From there it goes north to the hydro-electric power stations at Sigalda and Hrauneyjarfoss on the river Tungná.

A mountain road runs north across Sigalda, a range of hills on the edge of Sprengisandur. The road goes west of **Thórisvatn** which, at 70sq km (27sq miles), is the second largest lake in Iceland. There is a wonderful view of the glaciers Vatnajökull, Hofsjökull and Langjökull. The Icelandic Touring Club has a hut on this route which is situated in Nyidalur, southwest of Tungnafellsjökull, at 800m (2,624ft) above sea level. From Nyidalur it is possible to drive to Tómasarhagi, Fjórdungsalda and the north.

At Hreppar, instead of heading for Thjórsárdalur, drive north, crossing the river Stóra-Laxá to **Hrunamannahreppur**, an administrative district containing the settlements of Hreppholar, Flúdir and Hruni. Flúdir is an excellent place to stop for a meal of magnificent fish served by girls in national costume. There is also a residential school used as a summer hotel. From Flúdir, a road leads to the river Hvítá, which is crossed at Bruárhlöd, and then on a short distance to Gullfoss and Geysir and then back to Reykjavík.

Eastwards along the main road (No 1) is Iceland's longest river, Thjórsá, 230km (143 miles) long. Most of the river's water comes from Hofsjökull. South of Arnarfell, the river branches into several streams which cross a grassy plain known as Thjórsárver, which has the world's largest nesting colony of pink-footed geese. Thjórsá was first bridged in 1895. From here you can drive towards Hekla, the country's most famous volcano. Hekla is surrounded by lava sandmash and pumice. The last major eruption was in 1947-8 but there have been minor eruptions in 1970, 1980 and 1982.

The waterfalls Tröllkonuhlaup and Thjófafoss can be seen on the river Thjórsá near Búrfell, and the striking Fossabrekkur rapids on the river Ytri-Rangá. If Thjórsá is followed north, the road eventually joins the road leading to Sigalda. Before Sigalda is reached, however, a right turn leads to Landmannalaugar. There are hot streams to bathe in and a landscape with an unbelievable range of colours. The Icelandic Touring Club has a hut there and there is a campsite.

The road east from Landmannalaugar, called the North Mountain Road, passes many beauty spots, such as Eldgjá and Ófærufoss. There is another mountain route which travels farther south, nearer the Myrdals-jökull glacier, but it has to be approached from Rangárvellir, via Hvanngil and Maelifellssandur.

Another route is north across the river Tungná from Landmannalaugar

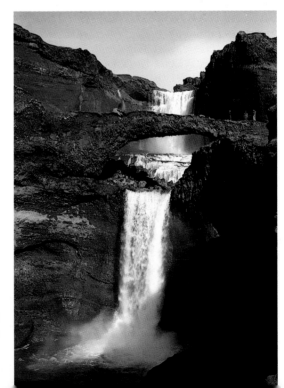

*Natural bridge and waterfall at Ófærufoss*

and then turn right just south of Thórisvatn. This leads to the Fishing Lakes, Veidivötn, an area of outstanding natural beauty. There is an Icelandic Touring Club hut at Tjaldvatn and it is quite easy to spend a couple of days walking around. There is also a mountain road up to another Icelandic Touring Club hut at Jökulheimar, on the western slopes of Vatnajökull.

The main road east from Vegamót leads to Raudilaekur and then Thykkvibaer, a village which dates back to the early settlers. Just west of the bridge over the Ytri-Rangá there is another farm of historical interest called Aegissída. There are twelve caves under one of the fields, with writing and symbols on the walls that have led some to believe that they were former dwelling places of Irish monks who inhabited Iceland before the arrival of the first Norsemen.

East of the Rangá bridge lies **Hella**, which has grown steadily since it became a trading centre in 1927. Being a market town, it has a wide range of services including guest house, restaurant and a campsite and it is possible to tour the area on a pony from a trekking centre. East of Hella are the farms Gunnarsholt and Keldur. The former is an experimental farm and plays a leading role in land reclamation projects, while the latter has a farmhouse dating back to 1200, the oldest building in Iceland. The road via these farms is only suitable for four-wheel drive vehicles.

Other interesting places in the Rangárvellir area are the wooded district of Hvannteigur and Oddi, one of the most famous farms in the country's history, where Saemundur the Learned founded his school in the Middle Ages. Saemundur's grandson Jón Loftsson, who died in 1197, was like an uncrowned king.

The next town on the route is **Hvolsvöllur**, with its restaurant, guest house, campsite and a range of other services. Hvolsvöllur is the business centre for the middle of Rangárvallasysla county, and again agriculture and allied industries is the main employer. From here many places familiar to Saga readers are within driving distance — for example, Hlídarendi, Gunnar Hámundarson's farm. There is an experimental arable farm at Sámsstadir which has specialised in corn growing since 1927, and a tree nursery at Tumastadir, founded in 1947.

Further up the valley is the farm Múlakot with its magnificent tree garden, and many waterfalls. The last farm in the valley has a youth hostel in an old farmhouse. There are also views of the glaciers and the highest mountain peaks in southern Iceland, and the Thórsmörk nature reserve, which has a campsite and hut accommodation. To reach it, drive east from Hvolsvöllur across the bridge over the Markarfljót, and then turn immediately left. There are several difficult rivers to cross on the way, including Krossá. The best way is by organised trip or with your own guide. A mountain road leads east from Fljótshlíd behind the glaciers to Skaftafellssysla. It is the continuation of the Thorsmörk road and is only suitable for four-wheel drive vehicles. The whole of this area is of interest to the backpacker or long distance walker, and there are interesting routes to Landmannalaugar and to Skógar, via Fimmvörduháls.

East of the main road from Markarfljót bridge, there is Eyjafjallajökull on the left and flat farmland on the right. This road leads to the waterfalls Gljúfrabúi and Seljalandsfoss, and another excellent place to stop. Nearby are caves which feature in the legends of Iceland, and one of them, near Fit Farm, is mentioned in the story of Anna from Stóruborg. Another is called Steinahellir, a short distance east of Holtsós. There is an open-air swimming pool at Seljavellir, fed from a warm spring. Travelling along the foot of the mountains, through fertile farmland, one comes to the village of Skógar, with its summer hotel and magnificent waterfall, Skógarfoss. There is a local museum here and swimming pool. East from the village, an area of black volcanic sands is soon reached. To the north is Sólheimajökull glacier, and to the south, the Atlantic.

As you drive across the river Jökulsá, there is a smell of sulphur in the air, an ever present reminder of the area's volcanic activity. East of Jökulsá, is Vestur-Skaftafellssysla, and more fertile country with the island of Pétursey, literally rising from the sand, on the right. There is a turn-off for the nature reserve at **Dyrhólaey**, and on the right, is a causeway on to the island itself. The view is staggering, with a sheer drop of 120m (400ft) from the top of the island down to the sea. The island (which literally means 'door-hole') gets its name from the massive arch that the sea has eroded from the headland. There is a lighthouse on the island, built in 1926. East along the main road, the valley is reached by crossing the mountain ridge. At the other side of the ridge is Reynisfjall mountain which must be crossed to get to Vík í Myrdal. If instead the route south into Reynishverfi is taken, the most southerly farm in Iceland at Gardar can be visited. On the beach there are interesting caves and basalt formations to see.

From Reynishverfi, the road leads to **Vík**, the only town in Vestur-Skaftafell county, which has a campsite, guest house, sleeping bag accommodation, summer houses and a number of services: from Vík, the road goes east past Víkurhamrar cliffs and out into the vast black Myrdal Sands, 700sq km (270sq miles) of sands washed down from the Katla eruptions. On a good day, the view stretches all the way to Vatnajökull. The southernmost point of Iceland is Kötlutangi 15km (9 miles) to the east of Vík. Once across the sands, the lavafield created in the Laki eruption of 1783 is reached. At 565sq km (218sq miles), this was the largest lava-flow recorded in historical times anywhere in the world.

From here it is only a short drive to **Kirkjubaejarklaustur**, where there is a hotel, restaurant, campsite and other tourist facilities. A short distance up the Skaftá river is Eldmessutangi, the point where the lava-flow stopped in the 1783 eruption, during the famous Fire Mass. Before the reformation there was a convent at Kirkjubaejarklaustur. There is a mountain road up to the Laki crater and many fine examples of columnar basalt may be seen.

From Kirkjubaejarklaustur, the route east is both beautiful and varied. There is a waterfall and interesting basalt formations at Dvergshamrar, and an attractive seventeenth-century turf church at Núpsstadur. It is here that the southern region ends; across Skeidarársandur the region leads into east Iceland. Ahead, the highest peak in the country, Hvannadalshnjúkur, at 2,119m (6,952ft), rises out of Öraefajökull glacier and then you are in Skaftafell National Park.

## Additional Information

### *Places to Visit in Reykjavík*

Many public buildings close on National Day, 17 June.

**American Library**
Laugavegur 26
☎ (91) 621022
Open: Monday to Friday 11.30am-6pm.

**Arbaer Folk Museum**
Arbaer
☎ (91) 814412
Open: indoor exhibits 1 June to 3 August, Tuesday to Sunday 10am-6pm, 1-30 September, Saturday and Sunday 10am to 6pm, rest of year by arrangement. The outdoor area is open all year.

**Arni Magnússon Institute**
Sudurgate
☎ (91) 25540
Open: 17 June to 1 September, Monday to Saturday 2-4pm. Groups by arrangement at other times.

**Asgrimur Jónsson Gallery**
Bergstadastraeti 74
☎ (91) 13644
Open: June to August, Tuesday to Sunday 1.30-4pm, closed Monday. September to May, Sunday, Tuesday, Thursday and Saturday 1-6pm.

**Ásmundur Sveinsson House**
Freyjugata 41
Hours vary ☎ (91) 32155

**Ásmundur Sveinsson Museum**
Sigtún
☎ (91) 32155
Open: 1 June to 14 September 1.30-4pm daily except Monday. 15 September to 30 November and 1 February to 31 May Saturday and Sunday 1.30-4pm. The gardens are open all year 11am-4pm.

**Einar Jónsson Museum**
Njardargata
☎ (91) 13797
Open: 1 June to 14 September 1.30-4pm daily except Mondays. 15 September to 30 November and 1 February to 31 May Saturday to Sunday 1.30-4pm. The garden is open all year 11am-5pm.

**Electric Museum**
Ellidaár Power Station
☎ (91) 679009
Open: Sunday 2-4pm and by arrangement.

**Geysir House**
Adalstraeti 2/Vesturgata 1
☎ (91) 628910
Open: daily 8am-8pm during the summer.

**Hafnarborg Art Centre**
Strandgata 34
Hafnarfjördur
☎ (91) 50080
Open: daily 12noon-6pm except Tuesday.

**Hafnarfjördur Folk Museum**
Vesturgata 6b
Hafnarfjördur
☎ (91) 54700
Open: 1 June to 30 September Tuesday to Sunday 2-6pm. 1 October to 31 May Saturday Sunday 2-6pm.

**Hallgrímskirkja**
Skólavörduholt
Open: Tuesday to Sunday 10am-6pm (lift to top of spire).

**Hladvarpinn (The Women's Centre)**
Vesturgata 3
☎ (91) 19055
Theatre, exhibition hall and arts and crafts gallery.
Open: Monday to Friday 12noon-6pm, Saturday 12noon-6pm.

**Kirkjumunir**
Kirkjustraeti 10
☎ (91) 15030
Permanent exhibition of textiles and
religious art.
Open: 9am-4pm.

**Kjarvalsstadir — Municipal Art
Gallery**
Miklatúm
☎ (91) 26131
Open: 11am-6pm.

**Labour Union's Art Gallery**
Grensávegur 16, top floor
☎ (91) 681770 for opening times.

**Maritime Museum**
Vesturgate 8
Hafnarfjördur
Open: 1 June to 3 September Tuesday to
Sunday 2-6pm. 1 October to 31 May
Saturday to Sunday 2-6pm.

**Maritime and Metalwork Museum**
J. Hinriksson
Súdarvogur 4
☎ (91) 814677
Open: Tuesday to Saturday 1-6pm.

**National Gallery**
Frikirkjuvegur 7
☎ (91) 621000
Open: 12noon-6pm daily except Mon-
days, public tours on Sunday 3-3.30pm.
Library open: Tuesday to Friday 1-4pm.

**National Library**
Hverfisgata
☎ (91) 13080
Open: Monday to Friday 9am-7pm, and
during winter only Saturday 10am-
12noon.

**National Museum of Iceland**
Sudurgata
☎ (91) 288888
Open: 16 May to 14 September daily
except Monday 11am-4pm. 15 May to 15
September, Sunday, Tuesday, Thursday
and Saturday 12noon-4pm.

**Natural History Museum**
Hlemmur
☎ (91) 298222

Open: Sunday, Tuesday, Thursday and
Saturday 1.30-4pm.

**Nature Study Centre**
Digranesvegur 12
Kópavogur
☎ (91) 40630
Open: Saturday 1.30-4.30pm.

**Nordic House**
Hringbraut
☎ (91) 17030
Open: 2-7pm during exhibitions.

**Numismatic Collection**
Einholt 4
☎ (91) 699964
Open: Sundays 2-4pm and by request
during the week.

**Post and Telecommunication History
Museum**
Austurgata 11
☎ (91) 54321
Open: Sunday and Tuesday 3-6pm.

**Reykjavík Photographic Museum**
Borgartún 1
☎ (91) 179222
Open: Monday to Friday 9am-5pm, and
during exhibitions Saturday to Sunday
2-6pm.

**Sigurjón Olafsson Museum**
Laugarnestangi 70
☎ (91) 32906
Open: 20 June to 31 August Monday to
Thursday 8-10pm, Saturday to Sunday
2-6pm. Concerts every Tuesday at 8.30pm.

**University Gallery**
At Oddi on the Campus
Open: daily 2-7pm.

**University Library**
Sudurgata
☎ (91) 25088
Open: Monday to Friday 9am-5pm
(until 7pm during winter).

## Reykjavík: Useful Information

**Theatre, Opera and Ballet**
City Theatre Lisdtabraut, Kringlan
☎ (91) 680680

National Theatre, Hverfisgata
☎ (91) 11200
Icelandic Opera Company, Gamla Bio,
Ingólfsstraeti ☎ (91) 622255
Icelandic Symphony Orchestra, Concerts at Háskólabió ☎ (91) 622255
Icelandic Orchestra ☎ (91) 626232
Summer Theatre, Tjarnarbió ☎ (91) 19181

## Cinemas
There are six multiple screen cinemas in Reykjavík. Shows normally start at 3pm and the last screening is normally around 11pm.
Bíóhöllin, Alfabakki 8 ☎ (91) 78900
Bíóborgin, Snorrabraut 37 ☎ (91) 11384
Laugarásbió, Laugras ☎ (91) 32075
Regnboggin, Hverfisgata 54 ☎ (91) 19000
Sagabío, Ifabakki ☎ (91) 78900
Störnubío, Laugavegur ☎ (91) 18936

## Emergency Numbers
Police ☎ (91) 0112
Fire ☎ (91) 11100
Ambulance ☎ (91) 11100
Rescue Squad ☎ (91) 627111

*Medical Help*
Emergency round the clock treatment is available at the City Hospital weekdays 8am-5pm ☎ (91) 69600, weekdays 5pm-8am and weekends ☎ (91) 21230.
The Medical Centre at Barónstígur 47, is open: 5-8pm on weekdays and 24 hours at weekends and on public holidays.

## Banks
Banking hours are Monday to Friday 9.15am-4pm. The following banks are open at the weekends: Landsbanki at the Hotel Loftleidir, weekdays 8.15am-4pm and 5-7.15pm, Saturday 8.15am-7.15pm, and Sundays 15 May to 15 September 12noon-5pm ☎ (91) 606690
Búnadarbanki Islands, Bankastraeti 2, currency exchange 1 June to 15 September weekdays 4.30-6pm, Saturday 9am-1pm ☎ (91) 623045

## Shopping
Shopping hours are Monday to Friday 9 or 10am-6pm, Saturday 10am-2pm although some shops stay open longer, and supermarkets stay open longer on Thursday and Friday.

Kringlan Shopping Mall Monday to Thursday 10am-6.30pm, Friday 10am-7pm, Saturday 10am-2pm.

*Markets*
Kolaportid Flea Market, Laekjargata, every Sunday 10am-4pm.

## Travel
*Airports*
Keflavík Airport handles all international flights, Reykjavík Airport handles internal flights, and flights to Greenland and the Faroes.

*Airport Terminals*
Hotel Loftleidir, at Reykjavík Airport for international flights, Reykjavík Airport terminal for all internal flights.

*Airline Information and Reservations*
Icelandair domestic flights ☎ (91) 690200
Icelandair international flights
☎ (91) 690300
Islandsflug, Reykjavík Airport
☎ (91) 616060

*Airport Buses*
Travel between Keflavík Airport and Hotel Loftleidir where there are further bus connections and taxis available. The Airport bus terminal is from Hotel Loftleidir.

*Public Transport*
*Buses*
BSI Bus Terminal
Vatnsmyrarvegur
Reykjavík
☎ (91) 22300

Reykjavík Public Transit (SVR) operates twenty bus routes in the city. The two main transfer points are Laekjargata and Hlemmur on the corner of Laugavegur and Raudarárstigur.

*Ferries*
Reykjavikurhöfn harbour for Akranes Akraborg car and passenger ferry
☎ (91) 16050
Sundahöfn harbour for Videy ferry
☎ 985-20099
Westman Islands, Herjólfur ferry, buses leave from BSI bus station ☎ (91) 686464

## Tourist Information Centres
Bankastraeti 2
☎ (91) 623045
Open: June to August, Monday to
Friday 8.30am-6pm. Saturday, 8.30am-
2pm. Sunday 10am-3pm. September to
May, Monday to Friday 10am-4pm.
Saturday 10am-2pm. Sunday closed.

City Hall
Vonarstraeti
☎ (91) 632005

**Campsite Laugardalur Service Centre**
Sundlaugavegur
☎ (91) 686944

## Accommodation
*Hotels*
City Hotel
Rámargata 4a
☎ (91) 18650

Hotel Borg
Rósthússtraeti 11
☎ (91) 11440

Hotel Esja
Sudurlandsbraut 2
☎ (91) 812200

Hotel Holiday Inn
Sigtún 38
☎ (91) 689000

Hotel Holt
Bergstadastraeti 37
☎ (91) 25700

Hotel Höfdi
Skipholt 27
☎ (91) 26477

Hotel Island
Armúli 9
☎ (91) 688999

Hotel Leifur Eiriksson
Skólavstraeti 45
☎ (91) 620800

Hotel Lind
Raudarárstigur 18
☎ (91) 623350

Hotel Loftleidir
Reykjavík Airport
☎ (91) 22322

Hotel Odinsvé
Thórsgata 1
☎ (91) 25640

Hotel Reykjavík
Raudarárstigur 37
☎ (91) 626250

Hotel Saga
Hagatorg
☎ (91) 29900

Hotel Sjómannaheimilid Orkin
Brautarholt 29
☎ (91) 680777

*Guesthouses/Hostels*
Laugavegur 101 ☎ (91) 626101
Baldursbrá Laufásvegur 41 ☎ (91) 26646
Bólstadahlid 8 ☎ (91) 612600
Egilsborg, Thverholt 20 ☎ (91) 612600
Eskihlid 3 ☎ (91) 24030
Flókagata 1 ☎ (91) 21155
Gudmundur Jónasson, Borgartún 34
    ☎ (91) 35870
Irisar, Vesturbrún 16 ☎ (91) 38534
Isafold, Bárugata 11 ☎ (91) 612294
Jöro, Slólavördustigur 13a ☎ (91) 621739
Mattheu, Bugdulaekur 13 ☎ (91) 33207
Miklabraut 1 ☎ (91) 622144
Perlan, Rámargata 10 ☎ (91) 626910
Royal Inn, Laugavegur 11 ☎ (91) 24513
Safamyri 77 ☎ (91) 37654
Skeggjagata 1 ☎ (91) 622240
Skólavördustigur 43 ☎ (91) 16614
Smárar, Snorrabraut 52 ☎ (91) 623330
Snorra, Snorrabraut ☎ (91) 20598
Svanurinn, Lokastigur 24a ☎ (91) 25318
Vikingur, Rámargata 120 ☎ (91) 621290
Salvation Army Guest House
(Gestaheimalid), Kirkjustraeti 2
    ☎ (91) 613203

**Hafnarfjördur**
Guesthouse Berg
Baerjarhraun 4
☎ (91) 652220

## Embassies and Consulates
UK, Laufásvegur 49 ☎ (91) 15883
USA, Laufásvegur 21 ☎ (91) 29100

**Chamber of Commerce**
Kringlan 7
☎ (91) 678910

**Motoring**
F.I.B. Iceland Automobile Association
(Féleg Islenskra Bifreidaeigenda)
Borgartún 33
☎ (91) 629999

*Parking*
Metred parking costs 50K per hour.
There are indoor garages at
Kalkofnsvegur 3, corner of
Bergstadastraeti and Skólavördustígur,
and Vesturgata 7. There is also a large
car park by the harbour at Tryggvagata.

*Car Hire*
Avis
Sigtún 5
☎ (91) 624433

Budget Rent a Car
Dalvegur 20
Kópav
☎ (91) 641296

InterRent/Europcar
Skeifan 9
☎ 686916

Hertz/Icelandair
Flugvallarvegur
Reykjavík Airport
☎ (91) 690500

**Post Offices**
Open: Monday to Friday 8.30am-4.30pm
unless otherwise stated.

Central Post Office
Rósthústraeti 5
☎ (91) 637010

Kringlan Shopping Mall
Open: Monday to Friday 8.30am-6pm.
☎ (91) 637030

BSI Bus Terminal
Vatnsmyrarvegur
☎ (91) 637060
Open: Monday to Friday 12noon-6pm,
Saturday 9am-1pm.

**State Liquor Stores**
There are seven State Monopoly Stores
in and around Reykjavík: Austurstaeti
10a, Kringlan Shopping Mall,
Mikligardur Shopping Centre,
Alfabakki 14, Studaháls 2, Hafnarfjördur
at Laekjargata, and in Seltjarnarnes at
the Eidistorg shopping centre.

*Other Places to Visit*

**Keflavík**
*Byggdasafn Sudurnes Folk Museum*
Vatnsnesvegur
Open: all year.

**Stokkseyri**
*Thurídarbúd*
Strandgötu 13
☎ (98) 31302
Open: daily June to August 9am-5pm,
open all year by appointment.

*Tourist Information Centres*

**Akranes**
☎ (93) 13327

**Bogarnes**
Hyrran Service Centre
☎ (93) 72100

**Keflavík**
Airport
Leifur Eiriksson Air Terminal
☎ (92) 50330
Hafnargata 12
☎ (92) 15575

**Selfoss**
Tryggvaskáli, by the bridge
☎ (98) 21704

# 3
# THE SOUTH AND SKAFTAFELL

The south of Iceland is dominated by the huge plain that sprawls, in places many miles wide, to the southern edge of Vatnajökull, Europe's largest glacier. The area is predominantly concerned with agriculture and associated industries, although there are a few fishing villages along the coast. It is criss-crossed by rivers, both freshwater and glacial, and there are many lakes.

It is always difficult to decide where the region starts, but having visited Thingvellir, Geysir and Gullfoss, the area known as the Southern Lands reaches from Reykjanes to Vatnajökull.

The ring road is a good metalled road — with just the occasional pot hole — until just about 9km (5½ miles) beyond Hvolsvöllur. It then alternates between a gravel surface and asphalt, and you have to concentrate hard on your driving. Although there is a maximum speed limit of 50km/h (30mph) in urban areas, 70km/h (40mph) in rural areas and 80-90km/h (50-60mph) on highways, the visitor is not likely to come near these speeds until he or she has built up a bit of confidence. The gravel roads, especially in the early summer, can still be potholed and cracked after the winter. Boulders often lie strewn across the road, and there is the risk of stones being thrown up from vehicles in front. Dust is another problem, and in the summer months you can normally spot another vehicle on the road miles away because of the dust cloud it throws up. All drivers in Iceland must use dipped headlights at all times, and because of the dirt, most filling stations have free high-powered water jets so that you can clean off your vehicles, especially the lights.

The drive from Holt, through Skógar to Vikand then on to Kirkjubaejar-klaustur, up round Kúdafljót, and across Eldhraun, is incredible. Then you have to cross another lunar desert landscape, skirting to the north of Skeidaráesandur to Skaftafell.

The glacier fingers from Myrdalsjökull creep down on your left, and the ice is blacked by the lava sand it has picked up. Stop for a few moments by the river Jökulsá in the summer and listen to the almost incessant calls of birds — curlew, redshank and oystercatchers and others. Thjórsáruer, south of Arnafell, is home to the world's largest nesting colony of pink-footed geese.

The road now passes very close to the sea and the towering cliffs play host to tens of thousands of sea birds, particularly large colonies of gannets. After the lava desert and Kirkjubaejarklaustur, the road follows the southern slopes of a number of mountain ranges. In many areas, sheltered from the north and easterly winds, clusters of trees huddle in the valleys, and everywhere along this route there are spectacular waterfalls cascading down the cliffs. At Skiedarár there is a very long single lane wooden bridge, with passing points at convenient intervals, and then it is only a short drive to the green oasis of Skaftafell.

Distances take longer than you expect, because you have to negotiate around pot holes, especially if you are not driving a four-wheel drive vehicle. It is just when your confidence starts to build up, and you put your foot down a little, that you hit the biggest pot hole on the road. On even rougher stretches of road, and there are miles upon miles of them, it is easy to upset the tracking of the vehicle because of the constant battering. It is worth having this checked out at the first opportunity, because if the tracking is bad you will be sliding all over some of the mud tracks, especially after wet weather, and even in a four-wheel drive vehicle.

The south is the most extensive area of lowland in the country, flanked by the sea on one side and mountains and glaciers on the other. In places the mountains are simply ridges that run for several hundred yards, and they are reminiscent of an American western landscape. The walls of these mesas are very steep and there are many spectacular waterfalls. Because there are so many faults in the rocks, it is quite common to see a raging torrent of water pouring out of a cave several hundred feet above the ground before it plunges down into a pool or river below.

Off the coast you can see the Vestmannaeyjar (Westman Islands) which had to be evacuated in 1973 when an eruption took place. Still further out to sea is the island of Surtsey, born of a submarine eruption in 1963 which lasted for more than 2 years.

There are many villages in the southern plains, and a comprehensive road network so travelling is easy. Progress is more difficult, but infinitely more rewarding, when vehicles are left behind, and a journey on foot is undertaken in the Skaftafell, one of Iceland's greenest areas, and now one of the country's three national parks. It is strange to walk in this oasis with the sea on one side and the Öraefajökull glacier behind. There are many walks both in the park and, with a guide, up on the glacier.

In the west of the region there are many geothermal areas, including the district known as 'Greenhouses' because the earth's hot water is used to heat glass-houses. The country's largest hydro-electric stations are also to be found in this region.

A most surprising fact is that Skaftafell had hardly any visitors before 1974, because it was so difficult to reach. It was not until 1974 that the final stretch of the national highway around the country was completed to commemorate the 1,100th anniversary of the country's first settlement. Before then, roads were built across the southern plains, but they were often washed away by the ice melt and floodwater coming down from the mountains and glaciers. Now, the road is elevated in places to allow the floodwater to pass underneath, and buses regularly visit the park; and Skaftafell, once a mystery, is now known and loved by thousands of visitors from both home and abroad. The journey across the great sands and rivers to get to the park is also unforgettable.

**Ingólfshöfdi**, on the edge of the region, is named after Iceland's first settler Ingólfur Arnarson, who spent his first winter there. It is a huge cliff which stands alone in a vast area of sand, close to the sea and about 10km (6 miles) from Fagurhólsmyri. The cliffs play host to thousands of nesting sea birds and it is possible to get very close to them. **Kirkjubaejarklaustur** is one of the largest farms in Skaftafell and a small village has grown up there recently. There is plenty to see including Kirkjuhólar, the remains of an old convent, and Systrastapi, which is an overhanging cliff to the west of the village. There is another cliff at **Hjörleifshöfdi** which can be climbed. The views from the top are stunning.

**Mount Reynisfjall**, 340m (1,115ft) high, is accessible by road from Vík in Myrdalur. There is a road which goes up to the top of the mountain, where there is a long-range radar navigation station. This is another good place for views and photographs. There are some unusual stone pillars called Reynisdrangar at the seaward foot of the mountain.

Not far away to the west is **Dyrhólaey**. It has a huge cliff overhanging the ocean, which has a hole in it. Large boats can pass through this hole in good weather. Nearby **Hekla**, at 1,491m (4,892ft), is Iceland's most famous volcano. Its first recorded eruption was in 1104; since then it has erupted fifteen times, the last time in 1990. In March 1947 when it erupted the column rose to 30,000m (100,000ft) while the lava flow covered 65sq km (25sq miles).

## The Fjallabak Nature Reserve

The reserve, established in 1979, covers 47,000 hectares and is more than 500m (1,640ft) above sea level. The land is very mountainous, rugged and spectacular. There are volcanoes and geothermal activity and the landscape is covered by lava fields, sands, rivers and many lakes. Geological activity is occurring almost before your eyes, and it is responsible for many of the magnificent colours of the minerals and rocks, and the incredible blue of the lake waters.

The aim of the nature reserve is to preserve the natural features and the desolate wilderness and tranquillity that thousands of visitors to Fjallabak enjoy every year.

### How to Get There

If you are driving in, there is the old horse track Landmannaleid, which runs between the settlements of Land and Skaftártunga, which crosses the reserve. The most popular route in, however, is F22 from Sigalda which joins the old Landmannaleid track (marked Dómadalseid on road signs) by Frostastadavatn.

Both roads are difficult to negotiate and four wheel drive vehicles are essential. The road surface is gravel at best and there are a number of rivers which have to be forded. The roads are only passable in July and August and are usually under snow or mud throughout the rest of the year.

Quicksands are another danger but do not pose a problem if you stick to the roads. As with all interior driving, never attempt to cross a river unless you know it is possible to wade across. Remember to take in with you everything you need such as fuel, oil and food, and as it is a nature reserve, it is illegal to drive or park off roads. BSI run coach tours which pass through the reserve on their way to and from Skaftafell through the summer.

## Walking

This is a great area for walking and backpacking. The most popular walks 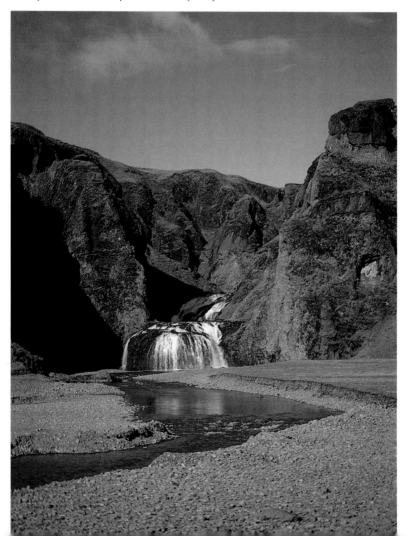 are to the summit of the steep Mount Bláhnúker 940m (3,083ft) and to the volcanic area around Brennisteinsalda (Burning Stones Ground) 855m (2,804ft) where gases come hissing out of the ground. Both walks take between one and two hours. Other interesting hikes include Háalda,

*Waterfall outside a campsite near Kirkjubaejarklaustur*

1,089m (3,572ft, 4-6 hours), around the blue lake Frostastadavatn (2-3 hours), Sudurnámur 951m (3,119ft, 1 hour), and Brandsgil (1-2 hours).

It is essential when walking in the area to have a good map and keep to the footpaths as it is easy to get lost. Wear sensible shoes or boots and even in summer be prepared for a sudden deterioration in the weather. Tell people where you are planning to go. Average annual temperature is around 1°C (34°F), with temperatures in July and August reaching between 5-14°C (41-57°F). Fog and mist are common. Winds from the south and south-east tend to bring rain and bad weather, while winds from the north and north-east usually signal cold but fine weather. Sandstorms can also be a hazard.

It is also important to note that none of the rock in the reserve is suitable for climbing and the best routes follow ridges and valley bottoms. Land around hot springs can be soft so must be approached cautiously.

**Fishing and Swimming**

If you want to fish for your supper, permits can be obtained from the farm at Skard, or from the warden at Landmannalaugar. The best trout lakes are Ljótipollur, Dómadalsvatn and Frostastadavatn. The hot springs at Landmannalaugar are suitable for swimming but avoid the hot mud pools.

**Accommodation**

The Touring Club of Iceland has a hut at Landmannalaugar which can accommodate 115 people. Space is allocated on a first come first served basis, and remember that about 15,000 people visit the reserve each summer. Most visitors belong to groups which have pre-booked their places. You must have your own sleeping bag and provisions. The club has another hut at Hrafntinnusker on the hiking route from Landmannalaugar to Thórsmörk (an incredible four day hike), which sleeps eighteen. It is locked in the summer and you must get a key either in Reykjavík, or from the warden at Landmannalaugar or Thórsmörk.

The campsite is at Landmannalaugar, either by the hut or beside the road junction to Landmannalaugar. Contact the ranger before pitching. Camping elsewhere is at the ranger's discretion.

**The Reserve**

Fjallabak, literally means 'Behind the Mountains', and is an area of wild and rugged mountains with deeply cut valleys, a result of volcanic and glacial action. The bed rock dates back only 8 to 10 million years. Torfajökull is still an active volcano although in decline, and is surrounded by numerous gas vents and hot springs. Vulcanologists believe Torfajökull is a caldera, the rim being Háalda, Sudurnámur, Nordur, Barmur, Torfajökull, Kaldaklofsjöll and Ljósártungur. The hot pools at Landmannalaugar illustrate the geothermal activity in the area. There are about 150 plants growing in the reserve even though the growing period is restricted to about two months. Birds are not common with snow buntings the most common species. The lakes play host to great northern divers, whooper swans and red necked phalaropes in the summer. Great northern divers nest by Frostastadavatn and Kirkjufellsvatn, and harlequin ducks are occasionally seen on the Jökulgilskvsi river. Brown trout and arctic char (introduced in 1970) are common in the lakes.

If you continue along F22 eastwards out of the park and back towards the ring road, it is worth detouring up the Eldgja (Fire Fissure) Valley, a 40km (25 mile) long volcanic rift valley, up to 200m (656ft) deep and 600m (1,968ft) wide in places. The 2km (1 mile) walk from the parking place to the spectacular Ofaerufoss is also worthwhile. The waterfall, with its natural stone arch, is one of Iceland's most famous.

The country's largest electrical plant is near Búrfell, and there is another to the north at Sigalda. At **Búrfell** you can visit the waterfalls Tröllkonuhlamp and Thjófafoss on the River Thjorsa, plus the striking rapids of Fossabrekkur on the River Ytri-Rangá. This area should not be confused with Búrfell in Hafnafjördur.

**Landmannalaugar** is a beautiful dale between the mountains east of Búrfell and is a very popular tourist spot in the summer. It must be remembered that it takes only a few people to constitute a crowd in Iceland's beauty spots. Visitors can take advantage of the hot pools and there is a rest house.

**Eyjafjöll** is a beautiful and impressive mountain range north-west of Vík and capped by the Eyjafjallajökull glacier, which is 1,660m (5,446ft) high. There are many waterfalls, the most remarkable of which are Skógarfoss and Seljalandsfoss. There are also caves which can be explored including Hrútshellir by Hrutafell, and Paradísarhellir, which literally means Paradise Cave. The valley is beautiful and so unspoilt that is has often been used by film companies, especially those making films about prehistoric times. There is also an open swimming pool in the mountains, only accessible by a steep pass. A cliff forms one side of the pool.

**Thórsmörk**, north of Eyjafjallajökull, can only be reached by four-wheel drive vehicles, or trucks, but the journey is worth it. Icelanders consider it to be one of their most beautiful places, but care is necessary. The journey can only be made when water levels are low, and many cars have been swept away when unsuspecting motorists tried to ford the rivers, not appreciating how strong the currents are. It is best to ask a guide to take you to visit this lovely place.

There are many historical places in the Rangárvallasysla district, including **Hlídarendi** in Fljótshlid and **Bergthórshvoll** in Landeyjar, both of which are dramatic settings for the *Njálasaga*. To the north of Eyjafjallajökull glacier is **Basar**, a weird and beautiful place.

## The Westman Islands

Vestmannaeyjar (The Westman Islands) is a chain of fifteen islands about 10km (6 miles) off the south coast of Iceland. There is a daily ferry service from Thorlákshöfn to Heimaey, which takes about 2½ hours. The ferry carries up to 500 passengers and 70 cars, and there is a daily 50-minute

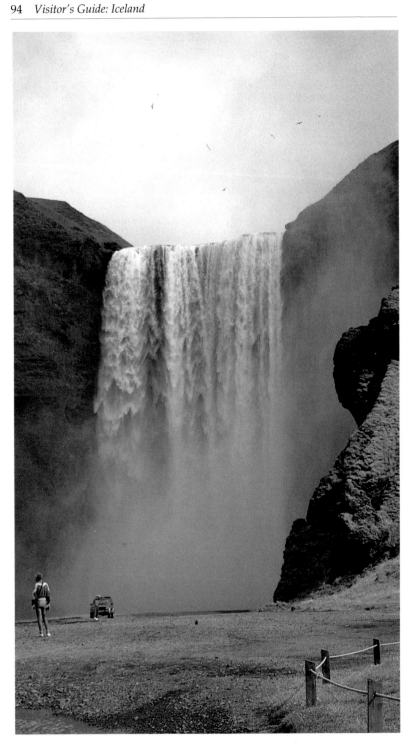

coach service from the BSI Bus Terminal in Reykjavík to connect with the ferry. The crossing can be rough and if you are not a good sailor, it is advisable to fly. There is a bustling little airport at Heimaey, the fourth busiest in Iceland, and regular flights to and from Reykjavík. It is possible to fly to Heimaey early in the morning, spend a day touring the island and then return to Reykjavík in the early evening. Some return air fares also include the cost of a guided tour on the island and this is well worth taking. As with all internal flights, the weather can severely disrupt schedules so do not visit the islands the day before you are due to leave the country, if the weather forecast is bad.

There is a surprising amount to see and do on the island, however, and if you have the time, a stay of a few days can be very rewarding. While a car is useful, the island is not large and there are some magnificent walks. The Westman Islands are exciting because they form the youngest archipelago in the world. All the island's were formed as a result of volcanic activity in the last 10,000 years. Heimaey itself was formed as a result of lava flows from several volcanoes. About 5,000 years ago, Helgafell on Heimaey erupted and Ofanleitishraun was formed. The latest subterranean eruption occurred in 1963 and resulted in the birth of Surtsey which continued to push itself out of the sea for four years.

*(Opposite) Skógarfoss*

*Heimaey*

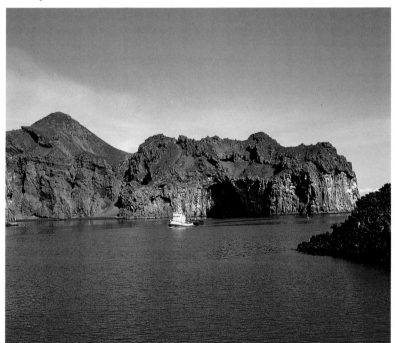

It is almost certain that the Westman Islands were populated before the mainland, and archaeologists have discovered the remains of settlements around Herjólfsdalur, probably built by Norwegians at the beginning of the ninth century, perhaps seventy years or so before Iceland itself was colonised. The origin of the name of the islands is also obscure, but it is generally believed to come from Irish monks, 'the men from the west', who settled there. There is a legend, however, that it was named after some Irish slaves who murdered their master, Hjörleifur, blood brother of Ingólfur Arnarson, and fled to the desolate islands thinking they would be safe; they were tracked down and killed within days. Even the translation of Vestmannaeyjar causes problems, and can appear as Westman, Westmen or Westmann Islands.

Apart from the fifteen islands there are many rocks and skerries, but
✳ **Heimaey**, the largest island in the group, is the only one to have a permanent human population, thus its name 'Home Island'. The geologic youth and volatility of Heimaey was brought home to them vividly on the night of 23 January 1973.

A massive eruption began at 2am in the eastern part of the island and continued until 3 July. The eruption from the new volcano Eldfell and subsequent lava flow caused massive damage. Many of the 5,300 inhabitants were evacuated to different places on the mainland, and at one stage it was thought the whole town might be destroyed. For five months the islanders fought to halt the advance of the lava. High pressure hoses poured millions of gallons of sea water on to the leading edge of the advancing lava in a bid to cool it down and divert it. By a miracle, the 5m (16ft) high lava wall stopped only yards from the island's hospital which was saved, although several feet of ash had to be swept from its flat roof. Less fortunate was a house close to the hospital. The lava wall stopped having engulfed half the house, and the remainder can still be seen poking from the towering wall of black lava. Altogether, almost 400 buildings were buried in ashes and lava, or destroyed by fire. The harbour and fish processing plants also escaped damage, and within a few weeks most of the population had returned to clean up and continue their lives. The eruption not only extended the size of the island by about 15 per cent but also produced an enormous amount of lava, an estimated 30 million tons, which has been utilised for building and road making.

Literally living on a volcanic island in one of the most inhospitable oceans in the world, means the Westman islanders are a very tough race who have always had to battle against the elements. Problems have not always been caused by the weather. In the fifteenth century, Heimaey was used as a base by British privateers, and they were followed by Danish traders. In 1627 a band of marauding North African pirates, led by a Danish bandit Jan Jantzen attacked the island killing forty people and taking 250 prisoners. The aim was to hold the prisoners hostage until the Danish king paid a ransom for them. For many months the Danish king refused to pay, and many of the prisoners were sold as slaves in Algiers.

It is said that only thirteen islanders returned after the ransom was eventually paid. In one blow, more than half the island's population had been murdered or sold into slavery.

Heimaey has the country's largest fishing fleet, and most of the population is engaged in fishing, fish processing or associated industries, although tourism is now an important and growing industry. Heimaey accounts for 12 per cent of Iceland's total exports because of its fishing, but has less than 2 per cent of its population.

Heimaey now has two hotels, five guest houses and a youth hostel (open 1 June to 15 September) next to the police station. There is a campsite on the north-western outskirts of the town. There are also cafés and restaurants, a cinema, hospital and a sports centre with a swimming pool, as well as an aquarium and natural history museum and Folk Museum.  The Aquarium and Natural History Museum was opened in 1964 and is an excellent place to while a few hours if the weather outside is inclement. The aquarium has a collection of very strange looking fish which can be found in local waters, and there is a very fine geology collection.

The Folk Museum, above the library, has a number of interesting exhibits including old maps and prints which give an impression of how the island has changed over the years, especially after the 1973 eruption. During the summer, the cinema screens a 'volcanic film' show two or three times daily. It features the volcanic eruptions in the Westman Islands in 1973, and includes fascinating scenes from daily life on the islands, both past and present, as well as fishing, birdlife, puffin hunting and the annual festivals.

The Westman islanders have a great zest for life and have had to make much of their own entertainment. One of the highlights of the year is the three-day festival during the first weekend of August, called the Independence Festival. One of the 'national' sports on the island is the 'sprang' above Skiphellar, where children and young men swing from a rope hanging over the top of the cliff. The aim is to grab as many eggs as possible from the puffins' nests. Although this is now regarded as a sport, the eggs are still eaten, and every year thousands are collected, especially the larger fulmars and guillemots eggs. For centuries, the islanders relied on egg gathering and bird hunting for food which was stored to see them through the winter when the sea was often too rough to fish. Bird eggs and the birds, particularly puffin, are still eaten on the island, although the very oily, fishy flesh is an acquired taste. Kelp is another staple ingredient, and it is usually gathered at low tide off the north coast of the island.

Hunting is still an important pastime, and 'huts' have been built on a number of the larger out-islands, as refuges for the hunting parties. Millions of sea birds nest on the islands and the puffins not only nest on the cliffs, but also on the grass banks on top of them as well. A good day out is to walk from Heimaey to the lighthouse at Stórhöfdavegur. It is about 7km (4 miles) north of town on the southern tip of the island. Just before you reach the lighthouse you pass Raeningjatangi, which is where the pirates swarmed ashore in 1627. The area is littered with caves and lava fields and many of the islanders hid among them until the pirates swarmed ashore in 1627. You can take in ascents of Eldfell (221m, 725ft) and nearby Helgafell (226m, 741ft), and try to imagine what the island would have looked like before the eruptions. Wear stout footwear as the ground is hot and steam and sulphur come out of vents around the summit. There are splendid walks all along the coastline with their spectacular cliffs and teeming bird life. Take care near the edges.

The annual festival is held at Herjólfsdalur, to the north-west of Heimaey. It has been held here every year since 1874, the year Iceland was granted independence. The weather was so bad that the islanders could not cross over to the mainland to take part in the celebrations, so they organised their own festival, and have done ever since. Huge bonfires are built and there is much dancing, music, singing and drinking. It is a true open-air festival because even the residents often pitch tents and camp out for the duration cooking over open fires.

❄ **Surtsey**

Named after the Norse fire god Surtur, Surtsey is not only one of the world's newest islands, but the most filmed and researched and one of the most restricted. Ever since the eruption in 1963 which heaved it up out of the waters 18km (11 miles) south-west of Heimaey, its progress has been monitored giving scientists a fascinating insight into how a new island evolves, how flora and fauna develop and so on. Because of this very few people are allowed to visit the island, and special permits are only granted for scientific research.

When the eruption first occurred, columns of ash were sent almost 9,146m (30,000ft) into the sky and could be seen on clear days as far away as Reykjavík. The birth of Surtsey took almost four years as eruption followed eruption until 1967, by which time the island stood 150m (492ft) above sea level and covered an area of almost 3sq km (2sq miles). Because of pounding seas, there was a considerable amount of early erosion, but the island core quickly solidified as rock and is now holding its own while the scientists watch everything.

Flights from Reykjavík fly over Surtsey if you want a closer look, while the excellent volcano show in the capital features the birth of an island, and makes you feel as if you are actually on the island.

## Skaftafell and Glacier Country

Although the north of Iceland has enormous beauty, especially the areas around Lake Myvatn, the national park of Skaftafell and the glacier country beyond is considered by many to be the most attractive region. It appeals because it offers everything the outdoor enthusiast wants. There are magnificent panoramas, walks of varying degrees of difficulty, and the most breathtaking views. In Skaftafell there is always the backdrop of the glaciers and up on the ice, one has the sensation of entering another world.

Skaftafell has been a national park since 1967 and it was created with the help of the World Wildlife Fund, now the World Wide Fund for Nature.

The glaciers have a silent power. They move relentlessly onwards and can crush everything in their path. Yet, when actually standing on them, there is a sense of enormous peace and tranquillity. Ice climbing is great fun though it can be dangerous and should not be undertaken unless experienced. There is enormous satisfaction in being able to climb, spider-like, up a vertical cliff face with just ice-axes and crampons for grip.

Then there are the walks over some of the most spectacular countryside in Iceland, where in the summer the greenness of it all is breathtaking. Skaftafell is an oasis in a desert of sand, and is the more spectacular because of this. It is less than 3½ hours by coach from Reykjavík, and should not be missed.

It is possible to camp at Skaftafell and there is a shop and warden service throughout the summer; camping is really the only way to see the national park and experience it properly. There is a marvellous feeling in being able to wake up in this huge area of spectacular countryside, with only the birds above for company. Even in the height of summer, the park rarely gets busy, and the campsite is large enough to allow everyone their privacy. The buses between Höfn and Reykjavík have a stopover in Skaftafell because there is now a filling station and café. For campers the weather forecast is posted daily in Icelandic and English, and the shop sells large-scale maps of the area. There is a full time warden in the park to help with any problems or enquiries, and there are charts available to help you identify the rich flora and fauna of the region. Bed and breakfast accommodation is quite new to Iceland, but a number of farmers now offer it, and a farm at Bólti, clearly signposted at Skaftafell, offers rooms if you want a few home comforts.

## Skaftafell National Park

The reserve was established on 15 September 1967 and covered an area of around 500sq km (310sq miles). In June 1984 a new regulation was approved increasing the park area more than threefold so that all three valley glaciers are now in the park. The reserve now covers an area of about 1,600sq km (992sq miles). The region has been deeply split by glacial and fluvial erosion, and many areas offer an Alpine type landscape. The highest point in the Skaftafell range is Midfellstindur (1,430m, 4,690ft), and close to it, a little to the west is Thumall (The Thumb) a 1,179m (3,867ft) tall basalt column. Other peaks in the area include Kristínartindar (1,126m, 3,693ft) and Skardatindur (1,385m, 4,543ft). The highest peaks, however, are to the east. Hvannadalshmúkur (2,119m, 6,950ft) juts out from the rim of Oraefajökull's ice-filled crater.

The three valley glaciers that run through the park include Skeidarár-jökull, Europe's largest valley glacier covering 1,600sq km (992sq miles). The lava sand desert at the head of the glacier covers a further 1,000sq km (620sq miles). The Morsárjökull descends in a series of spectacular waterfalls into the valley of the Morsá, and the third glacier is the Skaftafellsjökull, which is an arm of the Oraefajökull. Other glacier rivers in the park include Skeidará, Morsá and Skaftafellsá. Skeidará was the biggest obstacle to travel in the area until it was bridged in 1974. During the summer the volume of water discharged by the river is around 200 cubic metres a second, and the river is notorious for flooding over a vast area. The river's great floods occurred about every ten years when 40,000 cubic metres of strong sulphur-smelling water were being discharged every second. The frequency of the floods has increased in the past few decades although the volume of water discharged has decreased substantially. In the old days, it would regularly wash away all roads which is why travel in the region was so difficult, and, until the river was bridged, so perilous.

Skaftafell is a walker's, climber's paradise and if you are interested in wildlife and geology even better. It has numerous walks ranging in degree of difficulty from gentle to severe, and there is enough selection to keep you busy for a couple of weeks if you have time to spend here. The national park area has been the site of a farmstead for centuries, and for the most of this time, was very isolated. From the age of settlement there was a meeting place at Skaftafell but this has long since been buried under the sands.

The farmhouses were sited at the foot of the hills and traces of them can be seen east of Baerjargil, in an ancient area of pasture known as Gömlutún. As sands from Skeidará encroached on the farms, they were relocated about 100m (328ft) up the hill, and three new farms were built at Bölti, Sel and Haedir. Several hundred years ago there was also a farm called Jökulfell, after the mountain to the north under which it sheltered. A small church was attached to the farm as far back as 1343 but in the spring of 1362 an eruption on Oraefajökull devastated the area and buried most of the farms under lava. The eruption spewed out more pumice than any other eruption in Iceland's history. The region was renamed Oraefi, because translated this means 'devastated land'. Before then it was known either as Litla Hérad (Little District), or Hérad milli sanda (the land between the sands). Less than 100 years after the eruption, however, people returned to Skaftafell and the farm was resettled on the site it occupies today.

**Wildlife**

Inside the park there is an enormous diversity of flora and fauna. The park is very rich in insect life, and heath and upland birds such as redwing, snipe and meadow pipit are common. There are also many wrens, a special sub-species found only in Iceland, which are larger than their European cousins. Bramblings have become a more frequent visitor, and you can spot great and arctic skuas and greater black backed gulls, all of which breed on the reserve.

Because of the remoteness of Skaftafell, it was free of rodents until quite recently. It is thought that mice arrived only after road bridges were built to ford the rivers around Skaftafell. Arctic foxes and mink can occasionally be seen. More than 200 species of plants are found within the park with many flowers like harebell and saxifrage. The park is also host to many rare and protected species.

### Weather

Skaftafell enjoys a good climate most of the year, with higher temperatures than the rest of the southern half of the country, because of the protection afforded by mountains. Rainfall is at its lowest in the summer.

### Getting Around

Apart from the tracks to the farms and parking space below the campsite, there are no roads in the park. There is, however, a comprehensive network of footpaths throughout the park.

Some of the interesting walks (with round trip time from the campsite) are:

| | |
|---|---|
| Giljaleid to the waterfall Svartifoss | 1-1½ hrs |
| Sjómarsker | 1½-2 hrs |
| To the 'snout' of Skaftafellsjökull | 1-1½ hrs |
| Kristínartindar | 5½-6½ hrs |
| To the source of Skeidará | 7-8 hrs |
| Baejarstadarskógur | 5½-6½ hrs |
| Kjósarbotn | 10-12 hrs |
| Morsárjökull | 6-7 hrs |

### Maps

Good maps are essential even though most of the routes are well waymarked. Always check on conditions before setting out because most of the longer walks involve river crossings.

The best detailed maps of the area are published by the Iceland Geodetic Survey: General Map, sheet 9 scale 1:250,000 shows most of the park and the county of Austur-Skaftafellssyla.

Map of Iceland, sheet 87 Oraefajökull 1:100,000 shows most of the park and Oraefajökull together with parts of Breidamerkursandur.

Special map in 1:100,000 covers the same area as sheet 87 plus the area towards the sea, and on the reverse is a special 1:25,000 map of the park between Skaftafellsjökull and Skeidarárjökull.

### Accommodation

The campsite with excellent facilities, shop and snack bar is open from the beginning of June to mid-September. It is possible to stay in the park at other times of the year with special permission.

This part of Iceland also encompasses the most accessible parts of the glacier country. The district is known as **Öraefasveit**. It comprises the foot of the Öraefajökull glacier which forms the southern part of **Vatnajökull**,  the largest ice-cap in Europe, and the fertile strip that runs between the mountains and the coast. The word Öraefasveit comes from *sveit* which means a district, and *öraefi* which means an uninhabited wasteland. There are no ports or natural harbours along this shore, and the waves of the Atlantic pound it relentlessly, which could also account for part of the district's name.

Although the glaciers and ice-covering on Öraefasveit give an impression of cold, there is enormous power and turbulence just below the surface. This area is also called 'The Land of Fire'. **Öraefajökull** is a typical cone volcano and it has erupted more than once since Iceland was first settled in the ninth century. The last recorded eruption was in 1727 when it did considerable damage to stock and killed large numbers of animals trapped in the lava-flow. But it was the massive explosion of 1362 that did

*(Opposite) Road bridge at Eldvatn (picture taken after 10pm)*

*Vatnajökull*

the most damage, and devastated the entire region. Almost all the existing farmsteads here were wiped out, and a gigantic pillar of volcanic ash killed off all the vegetation, which meant that farmers could not return for many years. Records show that before this massive eruption there were six churches and at least twenty-four farms, whereas now there are only eight farmsteads and one church. Gröf is one of the old farmsteads. It has been excavated from the lava which buried it in 1362.

There are many rivers flowing through this region from the glaciers and mountains to the sea, and because of the intensity of the flood waters they are constantly changing their course. Due to this, engineers found it extremely difficult to complete the road around Iceland. Every time a section across this southern plain was completed flood waters washed it away.

The Öraefajökull glacier is not always visible; frequently it is hidden behind the mountains, but its presence is always felt. In places tongues of the glacier advance quite close to the road, often forming deep lagoons in which trapped icebergs bob about. Such a lake can be seen on the river Jökulsá, near the Breidamerkur Sands. This river was only bridged in 1967 and although it is less than one mile long, the river holds more water than many others which are much longer. The lagoon formed where it swells out is well over 90m (300ft) deep in places. At the farm of Svínafell in the west, the glacier encroaches almost to the door, although like most others in recent years, it has started to recede. The mountains consist mainly of volcanic tuff, although the rocks do contain a number of semi-precious stones such as opal, jasper, and Iceland spar.

The fertile grasslands of Öraefasveit are used mainly for cattle and sheep farming, although two or three centuries ago they were covered in the typical squat Icelandic brushwood. The slow advance of the glaciers and the constant overgrazing by sheep, however, killed off most of these woodlands, although areas still exist in and near the Skaftafell park.

The whole of this coastline is warmed by the Gulf Stream and this part of the country has one of the mildest climates in Iceland. Although it gets quite high rainfall, there is little snow and ice, and few frosts. The average temperature in January has for a number of years been above freezing and this special climate, especially in the summer, has led to a unique vegetation, especially in Skaftafell and Svínafell. Many plants and ferns, not found in any other part of Iceland, can be found growing in the national park, right at the very edge of the glacier.

In the sea to the south of Skaftafell, seals can be seen, and they are often hunted by the local farmers who see the pelts as a valuable addition to their incomes. Polar bears are reputed to have come ashore in Iceland in this area, having been swept across on ice floes from Greenland. There is a report of a polar bear being killed by farmers in this region in 1748. However, the only animal likely to be seen is the arctic fox, although there are hundreds of thousands of sea birds, the most common of which are puffins, fulmar, arctic tern, razorbill and oystercatcher. Beware of the fulmar, it has some very nasty habits. If its nesting site is approached too closely, or the bird is upset, it is likely to disgorge the oily, fishy contents of its stomach over the offender. After several baths the smell may be eliminated from the skin, but no matter how many times the affected clothes are cleaned, the smell will linger on. The largest breeding ground of the ferocious arctic skua in the northern hemisphere is on the Breida-merkur sands. It is a rapacious predator attacking other birds and their young, and stealing their eggs. The area is also interesting because it is on the migration route for a number of birds in the autumn and spring.

Apart from its present day interest as a national park, Skaftafell is also important because of the part it played in Iceland's history. It used to be the meeting place for the region's assembly and it is mentioned many times in the island's Sagas. Flosi, one of the characters in the *Njálasaga*, used to live at Svínafell, while another, Kári Sólmundarson, lived at a now abandoned farm at Breidá. Until the introduction of air flights, much of this region was truly isolated, almost the only communication with the outside world coming from the occasional freighters which plied along the coast. For centuries, the sturdy Icelandic horse was not only the pack animal but also the only way of travelling long distances. A few intrepid travellers would venture into this region on horseback but it could be a hazardous journey.

Because of the lack of good anchorages, the freighters would often try to unload their cargoes on the ice floes, or some way out to sea. The coast has many wrecks to show how dangerous this could be. A Dutch cargo vessel is reported to have foundered off this coast in 1667 with a valuable cargo on board, but all attempts to find her have failed. Although the name Iceland is a misnomer, as ice does not cover much of the country-side, anyone visiting the country must see the glaciers.

It is from this region that the best approaches to Öraefajökull and Vatnajökull can be made. Although there are many legends of islanders crossing the glacier from north to south, the first recorded crossing was in 1875 by the British explorer W.L. Watts. The first organised all-Iceland crossing was completed by three young men from Höfn in 1926. Since 1954 the Icelandic Geological Society has made many trips on to the glaciers, and travel has been made much easier by the use of snowmobiles.

The ascent of **Hvannadalshnjúkur**, the highest peak in Iceland at 2,119m(almost 7,000ft), is best attempted from Sandfell, an abandoned farm. At least 6 hours must be allowed for the reasonably fit, and May and June are considered the best months for climbing.

It is strongly advisable not to climb glaciers alone unless experienced. There are hundreds of crevices and cracks crisscrossing the glacier and it is very easy to become cut off. For instance, just after World War II, an American plane crashed into the glacier, and half the passengers and crew were killed outright. The remainder were unscathed and started to make their way down the glacier to safety. Not one of them survived, and the glacier continued to throw their bodies up at its feet for years afterwards.

It is possible to hire caravanettes and the like, or to stay in a neighbouring town, but the time taken to drive to the park each day cuts down the time left for sightseeing.

Perhaps the contrasts make Skaftafell so exciting. There is the roaring Atlantic on one side, and the vast white mass of the glacier on the other, and in between these, a paradise of lush grasses and flowers.

There are many walks in and around Skaftafell and most of them are well marked, not only with distances but also with the approximate times needed to complete them. It is possible to walk up to the base of the Kristínartindar peaks, which rise to about 1,130m (3,700ft), or down into the glacial valley of Morsárdalur. Another walk goes to Baejarstadaskógur, a veritable forest by Icelandic standards of willows, birches and rowans. One has to cross some rivers, and while it can be done by four-wheel drive vehicle, it is much more of an adventure to hike in.

There are wardens on duty throughout the summer months to advise on how best to see the park, and the campsite has a modern toilet block with washrooms and showers, a shop and café. Maps and guides of the park can be bought there.

Worth visiting while in the park is the **Svartifoss** waterfall, about half a mile from the three farms. The columnar basalt formations are said to have inspired the interior décor of the National Theatre in Reykjavík.

Two other places of interest to visit are **Hof** and **Kvisker** with its many rare flowers. *Hof* is the Icelandic word for 'temple' and you will see it cropping up on the map in several places. Hof used to be the site of a pagan temple but there is now a turf-roofed church, rebuilt in the 1880s. It can be inspected as can Gröf, an old farm that has been excavated from the pumice which covered it during the 1362 eruption. Kvisker is a resting post for travellers, especially in olden days for those on horseback.

*A view from the Kverkfjöll mountains*

# Additional Information

## Places to Visit

### Heimaey
*Town Hall and Cultural Centre*
Open: Monday to Friday 9.30am-3pm.

*Folk Museum*
Open: 1 June to 31 August 1-4pm daily,
1 September to 31 May Saturday/
Sunday 1-4pm.

*Aquarium*
Open: 1 May to 31 August Saturday/
Sunday 11am-5pm, 1 September to 30
April Saturday/Sunday 3-5pm.

### Keldur
*Folk Museum*
Open: 1 June to 15 September daily
10am-6pm, rest of year on request.
☎ (98) 78452

### Skógar
*Folk Museum*
Open: 1 May to 15 September 9am-
12noon and 1-6pm.

## Accommodation

Outside urban areas

### Fljótsdalur Youth Hostel
(summer only)
☎ (98) 78498

### Hrunamannahreppur
Hvítárholt
(sleeping bag accommodation)
☎ (98) 66758

Nátthagi Guesthouse
☎ (98) 66737

### Landsveit
Leirubakki Youth Hostel
(summer only)
☎ (98) 76591

### Skaftártunga
Flaga
☎ (98) 71377

### Skeid
Brautarholt
(sleeping bag accommodation)
☎ (98) 65508

### Skógar
In Rangárvallasysla
Hotel Edda
(summer only)
☎ (98) 78870

### Stóru-Versalir Guesthouse
(summer only)
By Sprengisandur road
☎ (98) 75058

### Nr Vík
Reynisbrekka Youth Hostel
☎ (98) 71106

*Campsites*
### Eyjafjallasveit
Skógar
Seljavellir
☎ (98) 78810

### Landssveit
Leirubakki

### Skaftártunga
Hrífunes

### Skeid
Brautarholt

### Stóru-Versalir
By Sprengisandur road
☎ (98) 75078

### Sydra-Langholt
In Hreppar
Alfaskeid
☎ (98) 66674

# 4

# THE SOUTH-EAST AND THE EASTERN FJORDS

The drive past Skaftafell leads into the south-east corner of Iceland. Behind is Europe's largest glacier and one of the world's most fascinating places. For although the ground is covered with ice in the hills, underneath the volcanoes still rumble on. Occasionally the heat rises close enough to the surface to melt the ice, and massive torrents of water sweep down across the plain into the sea. It was this kind of tidal wave, of greater volume than the Amazon estuary, that would frequently sweep away roads and bridges. Now, the road has been built to take you across the sand and flood plain, and beyond, to fishing towns like Höfn, and the east coast.

The horses of this region are reputed to be the most sturdy in Iceland, and they were nicknamed the 'water horses' because of their ability to cross the toughest ground, including fast-flowing rivers.

The whole of this region is still very active geologically speaking and it is possible to see how the country has, and is, being formed. Almost all the inhabited areas of Iceland, that is the coastal plains running between sea and mountain, were once covered by the oceans. The original coastline can still be spotted in many areas along the foothills of the mountains in the south-east.

About 10,000 years ago, the glaciers melted from the lowlands, and the island literally began to rise from the sea. Geologists think that the weight of the glaciers was so immense that it physically forced the island down. Proof of this can still be seen on the Hoffellsjökull glacier, near Höfn, which has been known to reveal sea shells from time to time, giving glimpses of its past. Eventually the upward movement of the land ceased, and the south-east corner began to sink back into the sea. At this south-east corner the land is thought to have submerged by as much as 5m (18ft), but this has to be balanced against the constant flow of silt from the glaciers which is extending the area of land around estuaries and in the fjords.

It is possible to fly to Höfn which saves a considerable amount of time, although the drive along the south coast from Reykjavík is an adventure. The road from Skaftafell, for example, to Hof is very potholed and care needs to be taken although it is quite passable by two-wheel drive vehicles. Most drivers try to stick to the centre of the road unless there is oncoming traffic, because the sides of the road can often be washed away, or the verges are soft and you may get stuck. The road deteriorates even more around Hof and you will be lucky to do more than 15-20km/h (9-12mph), so bear this in mind when trying to work out timings. There are incredible rock formations to your left, and the cloud ceiling can drop very quickly, obscuring everything in a blanket of mist. Inland, Öraefajökull dominates the landscape, with its peaks of Hvannadalshnjúkur (2,119m, 6,950ft) — the highest in Iceland — and Snaebreid (2,041m, 6,694ft), but these are often hidden by clouds.

From Hof, the gravel road follows the coast north-eastwards the 100km (62 miles) or so to Höfn, crossing the Breidamerkur sands which stretch for 25km (15 miles), and pass the spectacular finger glacier of Kvíarjökull, and then Fjallsjökull and Breidamerkurjökull. The farms here are separated by huge areas of mud and glacial silt.

The photographic possibilities in this area are tremendous, and it is a great place to get out and explore on foot. There are a number of walks in this area and you can discover many lakes formed by the glacier. The two best lakes are both near the road and you can drive right down to their edge. You will jump on the brakes when you first see Breidárlon with its icebergs and intense blue water, but don't take too much film, because the next lake, Jókulsárlón, is much bigger and far more spectacular. The glacier plunges into the water and the huge chunks of ice that break free and drift away are an amazing assortment of colours. Some are pure white, others black because of the lava sand they have collected, others are striped and yet more are vivid blue because of the way they reflect the sun's rays. Many of the icebergs have been trapped in the lake for years, while a few drift away out to sea. The sight is so spectacular that a local fisherman in Höfn now offers boat trips round the lake.

The gravel road then skirts the southern flanks of Sudursveit until it reaches the radio station at Smyrlabjórg. From here until Höfn, apart from a 4km (2½ miles) section around Bjarnanes, the road is metalled and fast. Suddenly the vegetation improves, there is rich farmland again with lots of cows, sheep and horses in the fields during the summer months, and then the road swings round Hornafjördur and you drop down into **Höfn**, sheltering under the backdrop of Vatnajökull to the north-west.

There is still a lot of building going on. The Youth Hostel is well signposted, although a bit of a walk from the bus stop. There is a campsite on the edge of town with washing and toilet facilities, but it can be very windy here so pick your site carefully. At the entrance to the campsite there is an information centre, and people using the campsite can use the shower and bathing facilities at the nearby swimming pool. There is also a large Hotel Edda on the outskirts of the town, a good hotel which is being extended, supermarkets, shops, restaurants, filling stations, cinema and  a museum. There is a pharmacist and facilities for hiring cars and horses. The Höfn airstrip is very close to the town, which is the largest in this

THE SOUTH-EAST AND
THE EASTERN FJORDS

Burstafell Museum

NESKAUPSTADUR
Natural History Museum

Vopnafjördur

Grimsstadir

Húsey

Kirkjubaer

ESKIFJÖRDUR
Folk and Maritime
Museum

Bakkagerdi

Klyppsstadur

Egilsstadir

Seydisfjördur

Neskaupstadur

Hengifoss
Eiríksstadir

Eskifjördur
Reydarfjördur

Narrow Tunnel
Gerpir
Headland

Askja

Fáskrúdsfjördur

Fáskrúdsfjördur

Kirkjuból
Stödvarfjördur
Breiddalsvík

Bulandstindur

Berufjördur
Djúpivogur

Papey

VATNAJÖKULL

Bjarnanes
Höfn

Stokksnes

STÖDVARFJÖRDUR
Petra Sveinsdóttir
Rocks and Minerals Collection
Ornithology Museum

Fjallsjökull    Jökulsárlón

Folk Museum

0                60km

0                40 miles

south-east corner. Höfn is a thriving fishing port with associated industries such as fish processing. It is also the commercial and market town for
a prosperous agriculture inland. In the last few years the town has grown
rapidly, again thanks to the completion of the road linking it with towns
to the west in 1974. Although it can be a bumpy and long journey there is
a regular bus service between Reykjavík and Höfn, and you can stop off

on the way to spend a night or two camped out in Skaftafell before continuing your journey. In Iceland, bus schedules are remarkably well adhered to.

Near the airport is Bjarnanes, a very old parsonage and manor that has  many close links with the island's history in the Middle Ages. From the Stapahólar hills, just to the south of Bjarnanes, there is a view across the  fjord Hornafjördur, to the surrounding mountains and glaciers. Like most other places in Iceland, the photographs almost take themselves, regardless of the quality of the photographer. On 2 August 1924, a plane piloted by the Swedish-American Nelson, who had flown to Iceland in 8½ hours from the Orkney Islands on his way west, landed at Höfn on the final stage of its journey. It was the first plane ever to fly around the world.

There are many things to see and do in Höfn, and there is a comfortable modern hotel to stay in as well as a Youth Hostel, campsite, and guesthouses. Since the road was built in 1974 linking Höfn to the rest of the south coast, there has been a massive increase in the number of travellers. The town used to get intrepid visitors in the past, but they had to arrive by steamer, on horseback, or after a long journey along the north coast and then down the east side of the country. Today, you can fly, or catch a scheduled bus. There are also many tours which take in Höfn and allow further exploration.

The area is good for walking and camping, and immensely attractive to naturalists, being rich in wildlife and rare plants. There are roads leading northwards to the Eastern Fjords and westwards to Öraefi. There is plenty

*Höfn Harbour*

of good sport available in the area, good cheap fishing in the lakes and rivers, and large numbers of plaice and flounders to catch in the fjords. Traditional Icelandic fishermen work here, using both nets and spears to catch the fish.

There is a greater variety of birdlife here than anywhere else in Iceland. The area is of special interest to ornithologists because many birds, swept in from western Europe on freak winds, have their first chance of landfall on this south-east outcrop of land. About forty species of birds from western Europe have been seen here in recent years, and it is thought that some species from mainland and northern Europe have established themselves in Iceland in this way. Certainly the starling and lapwing first settled and bred here before moving to colonise other parts of the island. The eider breeds in Hornafjördur and there are also large numbers of great skuas, great black-back gulls, fulmars, and arctic terns.

The area is also rich in plant life, and again, many species can be found here which do not appear elsewhere in Iceland. Flora such as the blue sesleria, the rosa dumalis and the green spleenwort can be found. Some of these species can only be found in Öraefi, but the locals, especially the farmers, have always taken a keen interest in the natural history of their area. It is true that until recently much of this region had not been scientifically explored, so new species are being discovered, not because they are new, but because they have not previously been catalogued.

From Höfn it is possible either to walk or to drive to the Almannaskard Pass, which is 11km (7 miles) away, and from here there are magnificent views of the coastline, glaciers and settlements. To the east of the pass there is the deeply indented Papafjördur with the estuary of the Papós. When the Norsemen first arrived in Iceland, they landed in this south-east corner, although it was to be several years before the first Norse settler Ingólfur Arnarson made his way along the coast to build his house on the site on which Reykjavík now stands. From the records of these earliest times it was clear that the first settlers on the island were Irish monks, who had chosen to live hermits' lives in the caves along the southern coast, but were gradually driven out by the heathens. It is not known where they went, but they left behind many artefacts, and there are still traces of their presence to be found in some of the place names. Some way north of the Hamarsfjördur, there has been a find that has still to be satisfactorily explained: three Roman coins, all dating from about AD300 were excavated from a field. There are no records of the Romans being here, but it is possible that a Roman ship, caught up in one of the terrible storms that sweep the area, may have been driven ashore, and some of its crew or at least some of its cargo, landed. Another theory is that the coins were brought in by the Vikings, who would certainly have had access to them during their raids in Britain and the Low Countries. However, no one really knows.

Farther around the coast is the US radar station at **Stokksnes**, which seems to attract all the seals in the area, of which there are large numbers.

There is much of interest to the geologist in this part of the country. The volcanic and glacial rocks contain many precious minerals, notably jasper  and opal, and there are many sub-species of rock which are peculiar to Iceland.

The road out of Höfn heading for Djúpivogur is lovely if the weather is fine, but can be hazardous if it is wet or there is a mist. The road follows the sea and hugs the mountains which tower above you on the right-hand side. There are many tight bends and in places, there is a sheer drop down to the sea. Massive scree slopes tower above you on the mountain side, and there are frequent landslides which throw debris across the road. The road is potholed and in wet weather can be very muddy, so drive at a safe speed to avoid sliding about.

Because of the deep fjords which penetrate well inland, you can eat up the miles getting to the various towns. It is a little frustrating when you turn a headland and can see the settlement you are driving to just a few kilometres across the water, but know that you have to drive 50km (30 or so miles) or more to get to it. Throughout the Eastern Fjords almost all the roads hug the coastline. There are a few roads through the mountains which can save you miles, but not necessarily time if the weather is bad. Always check before heading off for a mountain road. Ask the locals what the weather is like and what conditions you will face.

As you head towards Djúpivogur there is the sand bar enclosing Lónsfjördur, the waters of which provide the summer home for hundreds of whooper swans. Once round the headland which skirts Snjotindur, you  can see the even larger sand bank that nearly encircles Álftafjördur, with **Djúpivogur** in the distance on a promontory sticking out to sea.

As you approach the settlement, you will see the wooden fish racks where mostly cod are hung out to dry. These racks are a feature all along the coast, a sign that the population is so dependent on the sea for much of its living. It is one of the oldest trading centres in the region dating back to around 1600 and once served a huge area. The oldest house dates back to the arrival of Danish merchants in the area, around the end of the eighteenth century. The town has always prospered because of its good natural harbour. Fishing is the main industry and there is a large freezer plant.

It is also nice to see the trees just outside the town, and because this vegetation has been scarce on the island, great pains are taken to protect them. This often includes surrounding them with barbed wire to prevent the sheep from stripping off the bark. The 1,069m (3,506ft) pyramid-shaped Búlandstindur is reputed to be one of the most powerful 'spiritual power centres' on earth. This is excellent walking country through peaceful landscapes and you may come across wild reindeer.

Back westwards along the coast from Höfn there is a change in the geology, and a return to volcanic tuff. The change occurs about 87km (54 miles) from Höfn on the river Jökulsá on the **Breidamerkur Sands**. Here, glaciers constantly encroach and there is only a narrow strip between mountains and sea. In places the plain is only 5km (3 miles) wide and all the farms are separated by the mud and glacial silt deposits which are said to be more impressive here than anywhere else in the world.

There are many interesting places to visit such as the Hestgerdislón lagoon, just to the south of the Borgarhafnarfjall mountain. Many of the nearby place names are connected with the sea or fishing, reflecting the region's past. Until the end of the sixteenth century there was a small fishing port here known as Hálsar, but due to land subsidence, boats have not been able to use it since. There are also ruins of a fishing station at Kambstún, which now form a grassy plot just below the mountain.

During the fishing season, people used to come here from the north, having crossed Vatnajökull to get to the sea. The easiest northern approach to the glacier is from the farm of Kálfafellsstadur, through the Stadardalur Valley, and this part of the glacier is known as the Heinabergsjökull. Although this is the easiest route it is still fairly dangerous and it must have been quite an exciting trip in the Middle Ages, and a dire necessity that forced the fishermen to make such a trip. Other people from the north would go to fish off Ingólfshöfdi, but they would come down from the glacier in the Morsárdalur Valley in Skaftafell National Park. When at the end of the sixteenth century, the climate throughout Iceland turned colder, but especially so in the glacier region, the annual migration south ended. Other sites to visit are the mountains of Papylisfjall, and especially the Klukkugil ravine, and the breathtaking scenery at Járnhus, near Gardhvammur.

On the Breidamerkur Sands you can see some of the destruction

*Iceberg Lagoon*

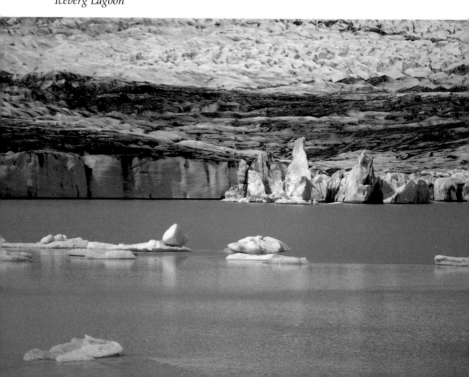

wreaked by the glaciers over the last two or three hundred years. The river Jökulsá flows out into a large lagoon which is often host to huge icebergs, which break off from the glacier towering behind. In the east there is now a wasteland, which was woodland before it was destroyed by the advancing glacier. Fortunately, the history of this time is well recorded in the *Njálasaga*. In many ways history is still being created here by the constant geological activity.

The eastern shoreline of Iceland is very reminiscent of Norway with its deeply indented coastline and mountains which plunge steeply straight into the sea. The Icelandic word for these inlets is *vík*, and presumably this is where the word Vikings comes from.

## The Eastern Fjords

The Eastern Fjords stretch from Berufjördur in the south which plunges north-westwards into the hinterland, to Borgarfjördur Eystri and Héradsflói in the north. Between these two places there are many coastal villages to visit, although much of the population has moved away from the countryside, and most of the farms are now abandoned.

In the Eastern Fjords (Austfirdir in Icelandic), there is little sign of the volcanic activity that can be seen in most other parts of the country. This is because the land here is the oldest in Iceland and it consists mostly of basalt, which contains spar, pearlite, quartz and fossils. Crystals of spar, with their special property of double refraction — known as Iceland spar — have been recovered in the past for use in the optical industry, and there

*Jökuldalur near Haukstadir Farm*

may be industrial possibilities for the pearlite as well.

Because many of the fjords are long and narrow, with towering sides, they are protected from the sea and make ideal shelters for vessels and wildlife. The coast above Húsey, at the end of highway 926, is home to a huge seal colony. There is also a Youth Hostel and horse riding is available from the nearby farm. In most of the inlets there is a fishing village, and the fishermen are some of the most skilled in the world. Not only do they have to contend with some of the most dangerous seas anywhere, their own coastline is littered with submerged rocks and reefs, which have caused many ships to founder.

Because the mountains inside the coast are so steep, travel used to be very difficult, but engineers solved the problem by building the roads wherever possible along the ridges of the hills, so that even though they are at high altitude, they do allow access.

There is no real coastal plain in this area because the mountains are so close to the sea, but behind the range is a plain, fertile enough for agriculture. Known as the **Fljótsdalshérad**, it reaches from a point just north of Austfirdir, and all the way south down the region, and encompasses some marvellous scenery. There are woods and lakes surrounded by lush vegetation and in the Fljótsdalshérad there are many farms. It has one of the most temperate climates in Iceland — not too cold in winter and quite warm in summer. The region is dominated by the market town of Egilsstadir, which has an airfield and a good road network which makes it ideal as a base for touring. From here, the wild, eerie world of Iceland's interior can be explored; not far away is **Askja**, a volcano that has erupted many times in the last hundred years. It has a caldera up to 50sq km (20sq miles) in size in the Dyngjiufjöll mountains. A lake called Öskjuvatn was formed after the massive eruption in 1875, and it is the deepest in Iceland at 220m (722ft) deep and with an area of 12sq km (4 ½sq miles). Beside the lake is the explosion crater Viti, formed on 29 March 1875; it is 100m (328ft) across, about 60m (200ft) deep and it is filled with water. Askja is a central volcano and it has erupted many times; 1961 was the last time. To reach the mountain a four-wheel drive vehicle is essential, and then a sturdy pair of walking boots. **Herdubreidarlindir** is an area of clear freshwater springs at the edge of the Ódádahraun, near the mountain of Herdubreid, often called the Queen of Iceland's Mountains. The area is lush and overgrown, and the springs were declared a nature reserve in 1974. This fertile region finally peters out in the south when it comes up against the northern edge of the Vatnajökull glacier.

The region can trace its history back to the earliest settlements of Iceland. Because it was the nearest coastline to Norway it was the first to be visited by the Norsemen in their explorations. They certainly landed here in the ninth century and some of them may have even come from the parts of Britain they had colonised. As in other parts of the south, there were Irish monks already living here in seclusion. The island off Berufjördur is called Papey, and is said to have derived its name from these Christians. It literally means Monks' Island.

There are even records that pirates from North Africa raided this coastline in the seventeenth century. Many records tell of the attacks by the 'Turks' on this coast and in other parts of south and east Iceland. Although the pickings cannot have been too rich, people were often taken away as slaves. There were two trading posts along this coast in the seventeenth and eighteenth centuries, at Reydarfjördur and Djúpivogur. This was at the time of the strict Danish trading monopoly and it is only in the last 100 years or so that the region has really developed. Like much of Iceland's prosperity, the wealth came from the sea. Until the late nineteenth century, there were few people living in the region and the small population was isolated with little chance of mixing, because travel between settlements was so difficult. Then the Norwegians arrived, searching for good fishing ground, and they established many of the small coastal villages which still thrive today.

The villages were set up to handle the herring catches, and then whaling stations were established. The coastline is the nearest part of Iceland to Norway, and Norway's influence can still be seen in the architecture and names used by the people of Austfirdir. In 1918 when Iceland received its independence from Denmark, it banned all foreign fishing interests from operating from its territory, and the fortunes of the Eastern Fjords began to decline. Some of the people moved inland and tried to farm, but better sea travel and the need for fish restored the fortunes of the region.

New ports were established at Neskaupstadur, in Nordfjördur, which were much closer to the fishing grounds, and the region's economy boomed after World War II when the herring returned in massive shoals off the coast. By then, there had been considerable advances in fishing techniques, not only in catching, but also in handling and processing. It is still worth visiting one of the fjords in the summer, when the catches are being landed, to see the bustle and activity. The arrival of the trawlers is presaged by armies of birds calling loudly and swooping overhead. Then, it seems that every member of the community joins in to help with the work of unloading.

Again, this coastline is a must for naturalists, for it teems with birdlife and seals. Like other parts of the south and east coast, the seals are still hunted for their skins, and the fishermen and farmers see this as a valuable source of extra income.

The best way to see the true splendour of the Eastern Fjords is to visit them by boat, provided sufficient time is available, and there are a number that ply around the coast, calling briefly at the villages in the fjords. If time is more pressing, it is possible to fly to Egilsstadir from either Reykjavík or Akureyri and then hire a car, to drive in. There are many hotels, guesthouses, and campsites throughout the region, and the more time you have to spend exploring here the better.

There are a number of islands off the coast of the Eastern Fjords, the most famous of which are **Skrudur** in the Fáskrúdsfjördur and **Papey**.

Both can be reached by ferry or local boat.

The eastern seashore has a very pleasant summer climate, and the landscape can be seen at its best during the summer months. **Búlandstindur**, which raises majestically to 1,069m (3,507ft), is thought by many to be the most beautiful summit in the east. It is best viewed from Djúpivogur or from the sea, but no matter from which direction you view it, it is magnificent.

Lagarfljót in Fljótsdalur is the second largest river in the east, running for about 140km (87 miles). The third largest lake in Iceland can be found in its upper reaches, and this 52sq km (20sq miles) wide stretch of water is said by legend to house the Lagarfljótsormur, a serpent-like creature, possibly Iceland's answer to the Loch Ness Monster. The lake is called **Lögurinn**.

**Hallormsstadur**, to the east of Lake Lögurinn, is the forest area which covers the site of an old manor house and church. The government decided to set up its experimental forestry centre here earlier this century. Scientists are trying to see which trees can cope best with the Icelandic climate and more than forty varieties from many countries have been planted. Varieties include mostly spruce and larch, but seeds and saplings have been brought in from the United States, Canada and Siberia.

Because of the forest, the country's largest, there is scenery here which is found almost nowhere else in Iceland, and because of this the area attracts many tourists. There is a very good camping ground at **Atlavík**, named after the pioneer settler Atli, on the shore of Lake Lögurinn. The river and lake are too cold to swim in, but there are many interesting walks in the area, and remember to look out for the 'monster'. There is a summer hotel. **Eidar** has a large district boarding school, which like most of the others in rural Iceland, is turned into a summer hotel during the 3-month-long vacation.

There are many tours of this area, and these can be arranged either locally or in Reykjavík. One of the best is a 5-hour tour which goes through the Hallormsstadur woods and round Lake Lögurinn and includes lunch. On the way it visits the Grímsá hydro-electric power station, the Valthjófsstadur church and the **Skriduklaustur** experimental farm.

The Valthjófsstadur church is famous for its carved wooden door which dates back to the turn of the twelfth century, although only a replica is to be seen, as the original is now preserved in the National Museum in Reykjavík. The experimental farm used to be the site of a fifteenth-century monastery, and some ruins of this can still be seen. It was here in the eighteenth century that the first reindeer were introduced into the country from Scandinavia by Hans Wium, the local sheriff. The reindeer still roam wild in the highlands of eastern Iceland and occasionally they are shot and their meat offered in local restaurants. The present buildings, designed by a German just before the outbreak of World War II, were the home of the famous Icelandic author Gunnar Gunnarsson, who donated them to the state. Part of them have been converted into a local folk museum.

*(Opposite) Litlanesfoss waterfall on the way to Hengifoss*

Nearby is the country's third largest waterfall **Hengifoss** (118m, 387ft) — a 3km (2 mile) walk from the road — and also on this tour you can see the remains of a stone-free church, and Mjóanes, the place where the warrior poet Helgi Arinbjörnsson lived many centuries ago.

While in the area the waterfall at **Lagarfoss** and the seal colony at **Húsey** in the north, should be visited. A stay in this region should also include a trip into the interior or on the Vatnajökull. There are many such tours organised and local guides to escort travellers. The best way in is either on horseback, or in a four-wheel drive vehicle.

The area is also good for bird watchers, and fly fishermen, and there is some excellent trout fishing to be had here. A licence is needed but it is not expensive.

**Egilsstadir** is a town that has mushroomed in the last two decades from a small market centre into a flourishing community with a lot of accommodation provided by a hotel, guest houses, sleeping bag accommodation and on farms nearby. There is a hospital, a number of restaurants and cafés, and a tourist information centre and travel bureau. Fishing permits can be obtained here, there is horse riding available, as well as a swimming pool and museum. You can hire bicycles, sea cats and play golf. It is also the site of the largest airport in the east, and is a natural touring centre, because from here you can travel in any direction. The town lies beside Lake Lögurinn and is at the main junction of the roads from Reykjavík and Akureyri with routes from them to all the fjords. There is a magnificent view of the whole area and the snow-capped peaks in the background, from the Seydisfjördur road just above Egilsstadir.

There is plenty of good accommodation in the region, including overnight accommodation on farms. The Hotel Valaskjálf holds traditional feats *(Héradsmót)* every Thursday evening during the summer, with Icelandic delicacies and lots of singing and dancing — everyone takes part! Also fun is the town's outdoor market held during the summer, known for its bargains and street entertainers. In Midhús, there is an artist's workshop specialising in woodcarving from Icelandic wood.

Interesting outings from Egilsstadir include trips to Hengifoss, the incredible rock formations around Stóraurd at Dryfjöll (the doors), and Fagradalsfoss on Fjardarheidi, where you walk behind the waterfall. You can also take short flights from the airstrip to Kverkfjöll, Askja and Herdubreid, as well as trips along the coast either by plane or boat. The Tourist Information Centre at the campsite, is very helpful, and buses leave from here for other parts of the region, north to Myvatn and Akuyeri, and south to Höfn and back to Reykjavík.

There are many organised tours of the area which leave from Egilsstadir. You can join a convoy of four wheel drive vehicles to Snaefell and the Eyjabakkajökull glacier, and to Kverkfjöll, from where you can walk up to Hveradalir. In 1992 the airport's runways were extended to accommodate international flights.

**Fellabaer**, on the western shore of Lagarfljót, across from Egilsstadir is a fast growing town. There is much to see and do, especially for those interested in nature or walking. It is possible to walk down into the Eyvindará ravine and also to visit **Gálgaklettur**, a small town where there is a stone marking the scene of the last execution in this district. In the eighteenth century, a man called Valtyr was put to death. The reason for his execution has been obscured by time, but local legend has it that he was innocent of any crime.

**Seydisfjördur** is a town standing on the fjord of the same name and for many years it was the largest town on the east coast. It is still the ferry port for ships arriving from the Faroes and the drive over the mountains to Egilsstadir is one of the most spectacular in Iceland, if not a little daunting if it is your first experience of driving in the country. As you climb away from the town, the valley is surrounded by sheer cliffs and scores of  plunging waterfalls. The mountains rise to 1,028m (3,371ft) and avalanches and rock slides are not uncommon. After climbing past the river which plunges in a series of spectacular falls, the road crosses a stark plateau with Heidarvatn on your right, a large, gaunt lake at 585m (1,918ft). It can be very cold and windy up here, but as you pass the lake you soon start your descent and can see Egilsstadir deep in the valley below.

Seydisfjördur is still a charming town, and the prettiest along the east coast. It began as a trading post in 1834 but it prospered in the latter part of the century. The town still has many wooden houses dating from the  turn of the century, showing the strong Norwegian influences in the area. Many Norwegian businessmen were attracted here last century because of the harbour, good weather and herring shoals. Otto Wathne was one of them and he is now regarded as the founder of the town. The decline of recent years has now been halted and there is a hotel, youth hostel, community centre, cinema and a campsite nearby at Fjardarsel. There is a good, but steep, footpath along the River Fjardará as it tumbles into town, and the walk to Lodmundarfjördur is easy. **Reydarfjördur** also started life as a trading post although its real name is Búdareyri. It grew in size with the completion of the highway in 1909, and during World War II was the home of one of the Allied Forces' largest bases. It is another useful place to stop and from which to explore the surrounding countryside. It has two hotels and a campsite, as well as all the usual facilities. Although industry is becoming important, the town's economy is still based on fishing. A coastal steamer calls here. You must try the hot springs.

Iceland's highest road suitable for motor vehicles travels through this area linking Eskifjördur and Nordfjördur using the Oddsskard Pass. In places the road is 660m, or more than 2,160ft above sea level.

**Eskifjördur** is another town named after the fjord on which it stands. The fjord is about 2km (1¼ miles) long and up to 6km (3¾ miles) wide.  Much of the surrounding area is protected because of its outstanding natural beauty and the wealth of natural history to be found there. The protected area is known as the Hólmanes, and this is the area between Eskifjördur and Reydarfjördur. The most easterly point in Iceland, the

**Gerpir Headland** can also be visited.

**Reydarfjördur** is the largest fjord on the eastern coast, 30km (19 miles) long and 7km (4 miles) wide in places. Eskifjördur is now reached by a good road but for centuries people either came in by boat or over the many mountain tracks, which now provide excellent summer walking.

The area around the town is known as Helgustadahreppur, named after the farm Helgustadir, the site of a spar mine worked from the seventeenth century until recently. Examples of Icelandic spar from the mine are now displayed in museums and galleries around the world, and the largest sample ever collected weighed 230kg and is now displayed in the British Museum in London. The site was declared a protected monument in 1975.

From Cape Hólmanes rises the 985m (3,230ft) high peak of Hólmatin-

*Seydisfjördur*

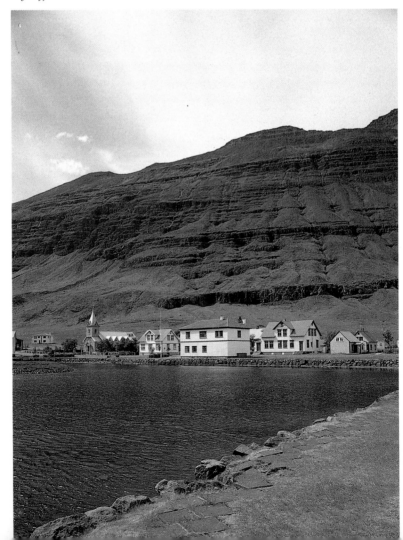

dur. Although it looks beautiful behind the town it is so high and so close it actually wipes out the daylight. Between the end of September until April it is very unusual to see the sun, which is masked behind the mountain. Fishing is the mainstay of the town and most of the other industries are associated with this, including a freezer plant. Dried fish is also produced and is very useful for campers or backpackers going into the interior. In the same way that American cowboys chewed strips of dried beef or jerky on the trail, the Icelanders chew dried fish. The fish has a number of advantages for backpackers; it is light, convenient, does not need heating and supplies plenty of nourishment. Although at first, when a piece is bitten off, it tastes just like a strip of wood, it gradually becomes softer, tastes fishier, and it is very enjoyable. The action also stimulates the salivary glands so it can be useful to bite a piece if you are feeling particularly dry. At Eskifjördur there is a hotel, a number of restaurants and all the services; there is also an interesting museum which has a ship's mast and rigging outside. There is also a very moving memorial to fishermen lost at sea. There is a well signposted campsite, swimming pool, filling station, garage and café.

It is worth the detour north to Neskaupstadur on Route 92. The road takes you through the Oddsskard Pass (at 632m, 2,073ft), the highest in Iceland) and through an eerie 600m long (1,968ft) tunnel guarded by massive pivoted metal gates. It is narrow and not too well lit and a lot of

*Breiddalsvík*

water seems to drip down from the roof, but there are spectacular views both just before and just after you pass through the tunnel. Snow lies in pockets all year round along the pass.

**Neskaupstadur** nestles on the left-hand side of Nordfjördur with the mountain finger of Bardsnes jutting out into the sea to the right giving the harbour a lot of protection. As you descend down the mountain, the valley opens up before you with its farms and fertile fields. Neskaupstadur is now the largest town in the east, again with fishing as the backbone of its economy, although there is some agriculture carried on inland. It became a trading post in 1882 and quickly prospered during the 'Herring years'. The town has a swimming pool and a community centre where you can get food and lodging. There is also a campsite and hotel, swimming pool, shops, restaurant, hospital and Natural History Museum.

Worth exploring is the lush broad valley of the River Nordflardará. The northern slopes of the valley are covered by woodland, which is thickest near the farm Krikjuból. To the north is Godaborg (1,132m, 3,713ft) the tallest peak in Nordafjórdur.

Other trips in the area include visits to the uninhabited fjords of Hellisfjórdur and Vidfjórdur from Oddsdalur. Vidfjórdur has already carved a name for itself in Iceland's mythology because it is alleged to be the site of some of the most frightening hauntings in the twentieth century. They have been recorded in a book written by Thórbergur Thórdarson. Nordfjadarnípa, which towers from the shore on the north side of Nordfjardarflói, is the tallest sea cliff in Iceland.

**Fáskrúdsfjördur** was established towards the end of the nineteenth century and became the main base for French fishermen operating in and around the Eastern Fjords. Its real name is Búdir, but this is rarely used. The French built their own hospital and chapel here but no trace of these buildings now remains, although there is the French seamen's graveyard. There is now no trace of the French because they left when the era of the sailing boats ended at the beginning of this century. The town is still charming with many different coloured houses, pretty gardens and lots of greenery. While fishing is the main occupation in the town, the hardships of farming can easily be seen by the number of deserted farms throughout the Eastern Fjords. Try to visit the huge 'evergreen' rock island of Skrúdur. Boat trips are available; and Sandfell, a magnificent laccolithic mountain, one of the world's finest examples of igneous intrusion.

**Stödvarfjördur** stands on the fjord which gives it its name, and is another of the bustling little fishing villages to be found all along this coast. There is a freezer plant which provides most of the area's employment. There is also a car repair shop, bank, store, and infirmary. Many of the houses bear paintings by local artists. The privately owned mineral museum is worth visiting.

**Breiddalsvík** stands by the cove bearing the same name and has only existed for a short time. It grew up a few decades ago when the fishing improved off the eastern coast and most of the inhabitants are now employed in the fishing industry. It has a new hotel and there is a small area of grass behind the hotel where you can camp for a small fee. The hotel is being extended and has a restaurant, and the small campsite has two small cabins, each containing washing facilities, water and toilet. There is a Hotel Edda at Stadaborg, about 7km (4 miles) west of the town.

The road out of Breiddalsvík heading for Stödvarfjördur, is spectacular with plunging cliffs on one side, and towering mountains with cascading waterfalls on the other. Great care is needed when driving, especially in wet weather when the pot holes fill with water and you cannot be sure how deep they are.

Borgarfjördur is the northernmost point of the Eastern Fjords, just south of Hérdasflói. This is a very fertile area with lush, green vegetation in the summer, surrounded by towering mountains.

The village of **Bakkagerdi** stands by the sea and has been a trading post since 1894. The church, consecrated in 1901, has a fine altar piece painted by Jóhannes S. Kjarval, depicting the *Sermon on the Mount*. The special importance of the painting is that it is based on the local landscape, with Christ standing on with Dryfjöll in the background. There is a guesthouse, café, campsite and community centre.

**Dryfjöll** (1,136m, 3,726ft) is regarded by many as the most magnificent mountain in eastern Iceland, but there are many others which can be visited from Borgarfjördur. Stadarfell is always impressive with its bright pink ravines and towering cliffs.

The area is noted for its unusual geological formulations and visitors can find many rare rock samples. For some years one company has specialised in making works of art using local rocks and stone, and there is a shop next to the works. If you have the time there is a very good trip to the uninhabited fjord of **Lodmundarfjördur**. Take the 946 out of the village to Hólaland, and then follow the track that runs over Húsavikur-heidi between the mountains of Hvítserkur and Náttmálsfjall. The track crosses Neshals and to the west is the imposing Skaelingur (832m, 2,729ft) which sailors have nicknamed the 'Chinese Temple'. From here you can follow the track north-eastwards to **Húsavík**, once a rich agricultural valley and now a deserted inlet. The old church remains, but parts of the churchyard have been lost to the sea. The area is very rich in minerals. There is a deserted farm on the northern shores of Lodmundarfjördur where the poet Páll Olafsson lived for a short time, but not too happily judging by his poetry written at the time.

There are many other deserted farms along the shores of the fjord. The author Helgi Valtysson was born in Nes, and the biggest farm was Stakkahlíd, finally abandoned in 1967. Not far from the farm and to the east are scree slopes of rhyolite deposited from Flatafjall, and close by you can see pieces of petrified wood. The farm is maintained as a summer refuge.

# Additional Information

## Places to Visit

**Borgarfjördur Eystri**
*Rock and Mineral Collection and Store*
Open: weekdays 9am-5pm, weekends 1-6pm.
☎ (97) 29977

**Egilsstadir**
*Safnastofnun Austurlands*
Skógarlöndum 4
Open: every afternoon during the summer.
☎ (97) 11451

**Eskifjördur**
*Folk and Maritime Museum*
Sjóminjasagfn Austerlands
Open: 15 June to 1 September daily 2-5pm.
☎ (97) 61179

**Höfn**
*Folk Museum*
Gömlu Búd
Hafnarbraut
Open: 15 June to 31 August, daily from 3-6pm and 8-9.30pm.
☎ (97) 81833

**Neskaupstadur**
*Natural History Museum*
Midstraeti 1
Open: 15 June to 31 August Monday to Friday 4-6pm, weekends 3-6pm by request during the winter.
☎ (97) 71454

**Stödvarfjördur**
*Petra Sveinsdöttir Rocks and Minerals Collection*
Fjardarbraut 21
Open: on request.
☎ (97) 58834

*Ornithology Museum*
(in the school)
Open: ask for details at Hotel Framtíd.

**Vopnafjördur**
*Burstafell Museum*
Open: 15 June to 15 September daily

10am-7pm.
☎ (97) 31466

## Useful Information

### Emergency Numbers
*Ambulance*
Höfn ☎ (97) 81919 (also police, fire and rescue squad)
Neskaupstadur ☎ (97) 71400
Eskifjördur ☎ (97) 61252
Reydarfjördur ☎ (97) 41248

*Fire*
Neskaupstadur ☎ (97) 71222
Eskifjördur ☎ (97) 61222
Reydarfjördur ☎ (97) 41222
Egilsstadir ☎ (97) 11222
Fellabaer ☎ (97) 11222
Seydisfjördur ☎ (97) 21222
Borgarfjördur ☎ (97) 29961

*Police*
Neskaustadur ☎ (97) 71332
Eskifjördur ☎ (97) 61106
Reydarfjördur ☎ (97) 61106
Egilsstadir ☎ (97) 11223
Seydisfjördur ☎ (97) 21334

### Hospitals
**Egilsstadir**
Health Centre
Lagarás 16
☎ (97) 11400

**Egilsstödum**
Health Centre and Hospital
Lagarási 17

**Neskaupstadur**
Fjórdungssjúkrah Austuri
Myrarg 20
☎ (97) 71400

**Seydisfjördur**
Heilsugaeslustöd Sjúkrahús
Sudurgata 8
☎ (97) 21406

## Motoring
Information on road conditions:
Vopnafjördur (97) 31302
Egilsstadir (97) 11343
Reydarfjördur (97) 41171

## Ferry Information
Seydisfjördur
Austrfarhf Information Centre
Fjardargötu 8
☎ (97) 21111

## Accommodation
A selection of hotels and guesthouses:
**Egilsstadir**
Hotel Valaskjálf
Skógarlöndum
☎ (97) 11500

Midhúsum Farm Holiday Centre
☎ (97) 11320

Guesthouse Egilsstadir
☎ (97) 81022

**Eidar**
Hotel Edda
(summer only)
☎ (97) 13803

**Fellabaer**
Skipalaekur Farm Holiday
☎ (97) 11324

Guesthouse Fellaskóli
☎ (97) 12264

**Hallormsstadur**
Hotel Edda
(summer only)
☎ (97) 11705

**Höfn**
Hotel Höfn
☎ (97) 81240

**Hólabrekku**
Hólabrekka Guesthouse
☎ (97) 81022

**Mjóifjördur**
Guesthouse Sólbrekka
☎ (97) 60002

**Nesjar**
Nr Höfn
Hotel Edda (summer only)
☎ (97) 81470
**Nesjaskóla**
Hotel Edda
(summer only)
☎ (97) 81470

**Neskaupstadur**
Hotel Egilsbúd
Egilsbraut 1
☎ (97) 71321

**Reydarfjördur**
Guesthouse KHB
Búdargata 4
☎ (97) 41447

**Seydisfjördur**
Hotel Snaefell
Austurvegi 3
☎ (97) 21460

**Thorsmörk**
Seydisfjördur
☎ (97) 21324

*Youth Hostels*
**Berunes**
(summer only)
☎ (97) 88988

**Höfn**
Farfuglaheimilid
☎ (97) 81736

**Hróarstunga**
Húsey
(summer only)
☎ (97) 13010

**Lón**
Stafafell
☎ (97) 81717

**Seydisfjördur**
Hafaldan
Ránargata 9
☎ (97) 21410

*Campsites*
**Berufjördur**
Nr Djúpivogur
Eyjólfsstadir
☎ (97) 88971

**Egilsstadir**
Campsite
☎ (97) 12001

**Eskifjördur**
Skrúdgard
☎ (97) 61170

**Hallormsstadarskógur**
Atlavík

**Höfn**
Hafnarbraut
☎ (97) 81701

Mánagardur
☎ (97) 81779

**Lón**
Stafafell
☎ (97) 81717

**Mjöifjördur**
Sólbrekka
☎ (97) 60007

**Neskaupstadur**
Bókkum
☎ (97) 71700

**Reydarfjördur**
Fagradalsbraut
☎ (985) 35556

**Seydisjördur**
Campsite
☎ (97) 21214

**Störa-Sandfell**
17km (11 miles) south of Egilsstadir
☎ (97) 11785

**Recreation**
*Swimming Pools*
**Höfn**
Hafnarbraut 11
☎ (97) 81157

**Eskifjördur**
Lambeyrarbraut 14
☎ (97) 61238

**Reydarfjördur**
Heidarvegi 14
☎ (97) 41331

**Neskaupstadur**
Midstraeti 17
☎ (97) 71243

*Golf*
**Neskaupstadur**
Graenanesbakki
☎ (97) 71700

**Eskifjördur**
Byggdaholt
☎ (97) 61170

*Salmon Fishing (permits)*
**Reydarfjördur**
Andapollur
☎ (985) 35556

**Neskaupstadur**
☎ (97) 71243

**Eskifjardará**
☎ (97) 61170

*Ski Centre*
**Oddskardi**
Oddskard
☎ (97) 71474

**Tourist Information Centres**

**Egilsstadir**
Kaupvangi 6c
☎ (97) 12001

**Höfn**
Hafnarbraut
☎ (97) 81701

**Seydisfjördur**
*Fjardargata 8*
☎ (97) 21111

# 5

# THE NORTH OF ICELAND

The north of Iceland is a lush farming area with broad valleys and some of the best rivers for salmon fishing. Transport around the area is relatively easy as there are good roads and some airstrips. There are many fishing villages along this stretch of coastline.

There are also many places to visit if you are interested in wildlife; of special note are the two islands of Málmey and Drangey which have interesting bird populations.

The northern and north-eastern regions contain some of the jewels of Iceland's rich treasure chest. Akureyri is the capital of this region and the the largest town in the north. To the east is Húsavík, another fishing town with a good hotel, which comes into its own during the winter because of its winter sports facilities. Lake Myvatn, however, is the area's greatest attraction, for its beauty, its internationally famous wildlife, and for its spectacular geological wonders.

The northern coast is divided into east and west by **Eyjafjördur**, the fjord that runs inland to Akureyri. It cuts through steep-sided mountains that split the region in two. The mouth of the fjord is 24km (15 miles) wide, with the headlands of Hvannadalabjarg on the west and Gjögur on the east. The sea runs inland for almost 60km (37 miles) to Akureyri. Near Akureyri the fjord narrows to approximately 2½km (1½ miles) wide. The northern part around the mouth of the fjord is dominated by the mountains which fall steeply into the sea, and there is little coastal land, especially in the region between the villages of Dalvík on the western shore and Grenivík on the eastern banks. To the south, the coastal plain widens, and there are fertile plains where a wide range of crops are grown, and animals are grazed.

There are many rivers running from the fjord and it is pleasant to explore them. There are now good roads in the area, and a new one to take travellers from Akureyri across the fjord and south to Lake Myvatn is now under construction. It includes a raised section over the fjord.

Eyjafjördur is separated from the Skagafjördur Valley to the west by a range of flat-topped mountains called the Tröllaskagi, mostly between

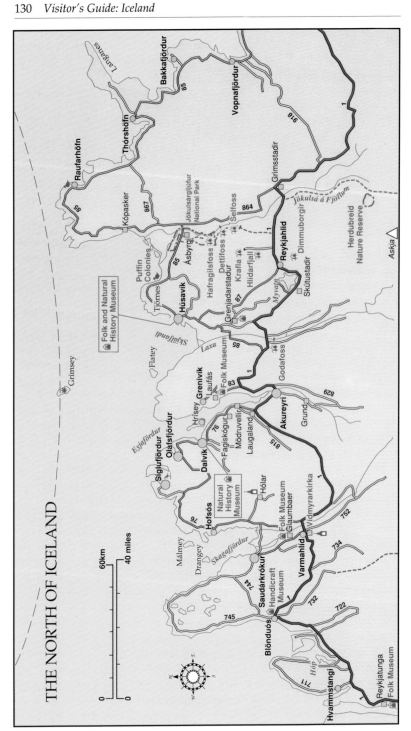

1,200 and 1,400m (3,937 and 4,593ft) high. When driving north round the island from Reykjavík to Akureyri, the Öxnadalur Pass at 550m (1,804ft) is crossed. Another route follows the western shores of Eyjafjördur round, through the village of Ólafsfjördur, and across the high moors of the Lágheidi (400m, 1,312ft) to Siglufjördur. A tunnel then takes the route to the eastern side of Skagafjördur.

Another, smaller mountain chain is to be found between Eyjafjördur and the Skjálfandi Bay to the east, dominated by the port of Húsavík. To the south is the main road to eastern Iceland, Lake Myvatn and Reykjavík.

You can drive some way up the Eyjafjördur, as far as the village of Grenivík, but beyond Grenivík the country is uninhabited and rugged, with the snow-capped coastline known as Látraströnd. Here you can see the 1,167m (3,828ft) high Kaldbakur mountain, and there are a number of small uninhabited fjords along this coast, but there is no access to them. South of Öxnadalur, which lies to the west of Akureyri, is the Kerling chain of  mountains, which at 1,538m (5,046ft) provides the highest peak in northern Iceland. The range also includes the small Vindheimajökull glacier. The best winter skiing can be found around here, near the Glerárdalur valley. The pyramid-shaped mountain of Súlur is another landmark.

Below Akureyri the valley gradually widens out before it climbs in altitude and is swamped by the foothills of the massive plateau which forms the uninhabited centre of the country. There are several tracks leading into the interior, including the Sprengisandur which can be used to traverse the island. It was used centuries ago by the farmers in the north, who would travel south to the fishing villages to work as part-time fishermen to eke out their living.

The area is very prosperous and there are many farms producing a wide range of crops. Many of the country's potatoes are grown here and in good years, Iceland is almost self-sufficient in this crop, but bad weather can, and often does, wipe out the entire yield.

The first settler to the Eyjafjördur is said to have been Helgi the Lean, who although a Norseman, came to Iceland via Ireland in the ninth century. Although he had been converted to Christianity he still prayed to the Scandinavian god Thor, like many of the islanders; when the island was swiftly converted to the Christian religion, most islanders simply moved their images of Norse gods into the houses and prayed to both them and their Christian God.

At the time of settlement, the valley ran much further inland, and some say Helgi came ashore at Festarklettur, a rock known now as the Mooring Rock, which is just to the south of Akureyri, while others say he chose the Gáseyri headland at the mouth of the Hörgá river, to the north of where the modern township started, to build his farmstead.

Fishing is still a major industry for the northern coastal villages, and there are fleets based at Akureyri, Hrísey Island, Dalvík, Ólafsfjördur, Siglufjördur and Grenivík. Unfortunately, the herring on which the northern fishing fleets based their economy have declined in recent years, and many of the herring processing plants in the region now lie idle.

**Hrísey**, the island in the mouth of Eyjafjördur, used to be the centre of shark fishing along the coast. The whole of this region is rich in wildlife, especially as you travel southwards towards Lake Myvatn. Along the coast, however, there are important breeding grounds of the ptarmigan, Iceland's most important game bird, and some of these areas have now been closed to visitors in order to undertake research. From the summit of Ólafsfjardarmúli there are breathtaking views northwards of the midnight sun during the summer and the island of Grímsey can be seen more than 50km (37 miles) away.

**Ólafsfjördur**, 63km (39 miles) from Akureyri, is a prosperous little fishing town and both its houses and swimming pool are heated by hot water from local springs. Ólafsfjördur used to be principally connected with agriculture, but since the turn of the century this has been superseded by fishing. An old fishing schooner is preserved here as a memorial to one of Iceland's most celebrated shipwrights. The campsite is by the swimming pool and there is a golf course at Skeggjabrekka to the west of the town.

At the northern tip of the fjord is **Siglufjördur**, a popular tourist spot both in summer and winter, for the mountains inland provide very good skiing. Siglufjördur was once the capital of the north coast's herring industry, but declined when the fish moved away. It is now regaining its popularity, and the fisheries now process other species of fish. The town used to be known as Thormódseyri after Thórmódur the Strong, who was the first settler there. There are now two hotels, a restaurant, swimming pool, community centre and hospital. The campsite is by Ithróttamidstödin Hóll. There is a herring museum.

**Dalvík** is another fishing village which can trace its roots back for centuries. The town gets its name from the large cove on the western side of Eyjafjördur, at the mouth of the valley Svarfadardalur. The cove is likely to be the last remnant of a fjord which followed the outlines of Svarfadardalur. Over the centuries silt from the many rivers flowing into the fjord, blocked it and the lush, verdant fertile valley was born. Farmers still turn up marine fossils while ploughing. Originally the area was known as Sandur and then Böggvisstadasandur, after the largest farm in the district.

Dalvík makes another good base for touring. The town is surrounded by magnificent mountain peaks, including the impressive wedge-shaped Stóll which divides the valley in two. The area to the east is known as Skídadalur with the mountain glacier Gljúfurárjökull. It covers an area of about 4sq km (2sq miles) and is surrounded by mountains between 1,200 and 1,300m (3,936 and 4,264ft) high. The number of small valleys and hollows found throughout the mountains show how much recent glacial activity in geological terms there has been.

There is an interesting range of vegetation in the valley, with typical wetland vegetation at the inner end of the valley, and grass, scrub and dwarf trees on the heath. This is also a favourite area with the locals because of the blueberries and crowberries. On the mountains the most common plant is whortleberry, which turns purple in the autumn bathing the mountainsides in brilliant colour. The marsh area at the mouth of the valley is a protected nature reserve with about thirty species of nesting birds, as well as diverse plant and animal life.

According to legend recorded in the Svarfdaelasaga, the first settler in the area was Thorsteinn Svörfudur who built a farm at Grund. His son, Karl the Red, lived at Karlsá, while a priest Ljótólfur, moved into the valley and built a farm at Hof. The two started to argue over who should be leader, and eventually Karl the Red was killed by the priest in a mighty battle.

Archaeologists have unearthed ancient graves in and around Dalvík where the battle is supposed to have taken place. In 1909 one of Iceland's most important grave discoveries was made while excavating around the town. In one burial mound, they found the remains of a boat, as well as the bones of a man and a dog. Everything accorded with the Saga's account of the burial of Karl the Red. In 1940, Kristján Eldjárn, later to become President of Iceland, discovered the remains of a hall dating back to the times of the Sagas. The hall was on the exact spot described in the Saga where Klaufi Snaekollsson built his home. Klaufi is one of the most famous ghosts to appear in all the Sagas. After his death, his brother-in-law beheaded Klaufi, and so he came back to seek his revenge.

For several hundred years the settlement has been noted for its boat-building skills. The farmers kept their boats on the coast but still lived inland, although they built temporary dwellings by the sea. The first permanent settlers in what is now Dalvík were Rósa Thorsteinsdóttir and her husband Jón Stefánsson, who built a turf house in the spring of 1897. In 1899 they built a wooden home called Nÿjabaer, which can still be seen today.

Originally the growth of the town was inhibited by the small harbour, which prevented large vessels from using it, but a new harbour was constructed shortly after the end of World War II. The people of the town pride themselves on their cultural heritage and will tell you that the first play was performed there in 1901 when there were just four families in residence. In 1934 the town was shaken by an earthquake, measuring 7.2 on the Richter Scale, 2,000 people lost their homes. There is a hotel, with the campsite alongside, and a swimming pool.

On the way down the western coast of the Eyjafjördur, there are many places of interest. The poet Davíd Stefánsson, for example, was born at a farm at **Fagriskogúr** and the historic farm at **Mödruvellir**, 12km (7½ miles) from Akureyri, was the site of a monastery and once one of the most important cultural and literary centres in Iceland. Other places of interest include the wooded glades of Vaglaskógur to the north-west of Akureyri and the farm of Baegisá on Öxnadalur where an Icelandic poet translated Milton's *Paradise Lost*. This area has excellent fishing. There are many geothermal areas in the region and you can enjoy a swim at **Laugaland**.

It is possible to drive up the eastern coast of Eyjafjördur only as far as Grenivík, about 47km (29 miles) from Akureyri, but the drive is worthwhile. There is an old turf and stone manor farm at **Laufás**, on the way, and it is now a famous museum with many exhibits of national importance.

You can travel out to the island of **Grímsey**, the most northerly part of Iceland; the Arctic Circle actually runs through the island. There is sleeping bag accommodation available in the community centre, so a trip of greater length than a day can be planned.

This northern strip generally has fine, dry summers, while the winters are cold and there can be blizzards. But, like all weather guidelines, there are massive variations. Some parts of the interior, around Lake Myvatn and up to Akureyri have recently experienced their hottest summer on record, while in the winter, if the wind is blowing from the south, the temperatures around Eyjafjördur can be several degrees higher than in the south of Iceland. The rule is to go prepared with warm woollens and waterproofs for winter and light woollens and warm jacket for summer, and always swimming costumes, because no matter what the weather, there will be a hot pool somewhere.

## Hvammstangi to Hofsós (to the west of Eyjafjördur)

The district of Vestur-Húnavatnssyla lies to the east of Midfjördur and Hrútafjördur, south of Húnaflói, and west of Gljúfurá, and north of the lakes of Arnarvatnsheidi. It covers an area of around 2,500sq km (1,550sq miles) most of which is very fertile lowland, lakes, meadows and woodlands, thanks to a widescale replanting programme. It is an area of geothermal activity which has been harnessed for industry and homes, and is very rich in flora and fauna. Highest points are Vatnsnesfjall (906m, 2,972ft) on Thraelsfell, and Krossdalskúla (980m, 3,214ft) on Vididalsfjall. The region needs time to explore. There are many historic sites, areas of great natural beauty, excellent salmon fishing, and some very good beaches. In addition, there are lakes, canyons, gorges, and miles of good walking.

The area of Midfjördur to the west includes the ancient farm at Melstadur, and Stadabakki, the birthplace of Gudbrandur, a famous bishop from the Middle Ages. To the north, the River Vesturá runs through an impressive gorge, and still further north, there is an anglers hostel at Laxahvammur. The region boasts three salmon rivers, which all rate among Iceland's best. It is worth the bumpy journey down the track alongside the Austurá river, which runs through a deep gorge, to the falls at Kambfoss. If you are really intrepid and have the right vehicle, you can continue along this road deep into the interior of the country to Lake Arnavatn, to the north of the Hallmundarhraun range and Eríksjökull (1,675m, 5,494ft).

Back in Midfjördur you can visit **Bjarg**, on highway 704, the birthplace of Grettir, one of the most popular and greatest of the Saga heroes. There is a memorial to his mother Asdis. Continue north and you come to **Laugarbakki** where there is a summer hotel. This is an area of hot springs, and water tapped here is used for homes both in Laugarbakki and **Hvammstangi**, the only town of the region. It is a service town and trading centre for both fishing and agricultural industries. There is a hotel and campsite close to the town, a health centre, bank, garage and swimming pool. If you drive up Vatnsnesfjall, there are views over seven counties on a good day. Most people travelling in the area tend to be going to and from

Akureyri or Myvatn, and do not spend enough time exploring here, especially north of Hvammstangi.

Highway 711 takes you along the Vatnsnes peninsula past Skard where you can laze on the beach or take a careful dip in the hot pools. Hamarsrétt is a well known beauty spot, and there is a breeding colony of eider at Illugastadir. From Tjörn you have a choice of tracks, one follows the river through a steep valley to Thorgrímsstadadalur, and the other heads for Hindisvik on the northernmost point of the peninsula where there is a seal colony. Other trips include a drive inland on highway 717 along Borgarvegur to Borgarvirki, a 177m (580ft) high volcano core. This is an area rich in both geology and archaeology. To the west of Vesturhópsvatn is Breidabólsstadur, where the first Icelandic laws were enacted, and where the country's first printing press was installed.

**Höfdakaupstadur** is also called **Skagaströnd**, and is an important port. Both English and German merchants traded here before 1660 and when the trade monopoly was established in 1602 it became a major port. It has a guesthouse, a campsite by the road leading into the village, and a sports field, community centre, swimming pool, and ski lifts servicing the Spákonfell mountain which dominates the town.

**Blönduós** stands at the delta of the river Blanda which runs north from the Hofsjökull glacier. As the river enters the valley its pace slows and huge volumes of the silt have been deposited to produce the delta. The town is the largest in the eastern county of Húnathing, yet still one of the newest in Iceland. Although it was officially declared a trading post in 1876, it was not granted full town status until 1988. There are records of merchants, however, using the settlement centuries ago. The town stands at a major crossroads, which makes it a good centre for touring the area. The ring road intersects with the highway leading to Skagastönd, and the road that runs to the south-east past Kleifar.

The bridge was completed in 1963 and just upstream there is the island of Hrútey which, in 1975, was declared a protected nature area because of its very special flora and fauna. There is a footbridge across to the island and a visit to what is now the Folkvangur Country Park, is a worthwhile experience, especially if you are interested in natural history. The town has an hotel, hospital and community centre, and the campsite is by Nordurlandsvegur, next to the river, looking over to Hrútey.

Other outings include a drive up to the source of the river. The river, as it crashes off the glacier, has dug a magnificent gorge, more than 18km (11 miles) long and up to 100m (328ft) wide in places. It is an area of contrast, with the powerful river and secluded areas of woodland and shrubbery. The new hydro-electric station at Blönduvirkin is also worth a visit simply because of the enormous scale of this engineering miracle.

Heading north into the Skagi peninsula also offers many good walking opportunities. The valleys of Vatnsdalur, Svínadalur, Langidalur and Blöndudalur, all to the south, are all worth visiting if you have the time.  **Vatnsdalur** is a very fertile valley about 25km (15½ miles) long. It is an area renowned for landslips and massive ones occurred in 1545 and 1720.

There is also a strange cluster of knolls at the mouth of the valley known as Vatnsdalshólar. Geologists believe these may have been caused by a colossal landslide more than 10,000 years ago.

**Vídidalur**, also south of the town, is worth visiting because of its waterfalls, gorges and cliffs. Borgarvikki is a towering cliff separating Vídidalur and Vesturhóp, formed of columnar basalt. Man-made stone walls surround the foot of the cliff but why they were built is not known. Kolgugljúfur is a gorge located further up the valley. It is named after the giantess Kola, who figures prominently in local folklore. She was supposed to have lived in the gorge.

**Varmahlíd** in Skagafjördur makes an excellent place to break your journey with its hotel and camping ground, swimming pool and beautiful turf-covered church at nearby Vídimyri.

The capital of Skagafjördur is **Saudárkrókur**, although the town did not exist before 1870. Its rapid expansion has taken place in the last few decades. Most of the population are involved with the fishing industry. The town has two hotels, restaurants, a campsite by the swimming pool, community centre, hospital and cinema. There is a golf course, tourist information centre and a library and art museum.

If spending some time in and around Saudárkrókur there are plenty of energetic walks. Molduxi (683m, 2,240ft) is behind the town and offers magnificent views over Skagafjördur from the top. It is a gentle stroll and takes about 2 hours.

A slightly higher, and steeper climb takes you to the summit of Tindastóll (976m, 3,201ft), while Maelifell is for the serious walker. The mountain is regarded by the locals as one of the most beautiful in the region. Situated deep in the fjord, it offers fantastic views from the top. The climb is not difficult but takes time, especially if you keep stopping to enjoy the views.

The walks on Tröllaskagi on the eastern side of the fjord are more strenuous and need planning. Allow plenty of time to complete them. If you venture across into Austurdalur, visit the church of **Arbaejar**, which lies some way off the road. Abaer farm is linked in folklore with Abaerjarskotta, a ghost who haunted the district. Although the farm is now deserted, there is a church service held once a year on the first Sunday in August. The parish has only one member. The church is close to the Merkigil ravine, and cable cars were erected many years ago, but only one is still in operation.

Two other 'musts' if in the area, are the beautiful turf church at **Vídimyrarkirka**, and the Glaumbaer Folk Museum. The church is just off the ringroad near Varmahlíd. It dates back to the nineteenth century and is one of the oldest in Iceland and is very carefully maintained. The church is open during the summer, and contains many interesting items from the past. The **Glaumbaer** Folk Museum is on highway 75 south of Saudárkrókur. It is an old turf farmhouse which was part of a working farm and occupied until 1940. It contains a marvellous collection of tools, furniture and artefacts and gives a fascinating insight into what life must have been like in days long past. The museum is open daily from June to the end of August. Glaumbaer is also famous because of its links with Snorri Thorfinnson, the first European to be born in America. He was the son of Thorfinnur Karlsefni, who led an expedition to America during the winter of 1002-3, two years after it had been discovered by Leif Eríksson, Snorri was born here, and he built the first church at Glaumbaer on his return to Iceland. Legend has it that he is also buried here.

**Hólar** in Hjaltadalur is in Skagafjördur county; it was the seat of the early bishops and the capital of the north from 1106 to 1798. Jón Arason was bishop here in the middle of the sixteenth century, losing both his seat and his head, when he was executed along with his two sons in 1550. The church is the oldest built in stone in the country and has recently been renovated.

**Hofsós** is one of the oldest trading centres in Iceland, based around fishing. The Gamla Hotel serves steaming hot coffee and piping hot home-baked bread. Visit the old log warehouse, the Pakkhus, built by the Danes in 1777, and one of the oldest buildings in Iceland.

## Húsavík to Vopnafjördur (to the east of Eyjafjördur)

**Húsavík** is a busy fishing and export harbour, with hotel, sleeping bag accommodation and camping and good tourist facilities. It received its name 'House Bay' from houses built by the Swedish Viking Gardar Svavarsson, who explored Iceland before the colonisation began. He discovered that Iceland was an island, and a memorial to him stands in the grounds of the primary school. There is a very unusual church which you should try to visit. It was consecrated in 1907 and is built of Norwegian timber in the shape of a cross. The steeple is 26m (85ft) high and the church contains fine murals, carvings and a large altar tablet. You can also visit a folk museum containing the 1584 Gudbrands Bible and a large polar bear shot in Grímsey after crossing from the Arctic on pack ice in the spring of 1969. There is a tourist information centre, and the campsite is at Hédinsbraut. An added bonus is that Húsavík also tops Iceland's sunshine league. Behind the town there is the mountain of Húsavík, and it is possible to drive or walk up to the summit to enjoy the views. The drive takes you through the magnificent scenery of the Tjörnes peninsula. The town boasts many winter sports facilities. From the top on a fine day, you can see as far as Grímsey in the north and Vatnajökull to the south.

Lake Botnsvatn lies to the south of the mountain. It is the source of the river Búdará which flows through the centre of the town. A public park by the river is rich in plant and bird life. Springs below the lake provide the town with its drinking water, while hot water is piped from the hot springs at Hveravellir, 18km (11 miles) to the south.

Boat rides are available from the harbour if you are interested in sea fishing or want to visit the islands of Flatey and Lundey. As Húsavík is just under the Arctic Circle it enjoys 24 hours daylight in the summer, and incredible midnight suns. During the winter, the days are short and the northern lights provide a natural picture show flashing across the horizon. There are numerous walks, both short and long distance, around Húsavik and Botnsvatn, where the trout fishing is free.

The county of Thingeyjarsysla has many natural wonders. About 30 minutes drive out of town is Hallbjarnarstadir, where you can see layers of fossilised seashells. There is a hydroelectric plant on the river Laxá close to the Brúarfossar falls, and close to the mouth of the river there is Laxamyri, a farm, which was the birthplace of Jóhann Sigurjónsson, one of Iceland's most famous playwrights. A memorial in his honour was erected here in 1980. A road leads from the farm to the Aervikurbjarg cliffs from where there are magnificent views of the Aedarfossar falls at the mouth of the Laxá. Travelling south you can take highway 87 through Reykjahverfi, an area of geothermal activity. At the farm Hveravellir, there are three geysirs, the most famous of which Ystihver, erupts regularly hurling a jet of water and steam 25m (82ft) into the air.

If you continue down the 87 you come to **Grenjadarstadur** where there is an old rectory and church. The old turf farmhouse is now a folk museum. Between the Laxá and the glacial river Skjálfandafljót, there is a lava desert called Adaldalshraun, which covers almost 100sq km (62sq miles). There are many craters and pseudo craters. At the farm Knútsstadir you can see a strange phenomenon created when steam trapped in the lava, caused it to rise like bubbles creating lots of small caves. Skjálfandafljót is Iceland's fourth longest river and contains many spectacular waterfalls.

If you do not want to stay in Akureyri, Húsavík also makes an excellent base for touring, with the magnificent horseshoe canyon at Asbyrgi only an hour away and Myvatn an easy drive to the south. It is also worth travelling north and exploring the Tjörnes peninsula. Apart from spectacular basalt columns, in many places you can see how the land has literally heaved itself up out of the sea with clearly discernible layers of lake, river and seabed sediment. Climatic changes over millions of years can also be determined because of these layers which show how flora and fauna adapted. At Hallbjarnarstadakambur, these layers, rich in marine fossils, are at their best.

The small town of **Kópasker** in Axarfjördur serves the local agricultural needs, but is now building up a successful fishing industry based on the shrimps found in the fjord. There is a hotel open all the year round, a restaurant, and a campsite by Söluskáli.

**Raufarhöfn** is very close to the Arctic Circle and an ideal site for viewing the midnight sun during the summer. It is a good birdwatching area, and there is fine salmon and trout fishing in the local rivers. There is a large hotel, community centre and swimming pool with the campsite alongside it. The church at Bakkafjördur, built in 1845 is the oldest in the eastern half of Iceland.

**Thórshöfn** is a small town that is less than a hundred years old. It has a guesthouse, campsite and swimming pool. The harbour has been used for centuries as a safe anchorage but the first houses were not built until 1875 when a shop and warehouse were established. In 1900 there were seventy-five inhabitants and now the village has more than 400 residents.  It is an excellent base for backpacking and walking with good trails over the surrounding heaths. The area is also rich in birdlife with large colonies  along the cliffs. The locals still practise the centuries-old custom of gathering the birds eggs for food. If you lean over the cliffs almost anywhere along this stretch of coast you will see birds nesting or resting just a few feet below you.

**Vopnafjördur** is mainly a fishing area, but agriculture and some other small industries also provide employment. The Burstafell farm and folk  museum contains buildings dating from 1770.

## A Drive along the North Coast

The roads are mostly gravel but quite passable and get a lot of traffic. Hrútafjördur marks the boundary between the Western Fjords and the northern coast and almost at its head there is a motel, one of the few in Iceland, which makes a good touring base. There is an exposed campsite by the river behind the motel but the rooms are very reasonable and there is a good round-the-clock restaurant.

About 12km (7½ miles) north, along the western bank of the fjord there is a marvellous little museum at **Reykjatunga**, which shows just how hard life was here a few decades ago. The museum is in the Hotel Edda complex, and is the building by the water's edge to the left of the hotel. There is a modest entrance fee which includes a guide, part of which is in English. The most interesting exhibits are to do with shark fishing, the principal occupation for centuries. The men used to go to sea in open rowing boats during the shark season which lasted from mid-January until late April. Each tour lasted up to a week, only cold food was eaten and there was little chance for sleep. The bait was horse flesh and seal. The shark flesh was processed by burying it, often for years and the longer the better. The liver was processed into oil at the end of each season and used for fuel in street lamps all over Europe — a market which died after the introduction of the gas lamp. The shark boats, one of which is beautifully preserved, would have a crew of nine to thirteen men and would weigh 7 tons when fully laden.

Another fascinating exhibit is a tiny, open row boat which was used to supply groceries to the fishermen living on the other side of the fjord. In winter, the boatman would sleep on a passing iceberg with the boat's hawser tied to his left foot to stop it drifting away.

At **Hvítserkur** there is a strange 15m high (49ft) basalt rock, and at Borgarvirki, a crag formation and basalt column which is thought once to have been used as a fortress. On the hill top at Bakkabrúnir, remains of alder trees and other plants have been found in the top layer of clay which dates back to the Tertiary period. Just a little to the south there are very picturesque waterfalls, the Kolufossar, in Kolugil, a great gully carved through the rock by the river Vididalsá. There is a remarkable cluster of hillocks at Vatnsdalshólar, at the mouth of the Vatnsdalur Valley. They were formed after a colossal landslide from Vididalsfjall.

The island's first monastery was founded at Thingeyrar in 1133 and it became a great seat of learning and education. At **Vidimyri**, near to Varmahlíd, there is a well preserved turf church, and at **Glaumbaer**, to the north, in Skagafjördur is a lovely collection of old turf buildings, and a beautifully preserved farmstead, with the rooms still in their original state. The oldest buildings date back to the eighteenth century and the rest were added in the nineteenth century. It is a fascinating glimpse into what life must have been like — tools, furniture, clothes and so on.

**Ölafsfjardarmúli**, to the south of Ölafsfjördur, is also worth exploring. It rises to about 400m and is famous for its perpendicular rock belts and scree slopes. In clear weather there are excellent views of the island of Grímsey and the midnight sun. Mödruvellir í Hörgárdal, south, has one of the country's finest country churches built in 1868, and the writer Nonni, otherwise known as Jón Sveinsson, and famous worldwide for his books for young people, was born in the parish.

South of Akureyri at **Grund** is Grundarkirkja, one of the most splendid churches in Iceland. Behind it is the 1,538m (5,044ft) Kerling mountain, the summit of which gives excellent views.

At **Saurbaer** there is the part turf church, now under national protection, and at **Leyningshólar**, there are glacial formations of moraines and hillocks, with scattered clusters of trees, surrounding the lake of Tjarnar-gerdisvatn. The old farm at Laufás is worth visiting, and is another national monument.

North of Myvatn is **Grenjadarstadur**, an ancient manor with vicarage and church. There is also an interesting folk museum, depicting local life of yesteryear. **Tjörnes** is the peninsula lying between the bays of Skjálfandi and Öxarfjördur, with strange and highly photogenic exposed rock strata dating back to the Iron Age.

## Ásbyrgi and Jökulsárgljúfur National Park

Ásbyrgi is one of the great wonders of Iceland but one that is missed by many visitors who stick to the ringroad when circumnavigating the island. The detour off the ringroad at Grimsstadir, if travelling up from Egilsstadir, or on to highway 85 north of Godafoss is really worthwhile, not just for the chance to see the fantastic horseshoe canyon of Ásbyrgi, but also for the drive round the coast with its spectacular cliffs, teeming bird life and sensational views. As you drive round the Tjörnes peninsula, on the road that hugs the cliffs, it is staggering just how much timber is washed up along the coast. On some beaches there are literally hundreds of tree trunks piled up on the sands, presumably having travelled thousands of miles across the ocean.

But if you are taking this detour you have to spend some time exploring Ásbyrgi, which is now part of the Jökulsárgljúfur National Park. The park was established in 1973 when the farm Svínadalur and parts of Asheidi were declared a protected area. In 1974, the As estate was added to the national park, and four years later, Ásbyrgi, which is owned by the State Forestry Commission, was also incorporated into the park. The park is situated on the west side of the glacial river Jökulsa á Fjöllum, and extends 35km (22 miles) northwards from the Dettifoss falls, covering an area of about 150sq km (93sq miles).

The Jökulsa Canyon is the largest in Iceland, more than 25km (15½ miles) long, up to ½km wide in places, and 100m (328ft) deep in several places. The upper canyon runs from Dettifoss to Sydrathórunnarfjall. Dettifoss is considered by many as the most spectacular waterfall in Europe. It is 45m (148ft) high and 100m (328ft) across, and a short distance downstream is the 27m (88ft) high Hafragilsfoss, with a third waterfall Selfoss, 10m (33ft) high, just to the south of Dettifoss and easily reached by a path close to the water's edge.

The central canyon is quite a large valley with many springs and incoming streams, and lush vegetation. The largest feeder rivers are Hölmá, Stallá and Melbugsá. There is an impressive rock outcrop at Vígabjarg, and Vígabjargfoss was an impressive waterfall until 1940 when the river suddenly changed its course. To the south is Réttarfoss.

By Svínadalur the valley turns and broadens again and then enters Vesterdalur, an area of towering cliffs. The grassy valley floor is sprinkled with lakes and rich vegetation, and runs into Hljódaklettar, an area of cliffs and caves. Karl of Kerling, opposite Tröllahellir, is the largest cave in the gorge.

Further north again, in Raudhólar the remnants of a number of craters can be seen. The river again forms a canyon which runs about 9km (6 miles) north to As. To the west is Asheidi, whose chief feature is Ásbyrgi, a 3½km (2 mile) long horseshoe canyon, more than 1km (½ mile) wide with cliffs rising more than 100m (328ft). Ásbyrgi is thought to have been formed as the result of colossal floods sweeping down from Vatnajökull. The waters washed away all but the hardest bedrock, leaving Ásbyrgi as it is today.

It is marvellous walking through the dwarf trees and heath vegetation in Ásbyrgi. As you walk deeper into the canyon there is more shelter, the vegetation becomes more dense and the trees grow taller. More than 220 plants grow in the park and there are many birds, especially moorland species such as golden plover, meadow pipit, ptarmigan and redwing. You can also see snow bunting, wren, redpoll, wheatear and snipe, and gyrfalcon and merlin nesting in the cliffs, together with raven. Many species of wader and duck can be found on the numerous ponds and lakes in the area. In 1970 fulmars started to nest on the cliffs at Ásbyrgi and there is now a thriving, and noisy colony. Arctic foxes and mink are the main animals, although a few long tailed mice occur. Reindeer, which were common in the area, have now disappeared.

## Maps

The best maps for the area, published by the Icelandic Survey Department, are: Atlast Sheet, scale 1:100,000, Sheet 82 Dettifoss; General Map scale 1:250,000 Sheet 7 NE Iceland; and Special map Húsavík/Myvatn scale 1:100,000.

## Walking

The park is ideal for walking and there are a number of well marked trails. In fact, most of the interesting things to see are only accessible by foot. The longest trail runs from Dettifoss, to the camping site at Ásbyrgi and mostly follows the course of the river through the gorges. You should allow at least two days for the walk. Special care should be taken if you suffer from vertigo or are carrying very heavy packs, as some of the descents are very steep and long.

The main hiking paths are:

| | |
|---|---|
| From Ásbyrgi to Ashöfda along the gorges | 2-3 hours |
| Eyjan (The Island) | 1-2 hours |
| Vesturdalue, along the gorges | 4-5 hours |
| Kvíar | 3-5 hours |
| From Vesturdalue around Hljódaklettar | ½-1 hour |
| to Raudhólar | 2 hours |

*Dettifoss*                    *(Opposite) Jökulsá Canyon just below Dettifoss*

| | |
|---|---|
| to Sýnadalur and Kallbjörg | 3 hours |
| to Hólmatungur | 3 hours |
| From Hólmatungur | |
| to Jökulsa and north to Hólmarfossar | 1 hour |
| Ytra Thórunnarfjall | ½ hour |

Further information about walking and riding paths can be obtained from the wardens at the information centre at Ásbyrgi.

Jökulsárgljúfur is famous as one of the largest and most rugged gorges in Iceland — a mini Grand Canyon, and the home of many spectacular waterfalls including Dettifoss, the most powerful waterfall in Europe, Hafragilsfoss and Selfoss. It is worth devoting some time to exploring the gorge with its caves, eerie rock formations and creeks. It is now a national park and camping is restricted to designated sites. **Dettifoss** is a spectacular waterfall on the river Jökulsá about 30km (18½ miles) north-east of Myvatn. The area in which it is situated has become the Jökulsá Canyon National Park, and the waterfall crashes down from a height of 44m (144ft). As you drive north from the Grímsstadir crossroads, you follow the Jökulsá á Fjöllum on your left. The river, the country's second longest, starts to widen its bank as it makes its way through the gravel-lined valley. The road is boulder-strewn and can be very muddy. The turn off on the right to Dettifoss is well signposted, but it is best to continue along the road for about 2km (about a mile), until you come to an unmarked track off to the left. If you follow this it will take you to **Hafragilsfoss**, even more spectacular than Dettifoss.

There is a parking area on the crest of the hill with stunning views of the falls and the canyon. The whole area is made up of red lava, and there are a number of paths affording even better views of the falls and the canyon. It can be very windy on top of the hill so be careful. The best views of the 27m high (88ft) falls can be got from a tall pyramid-shaped lump of lava, about 500m (1,640ft) to the left of the car park area. This is an area of canyons and water, with many gorges and rivers feeding into the main stream. The main canyon runs for 26m (85ft), and in places the sheer cliffs are more than 100m (328ft) high.

Having seen the splendours of Hafragilsfoss, you can retrace your route back to Dettifoss. The mud track to the falls can be quite slippery if it is wet, but most vehicles should manage it with care. The car park is well above the falls and as you make your way down through the rocks, the spray from the falls starts to hit you so keep your cameras protected. There is almost always a rainbow hanging over the river just to the north of the falls, and it makes for stunning photographs.

The river, which runs for 206km (127 miles), is suddenly compressed into a narrow channel which explains the ferocity of the falls. As you approach it is a good idea to keep to the path, because if you venture too near the edge you will see that the ground is rent with fissures, and every so often a chunk of cliff slides down into the canyon.

The Dettifoss falls are 45m (146ft) high and the flow of water, up to

1,500cu m (52,931cu ft) a second, makes it the most powerfall in Europe. It is possible to walk upstream for about a kilometre to the much smaller Selfoss (13m, 42ft) although the path is boulder-strewn and not easy to follow.

## A Drive from Egilsstadir to Myvatn

Driving in the eastern part of this region can be one of the great adventures of a trip to Iceland. If you leave Egilsstadir, over the wooden bridge and past the airport, the routes to Myvatn and Akureyri are well signposted. You travel through Fellabaer where you can go horse riding, and into lush green sheep pastures. It is worth a stop just beyond the bridge which crosses the Jökulsá á Brú, and walking back to see how the waters have carved out a deep canyon. The ring road heads roughly north and then swings south-west. Gradually the vegetation becomes more sparse, the number of abandoned farms increase and you get the feeling that you are heading out into a remote and desolate area.

Here the river has carved its way through hills of gravel, brought down over the centuries from Brúarjökull, a northern arm of Vatnajökull. In some places the gravel is tens of metres deep and it is grassing over, offering sparse grazing for the sheep. On the right there are steep cliffs and waterfalls, and you pass only a few very isolated farms. It is always a good idea to fill up with fuel when you get the chance, and there is a pump at Skjöldólfsstadir. After crossing the river Gilsá, the road starts to climb into the mountains before forking. You should take the right fork, still on the ring road and signposted to Myvatn and Akureyri.

The landscape is even more barren, with moss-covered rocks, lava and black sand. Beside the roads there are cairns, a reminder of days gone by when this was the only means of navigating. This area is notorious for dust storms and they can blow up very quickly, catching you unawares.

It is a lonely road with few vehicles, but you will spot the approach of another car miles away because of the dust it throws up. The road crosses this flat lava desert known as Geitasandur, and as you start to descend, you can see the even more imposing desert of Grjót in the valley below. The road heads north skirting the eastern flank of the desert, past Mödrudalur, at 469m (1,538ft) the highest farm in Iceland, until it hits Grimsstadir, and then you can either head south on Route 864 to visit Dettifoss, or west on Route 1 to Myvatn and Akureyri.

If you have a four-wheel drive vehicle and plan to drive to Askja, the road leads off south from the ring road, 7km (4 miles) after the Grimsstadir crossroad. Before making the journey, however, call in at the farmhouse at Grimsstadir and find out what the conditions are like and what the weather forecast is. There is a campsite opposite the farm with toilets and washing facilities, and is a good base for exploring north along the Route 864, if you don't want to have to keep retracing the road back to Myvatn.

## Herdubreid Nature Reserve and Askja

The journey to Askja is one of the great highlights of a trip to Iceland and should not be missed. The road is usually only open in July and August and it is sensible to check conditions before setting off. If you do not fancy the drive yourself, and you must have a four wheel drive vehicle, there are lots of organised tours from Akureyri, Myvatn, Egilsstadir and elsewhere. Most tours span a very long day and refreshments are not provided so you have to take in what you need.

The easiest way in if you are driving, is to follow the ringroad east from Myvatn, and then to take the mountain road heading south at Hrossaborg, before you cross the Jökulsa and reach Grimsstadir. An alternative is to continue round the ringroad through Grimsstadir and take mountain road F98. This allows you to visit other places en route, but it is a longer journey, with more rivers to cross. From Egilsstadir you can take the ringroad to just beyond Sköldólfsstadir, and then turn left on to highway 923 to Brú. Turn right on to the mountain road for about 3km (2 miles) then left on to the mountain road which takes you past the southern shores of Thrihyringsvatn to connect with mountain road F98.

On balance, if you simply want to get to Askja as quickly as possible from Egilsstadir under your own steam, drive west on the ringroad to Hrossaborg and take this route in. It is the quickest way and there is more traffic on this road just in case you run into trouble.

Askja is in the Herdubreid nature reserve, and an awe-inspiring, desolate place. Strong footwear and warm, waterproof, clothing is essential. The reserve was established in 1974 and includes Herdubreid mountain, the surrounding hot springs and Grafarlönd. It covers 175sq km (108sq miles). The reserve has 111 species of plants and ferns, including some pure alpines, about thirty species of birds, the most common of which are snow buntings. Purple sandpiper, long tailed ducks and red-necked phalaropes can all usually be seen on the lakes. Pink footed geese and harlequin ducks are also common.

Over the centuries the region was used widely by islanders wanting to travel from north to south during the summer. Ferjufjall (Ferry Mountain) is thought to have got its name because that is where people used to cross the Jökulsa. During the seventeenth and eighteenth centuries the area became the haunt of outlaws, and one of the most famous Fjalla-Eyvindur built his shelter at Herdubreidarlindir in 1774. A new shelter was built on the site of the old in 1922, about 100m north-west of the mountain hut owned by the Akureyri Touring Club.

This area is known as Odádahraun and is mostly covered in lava from a number of volcanoes in the region. When the land was covered with ice, the lava could not travel and so built up near the craters and vents creating new mountains such as Dyngjufjöll, Herdubreid, Upptyppingar, Herdubreidartögl and Hvammsfjöll. After the ice melted, lava flows created shield mountains like Vadalda and Kollóttadyngja. The area is a desert, albeit of land, and water is scarce. The main water supply is the Herdubreidalindir springs, and this is an oasis of vegetation. To the east are the floodplains of the Jökulsa, and plenty of signs of colossal floods over the millennium caused when massive eruptions of the glacier melted the ice.

Herdubreid was caused by a huge eruption under the Vatnajökull glacier. The heat was so intense that it melted a hole in the 1,000m (3,280ft) thick glacier filled with lava. The lava solidified on contact with the melted ice and when the glacier retreated, the mountain was left. The enormous Askja caldera, covering around 50sq km (35sq miles), was formed in 1875 when a massive eruption occurred blasting out the centre of the mountain. Over the next thirty years or so, subsequent eruptions took place within the rim of the caldera causing the surrounding lip to collapse inwards, in the deepest part of which is the intensely blue lake Oskjuvatn, which is 217m (712ft) deep, making it the deepest lake in Iceland.

To the north of the lake is Viti, formed after another explosion from a vent. As the vent collapsed it filled with hot water which is fine for swimming in although getting in and out of the water is a bit risky as it can be very slippery. The Herdubreid Nature Reserve is covered on Sheet 8 (Mid-Austurland) 1:250,000, and sheet 84 (Herdubreid) 1: 100,000.

If you are really feeling intrepid and have a lot of time at your disposal, you can drive west from Askja crossing the Jökulsa and then turn right down the mountain for Kverkjöll (1,920m, 6,297ft) on the northern flanks of Vatnajökull. The road is slow and tortuous, but it is worth the trip. The area is the source of the Jökulsa á Fjöllum. Although the water is flowing off the glacier, the area is such an active geothermal one, that the ground is warm and the river steams. The water does not erode the ice, it melts it in places. The major attraction is the ice cave filled with water from the hot springs, about 5km (3 miles) from the end of the mountain track. If you do not fancy making the trip yourself, there are tours arranged by BSI leaving from Húsavík and Myvatn, and others. You must allow at least three days for the trip and supply your own food for the duration.

## Lake Myvatn and the Surrounding Area

The area around Lake Myvatn is not only Iceland's most beautiful countryside, but some of its most interesting. It is a geological paradise and everywhere has something new and exciting to see.

Lake Myvatn is the fifth largest lake in Iceland, with an area of about 37sq km (14sq miles) and it lies 278m (912ft) above sea level. The lake has literally hundreds of inlets and creeks, each one the home of ducks and waders. The lake is in two parts — Ytritflói and Sydriflói. The average depth is only 2.5m (9ft) and the maximum depth is 4.5m (15ft). There are more than fifty islands, and the largest are clusters of pseudo-craters — explosion craters formed by hot lava flowing into the lake. Almost all the water flowing into the lake comes from springs along the eastern shore. The river Graenilaekur, which flows from the spring-fed Lake Graenavatn in the south, is the only surface flowing stream of any note running into Myvatn.

There are more varieties of duck on Lake Myvatn than anywhere else in the world, which is why it is of such importance to ornithologists. Geologically it is very interesting because the land is so new. It is actually being altered all the time, and eruptions occur frequently, although few are violent. In the last few years, however, the amount of geo-thermal activity has increased enormously, and there are now many columns of steam rising from fissures to the north and east of the lake. Experts are convinced that there will be more major eruptions here but they cannot say how soon.

The lake gets its name from the midges and black-flies which can prove a nuisance in summer. At certain times the midges swarm and unless you are well protected, it is almost impossible to breathe without inhaling large numbers into your nose and mouth. It is only the female black-fly that bites, and usually only in damp and calm weather. They are not supposed to bite indoors! The presence of the midges give a clue to the area's climate; in the lee of the Vatnajökull glacier it gets little rain, making it one of the driest and sunniest places in Iceland. Summer temperatures of over 20°C (68°F) have often been recorded, and summers often consist of many warm, dry days strung together. Annual rainfall is about 40cm (16in), ten times less than on the glacier to the south. Because of its position and climate, Lake Myvatn is considered to be the most fertile place of any on its latitude.

The district was formed about 3,800 years ago from the older Laxá lava, and lava flows have been adding to it ever since. In some places the earth's crust is only inches thick, and many unsuspecting people have been badly burned by breaking the surface; their feet having been scalded by the underlying hot sulphur pools, so please follow the notices in these areas which advise travellers of where to walk in safety.

The lake in the summer plays host to up to 150,000 ducks as well as thousands of geese and waders. The Barrow's goldeneye, an American species, is found nowhere else in Europe, and the harlequin, also a North American native, does not breed anywhere east of Iceland. The most common duck to be seen is the scaup. There are approximately 3,500 pairs of tufted duck, 1,800 pairs of scaup, 1,000 pairs of wigeon and 500 pairs of Barrow's goldeneye.

There are red-breasted merganser, common scoter, long-tailed duck, mallard, and teal, and less frequently gadall, pintail, shoveller, and goosander. Large numbers of eider breed along the Laxá, and about 600 whooper swans choose the lake to moult. There are numerous horned grebe, red necked phalarope, great northern and red throated divers, greylag geese, gyr falcons, ptarmigan, assorted plovers, gulls and terns. There are also snow buntings, pied wagtail, wheatear, raven and redwing. Mink which escaped into the wild, were first seen in the 1960s but are now common, while the arctic fox has become rare. The other animal to be seen is the long-tailed field mouse which is plentiful. The birds are protected by law, and the countryside is protected by the Icelanders ever mindful of the wonders of Myvatn which they hold in trust for mankind. One writer described Myvatn as an open book detailing the world's creation. Arctic char live in the lake and trout migrate from Laxá so that they can spawn near the springs on the eastern side of the lake. A dwarf char has evolved which lives in subterranean caves and the three-spined stickleback is very common. Salmon migrate up the Laxá in the spring.

Myvatn is a paradox, because it is a small area, with enormous contrasts, in which one can get lost because it is unspoilt and unpopulated. Here the vegetation is strange, and on the newest lava there is no vegetation at all. This is the wonder of Myvatn; the land is so new that it is possible to watch the evolution of land through its various stages, from bare new lavafields to those which have been colonised, first by moss and lichens, then by plants and shrubs, and then finally by the squat Icelandic trees. The most luxuriant growth will usually be found inside the crevices, where the plants get maximum protection from the weather and enjoy their own freak micro-climate.

The vegetation around Myvatn and the Laxá river running from it is particularly lush and contains many rare plants; there is even one named the Queen of Myvatn. There are birch woodlands to the north and east of the lake, and bogs and moors to the south and west. Bottle sedge forms many of the reed beds, while the string sedge dominates the marshy areas. Other vegetation includes dwarf birch, tea-leaved willows, and willow. There is angelica and meadow buttercup, marsh marigold and wood cranesbill. Lichens are very common and the vegetation of the lake includes two species of watermilfoil, the water crowfoot and sago pondweed. Because of the algae in the lake, the water often turns opaque blue-green in July. Other common vascular plants in the area include: woolly willow, sorrel, alpine mouse-ear, hairy stonecrop, marsh cinquefoil, water and mountain avens, field gentian, thyme, butterwort, ladies' bedstraw, boreal fleabane and yarrow. The lake itself is shallow, and in places is edged by reed beds and small marshy areas. In most places it is between 1 and 3m (3 to 7ft) deep.

Two types of midges live around the lake, the true midge, and the black-fly which is a real scourge as it is the only one which bites. In some summers thick clouds composed of hundreds of thousands of midges can be seen, and for some reason, they travel to only one or two special islands to die. These islands are much greener with vegetation than the others because they are being fertilised by the bodies of millions of midges. Scientists do not yet know why the midges should choose these particular islands on which to die. Some midges die before they reach either of the islands and drop into the water. They help fertilise the marine plant life which attracts the birds, and so the cycle continues.

The area has been protected by the country's Nature Conservation Council since 1974 and is considered by the World Wildlife Fund to be one

*Lake Myvatn and Ásbyrgi*

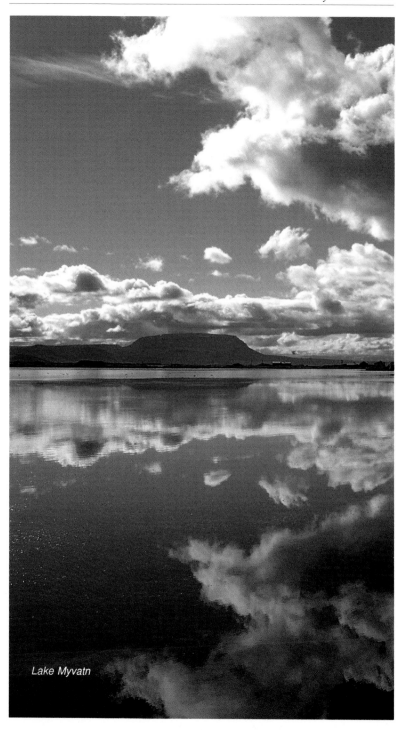

Lake Myvatn

of the most important bird habitats on earth. There is also a research centre at Reykjahlíd run by the Nordic Volcanological Institute.

---

**Help To Protect Myvatn**

The Myvatn region is a specially protected area covered by a special law passed in 1974. The area includes the whole of the Myvatn area and both banks of the Laxá river for a distance of at least 200m (656ft). The aim of the law is to protect the natural environment and the flora and fauna particular to the region, and to facilitate research. The limits of the protected area, where it borders on habited areas, are clearly marked by signs.

In order to help protect the region, visitors are urged to take note of the following points: camping sites are at Reykjahlíd and Skútustadir. Camping or staying in vehicles outside these areas is forbidden, and no matter how well tucked away you think you may be, the wardens will find and move you as they patrol throughout the night; during the nesting period, from 15 May to 20 July, the northern banks of the lake are a protected area, and all off-road traffic is banned; motor vehicles are only allowed on roads and officially marked tracks. Many farm tracks are private and have locked gates. Walkers should keep to the officially marked paths in Dimmuborgir and at Skútstadir to prevent erosion damage. The use of private boats on Lake Myvatn is not allowed.

The Höfdi Nature Park is open to visitors although a small admission price is charged. The park is open between 9am-7pm daily and there are hides and observation posts where you can spend the whole day if you wish. There is a parking area immediately outside the park entrance. Fishing permits for Lake Myvatn can be obtained from local farmers, and permits for the Laxá and Kráká can be obtained at Arnarvatn.

**Warning:** Do not ignore the warning notices at geothermal sites. If it says the water is too hot to bathe in, or that the ground is too soft to walk on, do not try to prove them wrong. People have received very serious scalds because of this.

The ground at Bjarnarflag, Námafjall and Hverarönd is extremely hot in places, fissured and dangerous to cross. Avoid light, white and yellow areas, and only walk on dark clay. The water at Grjótagjá is now around 50°C so far too hot to bathe in, while the water in Stóragjá has a high bacteria count, and it is not advisable to bathe in it. However you may consider Stóragjá not worth the effort, especially if the midges are flying! Studies in other parts of the world show that bathing in bacteria-laden waters like this may cause meningitis.

The area around Krafla is an active volcanic zone, it is therefore highly inadvisable to get anywhere near Leirhnjúkur.

**Wardens:** There are wardens throughout Myvatn and you will spot them on patrol. They are always very helpful and will offer assistance and information. They are based at the Reykjahlíd camping site (☎ (96) 44103.

There are less than 600 people living in the area, and farming is the main occupation as it has been for centuries. Tourism, however, is becoming very important and facilities to cope with the growing number of visitors are being provided. Again, however, it must be stressed that although tourism is growing for obvious reasons, there are no crowds. There is so much open space, and the number of visitors at any one time is still relatively small, so it is possible to spend whole days and see only a handful of people. Most of the population is concentrated at Reykjahlíd with its hotels, camping site and other services.

Most of the farmers raise sheep which graze along the edges of the lake, but there is excellent fishing in this area, and this has helped supplement the diets of the local people, as have eggs from the nesting water birds. Although agriculture is now the major industry, there are others.

Mining, especially, has played a role in the region for centuries. Hundreds of years ago there were sulphur mines here; as this industry died out, the lava came into its own. It was taken to factories where it was crushed and pressed into building blocks, and there are still plants doing this today. The major mining enterprise, however, is the plant which opened in 1966. It extracts the mineral from material dredged up from the shallow bed of Lake Myvatn. Diatomite is used in a number of industrial processes, including making photographic film. Because of the growing popularity of the area there is quite a lot of building work going on in the towns, and the construction industry is the second largest industrial employer after the mining.

As you travel into the area from the west, especially in the Fnjóskárdalur Valley, remnants of the birch forests that once covered the whole of northern Iceland can be seen. In the Ljósavatn Pass, which passes through the basalt mountain range, there are the remnants of a massive earthslip from the Stóradalsfjall mountain, which took place at the end of the Ice Age after the ice had melted. On the journey from Akureyri to the lake, a convenient stop is at the farm at **Ljósavatn**, where Thorgeir Godi, the ✳ warrior priest lived. It was he who, in AD1000, decreed that Iceland should change to Christianity, and that the Nordic idols should be thrown out. Around this farm the landscape changes away from jagged mountains and plunging valleys to the lavafields and moors, and glacial hills that make up the scenery of Myvatn.

There is the lava of **Bárdardalur**, already clad in shrubs and mosses, which came 8,000 years ago from the Trölladyngjur. It is the longest shield volcano lavafield in Iceland, running for over 100km (62 miles).

The Myvatn moor is dominated in the south by the tall volcanic mountains, and the special colouring on Námafjall caused by the hot springs and sulphur wells is striking. It was here that the sulphur was mined in the Middle Ages. All around, the landscape is marked by the effects of glaciers, earthquakes and volcanoes, but the view is dominated by the volcano, Krafla.

**Arnarbaeli** is a closed lava knoll just by the road to the south of Myvatn and east of Skutustadir. From the road it looks like a small solid hill, but from the top it can be seen that the structure is hollow. There is also a pseudo-crater beside the road.

**Dimmuborgir** is a large lava pile east of Myvatn, now rich in plant life and with many trees. Known to the locals as the Land of Dark Castles, the lava has been formed and eroded into many strange and wonderful shapes, many of which look as if they have been built by man. There are caves and holes in the cliff; the most famous cave is known as the Church of the Fortress (Kirkjan) and it has what appears to be a large Gothic-style vault.

Many of the lava formations tower 15 to 25m (49 to 82ft) high; and were formed by lava-flow some 2,000 years ago. The younger Laxá lava came from Threngslaborgir which can be seen from the small hill as you enter the enclosure. The castles, best viewed just before sunset, are at their finest near Valsbjarg which has become a nesting-place for falcons. It is possible to spend several hours in this fascinating area of lava architecture which is enclosed behind a fence. Although there are footpaths it is very easy to get lost; if this happens, do not cross the fence, but simply follow it around until the only gate is reached. The area of lava between Reykjahlíd and Grímsstadir that flowed from Leirhnjúkur during the Myvatn Fires of 1729 is called **Eldhraun**. The flow extends for several kilometres.

**Grjótagjá** is the name of a ground fissure to the east of Myvatn that runs for several kilometres. There are many pools in the fissure, and they get warmer the farther to the north they are. Many of the pools used to be popular for bathing, but since the volcanic activity in the area has considerably increased, they have now become too hot to swim in. In 1977 the magma intrusion north of Krafla pushed the temperatures up to 50°C.

About 4km (2½ miles) to the north-east of Reykjahlíd is a cone-shaped mountain called **Hlídarfjall**. It is 771m (2,529ft) high, and forms a good vantage point to survey the surrounding countryside. **Hverfjall** is claimed to be the most famous crater in the Myvatn region. It was formed about 2,500 years ago during an explosive eruption and there is now a large tuff ring to be seen east of Myvatn. It is more than one kilometre across and rises about 150m (492ft) above the surrounding land. It is called 'the perfect mountain' because its shape is so symmetrical.

There is an area of unusual lava flow running eastwards from Myvatn towards Kálfastrandarvogur called **Höfdi**. It is considered to be one of the most beautiful spots beside the lake. For many years it has been a public park because of its rich vegetation and strange lava shapes. This whole area is well worth a visit and is a paradise for photographers.

**Jardbadshólar** has a steam bath where locals have taken healing baths for centuries. Kálfastrandarstrípar, near Höfdi, a short walk away, is also worth exploring because of its strangely-shaped lava rocks. The reason for the strange formations is that there was once a lava pool here whose level suddenly dropped, leaving behind lava columns that solidified.

About 10km (6 miles) north-east of Myvatn, the great volcano, **Krafla**, has become a regular tourist attraction because of its frequent eruptions. The latest and most powerful in recent years occurred in September 1984 when a 9km (5½ mile) long fissure opened up and lava started to flow. The force of the eruption was so great that at about 2am it could be seen more than 300km (186 miles) away, lighting up the sky.

The central volcano is 20km (12 miles) wide, and the caldera is about 8km (5 miles) in diameter. A large fissure runs north and south about the caldera, and there is thought to be a magma chamber underneath the centre of the caldera about 7km (4 miles) down. Its longest eruption ever took place during the 5 years from 1724, when so much lava flowed that at the time it became known as the Myvatn Fires. In 1975 volcanic activity started again, and there has been an eruption every year since, although some have lasted for only a few hours, while others rumbled on for some days. At the same time there have been a number of earth tremors in this area which have caused land movements and earth slips. There is some concern at the increased activity because a hugely expensive geothermal power station has been built on Krafla, and the first of the recent eruptions occurred during the first year of construction. You can drive up the mountain and notice boards point out the various things to see.

Laxá is a magnificent river rising in Lake Myvatn and flowing north for about 50km (31 miles) to the sea. It is one of Iceland's most popular salmon rivers and between 1954 and 1963 more than 1,150 salmon, with an average weight of 10lb, were caught annually. A new fishing lodge has been built on the river, at which it is possible to stay on full board or self-catering terms. A bed can be obtained at a cost which is insignificant in comparison with what is paid on some of the top English and Welsh rivers.

There is a large geothermal area to the west of Krafla called **Leirhjnúkur**, dominated by a rounded volcanic hill. You can see a variety of craters and boiling mud holes, or mudpots, and the area is carpeted with flowers in the summer. The ground is so warm that spring comes here earlier almost than anywhere else in Iceland, even though it is 600m (1,970ft) above sea level.

**Lúdent** is a large crater about 6km (3½ miles) east of Myvatn, and formed more than 6,000 years ago. It is almost 1km (1,000yd) wide and to the south and east you can see a number of spatter cones that stretch for many kilometres. The area is known as Lúdentsborgir.

There is another geothermal area called **Námaskard**, and here caution must be exercised when walking round it — the earth's crust is only inches thick, and so it is essential to keep to the areas indicated. There are bubbling mudpots, sulphur wells and hot springs. The earth is multi-coloured because of the sulphur and other chemicals in it. You can cross from the road, through the geothermal area to Námafjall which rises to 482m (1,580ft), and there are excellent views from the top of the mountain. Just beyond this area is the first geothermal plant, built in 1968, and the diatomite plant.

**Neslandavík** is a shallow cove, almost 3km (1½ miles) long and up to 1km (1,000yd) wide, in the north-west shore of Lake Myvatn. It is one of the best breeding grounds in the area and has been proclaimed a nature reserve, so no cars are permitted on the road here between 15 May and 20 July.

There is a 20sq km (7¾sq mile) area north of Reykjahlíd called **Reykjahlídarheidi** full of kettle holes and moraines, and overgrown with birch, willow and rowan. It was formed about 10,000 years ago, by water when the glaciers melted at the end of the last Ice Age. In winter it is ideal for cross-country skiing.

**Reykjahlíd** is the tourist centre for the region with hotels and campsites. According to legend, the first man to live here was Arnór Thorgrímsson. There is believed to have been a church on the hill overlooking the town ever since the country turned to Christianity in AD1000. During the Myvatn Fires on 21 August 1729, lava from Eldhraun flowed round the church, and although it piled up against the walls, it did not enter the building. The foundations of that old church are still preserved, although there have been two churches on the site since then, the last being built in 1962.

In Reykjahlíd town there is a lava core called Saudahellir, it is about 70m (230ft) long, and in places it is tall enough for a person to stand upright. It is named after the sheep which used to be sheltered here, although it is now used as a potato store.

West of Bláfjall there is a breathtaking ravine called **Seljahallagil**, about 7km (4 ¼ miles) south-east of Myvatn. There are magnificent columnar basalt formations at the end, formed when a lava flow entered the ravine about 3,800 years ago.

**Skútustadagígar** is an area of pseudo-craters beside the lake. They can be inspected but visitors are asked to keep to the clearly marked footpaths. Pseudo-craters are formed when lava flows into a lake or waterlogged area. The heat of the lava causes the water below to boil, and steam bursts through. Cinders and ash are forced up thus building the craters. It was here, at Thangbrand's Pool, in 998, that a German missionary baptised the inhabitants of Myvatn into the Christian religion. A large number of nesting birds can be seen at **Slútnes**, which is a lowland and fertile island in the north-east corner of Myvatn.

**Stóragjá** is another fissure to the south of Reykjahlíd which used to have pools popular with bathers. Again, the waters have become considerably hotter with the recent volcanic action, and bathing is no longer advised. **Sydrivogar** is a variegated lava cove in the south-east corner of Lake Myvatn. The water comes mainly from the freshwater springs along the east shore. **Vindbelgur** is a volcanic mountain about 240m (78ft) high, west of Myvatn and about a mile from the road. There is an easy path up the west side, and it is worth the climb for the views from the top. About 5km (3 miles) south-east of Myvatn there is **Threngslaborgir**, an 8½km (5 ¼ mile) long row of spatter and scoria cones. There are water-filled craters, and some fissures are so deep and sheltered that snow is trapped here throughout the summer.

The attractions of the area for the ornithologist are obvious but there are strict rules preventing the birds being disturbed between 15 May and 20

July. Boats can be hired for trips on the lake, for fun or for fishing. Fishing permits for the Laxá are sold in Arnarvatn, and fishing is also allowed on Myvatn, where there are char.

The area is a walker's paradise and there are many local trails, although few have been waymarked. There are many short and long distance walks  in the Myvatn area. One of the most popular walks is between Grjótagjá and Dimmuborgir, with a stop at the top of Hverfjall where there are spectacular views over the whole area. The walk takes between 3-4 hours.

The walk around Dimmuborgir takes about 1½ hours but you can spend very much longer exploring this fascinating area if you wish. A climb to the top of Vindbelgjarfjall (529m, 1,735ft) takes between 1-1½ hours but from the summit there are views over the whole of Myvatn. The descent takes about ½ hour.

In the winter there is good cross-country skiing, and of course, there is  all-the-year-round swimming in some of the hot pools. There are regular flights from Reykjavík to either Akureyri or Húsavík, and a shuttle bus runs from the latter to Myvatn in the summer. There is an airstrip at Reykjahlíd, and small planes can land there, opposite the hotel. During the summer, there are bus trips to Myvatn from Reykjavík travelling over the interior highlands. There are daily summer buses between Akureyri and Myvatn, and four trips a week between Húsavík and Myvatn, although during the summer peak period, there are daily trips. There are also three trips during the summer between Myvatn and Egilsstadir.

There are many tours organised in and around Myvatn taking in all the places of interest. Details can be obtained from hotels, travel agents, Icelandair, or Eldá Lake Myvatn (which runs many of them).

The Myvatn area has its own cuisine, with trout and lamb as the favourite dishes. Reindeer, which roam the eastern highlands is often offered on the menu. The locals bake a rye bread in the volcanic earth and it goes particularly well with smoked trout. There is also *grasamjólk*, a rather special dessert made from milk and Icelandic moss.

One other delicacy, which may not appeal, is rotten eggs. The locals gather them in the spring, and bury them in ashes before hardboiling them. They are eaten for Thorrablót, the traditional late January feast, and are said to taste like ripe cheese!

When it is time to leave Myvatn and head for Akureyri stop off at **Godafoss**, another of Iceland's wonders. From Reykjahlíd drive south down the western shore of Myvatn on Route 1. The road then turns north-westerly, past Másvatn and on to Einarsstadir. Stay on the ring road until Fosshóll where the river is bridged. It is possible to approach the falls on either side of the road, down the east bank on the 844 and the west bank using the 842. The west bank has the better car park, but the east bank gives the best views. The 10m-high (33ft) falls carry huge volumes of water and are known as the Falls of the Gods, because when Iceland adopted Christianity, the deed was celebrated by the symbolic casting of the pagan gods into the waters of the falls.

*Godafoss*

## ✳ Akureyri: the Jewel of the North

Akureyri, the third largest town in Iceland, nestles between mountains on an inlet on the northern shore of Iceland. On fine days you can see ships at sea that are inside the Arctic Circle, yet the town, the largest in the north, enjoys a warm climate, frequently with hot summers.

For almost 500 years, the perfect natural harbour attracted trading ships, but it was not until 1777 that the town began to grow. In 1785 the official register still only recorded ten inhabitants, all of them Danish.

The river mouth, which was originally used as the harbour, gradually silted up, and the trading post was moved to the end of the fjord, in the shelter of the Oddeyri peninsula. Shops, warehouses and stockpens for animals were built, but it was not until the late eighteenth century that Akureyri really became established. This was at the time of the repressive Danish trading laws and the King of Denmark ordained that all merchants with trading monopolies in Iceland must live there.

Due to this decree, Friarik Lynge built his home near the warehouses, and the first home in Akureyri was thus erected. The first house on the Oddeyri peninsula was built in about 1858, and within 8 years this district had been merged with the now established Akureyri. The town received its charter as a trading post in 1862 when the population is believed to have been about 286. Since then it has grown gradually, and now has about 14,000 inhabitants.

Because of its close links with trading ships from Denmark, Akureyri

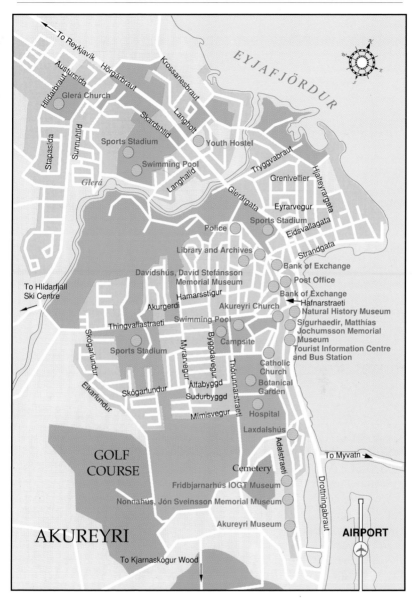

was very similar to many Danish villages, and this character and charm was preserved for many years, but unfortunately, little remains today. However, Akureyri's roots as a trading settlement still remain and it is the centre for the very prosperous northern region. The town houses most of the commercial and service needs of the region, and has a thriving port and shipyard.

In 1870 the Grána Trading Company was founded in Akureyri, as a co-operative business, and for many years it was the most successful commercial enterprise in Iceland with branches in many districts. At the height of its prosperity the company was based in Oddeyri. When the company began to lose its influence, it was replaced by the Akureyri Co-operative Society (KEA). The Society opened the first general store owned by the Association of Icelandic Co-operatives (SIS) in Akureyri in 1906 and for many years it has been the largest and most successful co-operative in the country.

While the rich land to the south contributes to the prosperity of farming, the richness of the sea is also another factor in Akureyri's success. It has long had a fishing fleet and its herring factories were once famous. The herring salting factory at Krossanes was built by the Norwegians, but bought by the town in 1946 and has been run by the municipal authorities since then. Herring is still caught, and salted, or processed, but the decline in the catch has hit the industry.

For the last 130 years Akureyri has also been a thriving industrial centre. Records show that in 1853, when there were only 230 inhabitants, Akureyri had a printer, a bookbinder, four gold and silversmiths, five carpenters, one saddler, one mason and one cobbler apart from several others who were part-time tradesmen. Today there are many more industries as diverse as bakeries and breweries, candy makers and shipbuilding. The shipyard is the largest in Iceland.

Akureyri also has a thriving cultural life, and the national poet Matthías Jochumsson, who lived in the town for 34 years, said, 'Schools are and will be crucial in endowing this town with the aura of a capital, success and respect'. It is perhaps because of this that Akureyri is known not only as the 'Jewel of the North', but also as the 'Capital of the North'.

It is surprising just how many museums and places of interest Akureyri has to offer. Akureyrarkirkja, the Lutheran State Church with its twin towers, dominates the town skyline. The church was completed in 1940 and designed by Gudjón Samúelsson, the architect of many of Iceland's finest buildings. One of the decorated stone frames came from Coventry Cathedral in England which was destroyed during World War II. Services are conducted June to September every Sunday at 11am and October to May at 2pm. It is open to visitors 9.30-11am and 2-3pm daily.

Amtsbókasafnid (Town Library) was established in 1827 and has been operated by the municipality since 1906. It contains 83,000 volumes. The archives was founded in 1967 and contains documents about the town, its institutions and families.

Davídshús (Davíd Stefánsson Memorial Museum) was built in 1944 by the poet Davíd Stefánsson (1895-1964) and he lived there until his death. The house contains his personal property, including his personal library, and it remains in the condition he left it. The house is typical of private homes built in the 1940s.

Fridbjarnarhús (the Order of Good Templars Museum) is housed in the home of Fridbjörn Steinsson, a bookbinder and bookseller (1838-1918). The house was built in 1856. The first IOGT order in Iceland, the Order of

Isafold No. 1 was founded in the building on 10 January 1884. The house is now a museum preserving many of the objects used in the activities of the Order.

The Lystigardur Akureyri (Botanical Gardens) were founded in 1912 and represent almost all the plants that can be grown in northern latitudes. A living collection of almost all Iceland's native plants has been maintained since 1957. Most of the 2,000 plant species on display are labelled.

Minjasafnid (Municipal Museum) illustrates what life used to be like in Akureyri and the surrounding area, with exhibits of work tools, culture and art. There are splendid examples of artistic needlework by the women-folk, their unique national costume, as well as fine silver work and wood carvings by the men. An old church, dating from 1846, stands next to the museum and is open during the same hours. It was built at Svalbard, east of Eyjafjördur and transferred to its new site in 1970.

Náttúrugripasafnid (Akureyri Natural History Museum) was founded in 1951. It houses extensive collections of Icelandic and European plants, animals from Iceland and a world-wide collection of sea shells. It is a centre for mycology (the study of fungi) in the area. The oldest and most complete collection is a display of native birds and eggs, containing all the country's nesting birds. The flora of the country is represented in a series of pressed plants arranged in folders.

Nonnahús, was the childhood home of Nonni, the Reverend Jón Sveinsson (1857-1944) a Jesuit priest and writer of children's books which have been translated into more than forty languages. The house was opened to the public as a museum on the 100th anniversary of his birth. It displays copies of his books, and their translations, as well as original illustrations. The house is one of the older properties in the town, built in 1850.

Sigurhaedir (Matthías Jochumsson Memorial Museum) was the home of the national poet and pastor who lived from 1835-1920. He had the house built in 1902 and lived in it until his death. He composed the words for the *Icelandic National Anthem*, and translated many of the works of Shakespeare and Shelley. The house contains some of his personal property and his literary works.

A visit to Akureyri is essential for anyone who wants to see the 'other Iceland'. It is only 45 minutes flying time away from Reykjavík and the flight alone, over mountains and glaciers, is well worth it.

It seems strange to see beautifully coloured gardens in Akureyri, with snow-capped mountains beyond, but the people have always taken a pride in their gardens, and even though the summer is relatively short they always seem to produce a marvellous array of flowers. The ease with which one can get to Akureyri can also be a blessing when one remembers that the weather in the south is often the exact opposite to that in the north.

Although Akureyri and its surrounding area sees a lot of snow during the winter, the summers are generally mild, and there can be spells of several days of hot, windless weather. The 1984 summer will go on record as one of the hottest ever, with temperatures on some days rivalling those of the Mediterranean. It is this warm summer weather, and the town's love

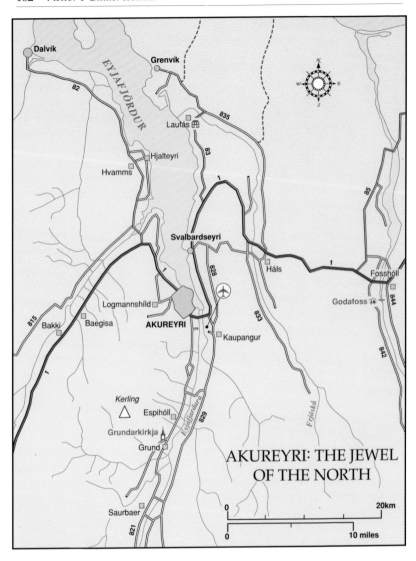

AKUREYRI: THE JEWEL
OF THE NORTH

of gardening, that led to the opening in 1912 of the town's park. It began as the idea of a few townswomen, but now has an important place as a living collection of Iceland's flora. The collection contains a specimen of every flower and plant that grows in the country. Equally, the weather can bring surprises and July, 1992 saw the worst summer snow storms for 100 years.

Because of Akureyri's growing popularity as a tourist centre, there has been a determined effort to provide more accommodation and now there are hotels and hostels to suit all needs. There are also three campsites, two on the outskirts of the town and one by the pool. Akureyri is worth visiting not only in its own right, but because it is the perfect springboard for

*Unusual summer snow at Akureyri*

*Hafnarstraeti in Akureyri*

discovering the rest of the region, especially Lake Myvatn.

 In the winter, the area is also popular with skiers, and Iceland's main winter sports centre is to be found near Akureyri. On the mountain slopes above the town at Hlídarfjall, there are ski slopes both for experts and beginners, with a modern ski hotel and lifts.

The tops of the mountains are capped with snow all year round and it is possible to ski here during the summer if you are experienced. During the winter the best skiing is between 500m and 1,000m (1,640ft and 3,280ft) above sea level, about 11¼km (7 miles) out of town. There are heavy falls of snow from mid-December right through to the end of May. A bus service runs three times a day from the centre of town.

The ski hotel, which is at an altitude of 500m (1,640ft), has eleven double rooms, and sleeping bag accommodation for up to seventy people. There is a sauna to get rid of the day's aches and pains, and ski equipment can be hired. The hotel is open during the peak season, from January to May; it also offers ski instruction. The longest lift goes up to the 1,000m (3,280ft) level, and the longest slope down runs for about 3km (1.8 miles). All the ski routes are compressed by snow tractors, and are floodlit during the evenings for the romantics. There is some marvellous walking in this area, and many walks can be started from the hotel. They are waymarked.

During the summer months, there is still a lot of sport to be had in Akureyri. Like everywhere else in Iceland, swimming is very popular and the town pool is open from June to the end of September. There is a good golf course on the outskirts of the town, and pony trekking trips, on the sturdy Icelandic ponies, are available and becoming increasingly popular. One of the sporting highlights of the year is the Arctic Open, the most northerly international golf tournament in the world. Open to professionals and amateurs alike, the competition tees off at midnight to take full advantage of the 24 hour daylight.

There are ten restaurants, four dance halls and a disco and the usual shops and facilities. You can wander around several museums, visit the public library, enjoy a sauna, go to the cinema or theatre, or loosen up at one of the town's ten athletic clubs. Like all Icelanders, the people of Akureyri love football and hold matches at one of four grounds. In addition there are six community centres, most of which visitors are made welcome. Akureyri church is noted for its stained glass windows.

There are four or five flights a day between Reykjavík and Akureyri during the summer and three or four flights daily over the winter months. Flights are operated four to five times a week to the following localities in eastern Iceland: Vopnafjördur, Raufarhöfn, Thórshöfn, and Kópasker. From the east coast: Seydisfjördur-Egilsstadir-Akureyri daily except Sundays. There is a daily flight to the Western Fjords (Isafjördur) except Sundays. There are five to six flights a week to Ólafsfjördur, Siglufjördur and Grímsey. There is a regular bus service to the south and east and to the villages north of Akureyri: Dalvík, Ólafsfjördur, Hrísey and Árskógsströnd to Hrísey.

Some of Iceland's most beautiful places are to be found around Akureyri. One can travel to see the old farm at Laufás and the old-style church at Saurbaer in the valley south of Akureyri. At Grund there is another unusual church which looks as if it has been built along Byzantine architectural lines. Across the mountain to the east there is the famous waterfall, Godafoss, on the way to Lake Myvatn, which is rapidly becoming one of the country's most popular resorts. The whole area to the south and east of Akureyri is volcanic and eruptions can be expected at almost any time. While there have not been any eruptions in recent years that have been dangerous to life, there have been some quite spectacular things to see including the volcano Krafla.

## Additional Information

### Places to Visit

**Akureyri**
*Akureyri Museum*
Adalstraeti
Open: 1 June to 15 September 11am-5pm, rest of year Sunday 2-4pm.
☎ (96) 24162

*Akureyri Natural History Museum*
Hafnarstraeti
Open: 1 June to 15 September, Sunday to Friday 1-4pm, 1 July to 15 August 10am-5pm.
☎ (96) 22983

*Davídshús*
Bjarkarstíf
Open: 15 June to 15 September 3-5pm.
☎ (96) 27498

*Fridbjarnarhús*
Adalstraeti
Open: July and August, Sunday 2-5pm.
☎ (96) 24459

*Laxdalshús*
Hafnarstraeti
Open: 1 June to 1 September 11am-5pm.
☎ (96) 24490

*Mineral Museum*
Hafnarstraeti
Open: Monday to Saturday 15 to 30 June 1-4pm, 1 July to 15 August 10am-5pm, 16 to 31 August 1-4pm.

*Town Library and Archives*
Brekkugötu
Open: Monday to Friday 1-7pm, and on Saturday 10am-3pm during winter.
☎ (96) 24141

*Nonnahús*
Adalstraeti
Open: 1 June to 31 August 10am-5pm.
☎ (96) 22777

*Sigurhaedir*
Eyrarlandsvegur
(entrance from the church steps)
Open: 15 June to 15 September daily 2-4pm.
☎ (96) 21030

*Lystigardur Akureyri*
Open: daily 9am-10pm during the summer.

### Useful Information: Akureyri

**Emergency Numbers**
Police ☎ (96) 23222
Fire & Ambulance ☎ (96) 22222
Doctor ☎ (985) 23221 (on duty evenings and weekends)

**Hospital**
Sjúkrahúsid
☎ (96) 22100

**Travel**
Akureyri airport ☎ (96) 12200

**Tourist Information**
Hafnarstraeti 82
Open: June to August, Monday to
Friday 8am-7pm,weekends 7.30-11.30,
winter weekdays 9am-5pm.
☎ (96) 27733

**Accommodation**
In and around Akureyri
**Hotel Kea**
Hafnarstraeti
☎ (96) 22200

**Hotel Harpa**
Hafnarstraeti
☎ (96) 11400

**Hotel Nordurland**
Geislagata
☎ (96) 22600

**Hotel Edda**
Hrafnagilsstraeti
☎ (96) 24055

**Hotel Edda**
Stórutjarnir
☎ (96) 43221

**As**
Skipgata
☎ (96) 26110

**Bakki**
(sleeping bag accommodation)
Bakkahlíd
☎ (96) 25774

**Dalkakoffin**
(sleeping bag accommodation)
Lyngholt
☎ (96) 23035

**Salka**
Skipagata
☎ (96) 22697

**Thelamörk**
Hotel Edda
☎ (96) 21772

**Hrafnagil**
Hotel Vin
☎ (96) 31399

*Youth Hostels*
**Akureyri**
Stórholt
☎ (96) 23657

**Lónsá**
3km (2 miles) from Akureyri
☎ (96) 25037

**Alda**
(sleeping bag accommodation and
    camping)
Melgerdi
☎ (96) 31267

*Camping*
**Akureyri**
Campsite Off Thórunnarstraeti
Open: 10 June to 1 September.
☎ (96) 23379

**Svalbardsströnd**
☎ (96) 24921

**Recreation**
*Swimming*
Thingvallastraeti
☎ (96) 23260

*Golf*
The world's most northerly course.
☎ (96) 22974

*Horse Riding*
Alda, Eyjafirdi (south of Akureyri)
☎ (96) 31267
Polar Hourse, Gytubakka ☎ (96) 33179

## Other Places To Visit

**Blönduós**
*Heimilisidnadarsafnid (Handicraft
    Museum)*
Arbraut 31
Open: 20 June to 31 August, Tuesday,
Wednesday and Thursday 4-6pm.
☎ (95) 24067

**Dalvík**
*Natural History Museum*
Open: daily 1-6pm.
☎ (96) 61353

**Glaumbaer**
*Folk Museum*
Open: 1 June to 1 September daily 10am-
12noon and 1-6pm.
☎ (95) 38266

**Grenjadarstadur**
*Folk Museum*
Adaldalur
Open: June to August daily 10am-6pm.
Guides available.
☎ (96) 43545

**Húsavík**
*Folk and Natural History Museum*
Open: 22 June to 22 August 10am-
12noon and 2-5pm.
☎ (96) 41860

**Laufás**
*Church and Folk Museum*
Eyjafjördur
Open: 1 June to 31 August daily except
Monday, 10am-6pm.
☎ (96) 33106

**Reykjatanga**
*Folk Museum*
Open: June to August 10am-12noon and
1-6pm.

**Saudárkrókur**
*Art Museum and Library*
Open: daily.
☎ (95) 35424

**Skagafjördur**
*Vidimymri Church*
Open: 1 June to 31 August 9am-6pm
(closed during services).
☎ (95) 38167

**Varmahlíd**
*Natural History Museum*
Open: daily during the summer.

## Useful Information

### Emergency Numbers
*Fire*
Nordurlandsbraut ☎ (95) 24327
Slökkvistödín ☎ (95) 12411

*Police*
Blönduós ☎ (95) 24377
Húsavík ☎ (96) 41630
Saudárkrókur ☎ (95) 36666
Hvammstangi ☎ (95) 12365

### Hospitals
**Saudárkrókur**
Emergency service open 24 hours.
☎ (95) 35270

**Hvammstangi**
☎ (95) 12345

**Húsavík**
☎ (96) 41333

**Blönduós**
Health Clinic and Hospital
Open: 8am-5pm.
☎ (95) 24206

### Motoring
Information on road conditions
Blönduós ☎ (95) 24152
Hvammstangi ☎ (95) 12455
Saudárkrókur ☎ (95) 35500
Akureyri ☎ (96) 26700
Thórshöfn ☎ (96) 81180

### Airports
**Húsavík**
☎ (96) 41140

**Blönduós**
☎ (95) 24289

### Accommodation
*A selection of Hotels and Guesthouses*
**Stóru-Tjarnir**
Hotel Edda
☎ (96) 43221

**Reykjum**
Hotel Edda
☎ (95) 10004

**Hörgárdalur**
Hotel Edda
☎ (96) 21772

**Húnavöllum**
Hotel Edda
☎ (95) 24370

**Laugarbakki**
Hotel Edda
☎ (95) 12904

**Húnavellir**
Hotel Edda
☎ (95) 4370

**Hrútafjördur**
Hotel Stadarskáli
☎ (95) 11150

**Saudárkrókur**
Hotel Aning
(summer only)
☎ (95) 36087

**Eyjafjördur**
Hotel Vin
☎ (96) 31136

**Saudárkrókur**
Hotel Maelifell
☎ (95) 35265

**Myvatn**
Hotel Reynihlíd
☎ (96) 44170

**Varmahlíd**
Hotel Varmahlíd
☎ (95) 38170

**Hvammstangi**
Hotel Vertshúsid
☎ (95) 1717

**Hvammstanga**
Hotel Vertshús
Nordurbraut 1
☎ (95) 12717

**Húsavík**
Hotel Kidagil
On the Sprengisands road
☎ (96) 43290

**Blönduós**
Hotel Blönduós
Adalgata 6
☎ (95) 24126

Jónas Skaftason
(sleeping bag accommodation)
Blöndubyggth 10
☎ (95) 24535

**Asar**
Stóra Giljá (farmhouse)
On Highway 1
☎ (95) 24294

*Youth Hostels*
**Akureyri**
Lonsá
☎ (96) 25037

**Hosfós**
Lónkot
☎ (95) 37432

**Hvammstangi**
Osar
☎ (95) 37432

**Reykir**
Saeberg
☎ (95) 10015

**Bárdardalur**
Fosshóll
☎ (96) 43108

*Campsites*
**Asbyrgi**

**Saudárkrókur**

**Hvammstangi**
☎ (95) 11150

**Stadarskáli**
☎ (95) 11150

**Húsavík**
Hédinsbraut

**Recreation**
*Golf*
**Blönduós**
Vatnahverfli
☎ (95) 24980

*Swimming Pools*
**Reykir**
☎ (95) 10003

**Blönduós**
☎ (95) 24451

**Varmahlid**
☎ (95) 38125

**Husabakki**
☎ (96) 61551

**Arskógsskóli**
☎ (96) 61970

**Bakkaflöt**
☎ (95) 38245

**Steinsstadskóli**
Skagafjördur
☎ (95) 38812

**Hólar**
Hjaltadalur
☎ (95) 35962

**Húsavík**
(hot tubs/sauna)
☎ (96) 41144

**Hvammstanga**
☎ (95) 12532

## Tourist Information Centres

**Blönduós**
☎ (95) 24520

**Húsavík**
☎ (96) 42100

**Hvammstangi**
☎ (95) 12434

**Stadarskáli**
☎ (95) 11150

**Varmahlíd**
Open: 15 June to 31 August 10am-9pm.
☎ (95) 38860

# 6
## THE WEST COAST AND WESTERN FJORDS

The western coast really comprises the districts of Borgarfjördur, Snaefellsnes, and Dalir. In this region can be found almost every type of geological formation and it is extremely attractive to bird watchers.

Off the **Borgarfjördur Bay**, there is a lowland plain whose fingers reach between the mountains in a series of valleys. Here you will find fast running rivers and some of the best salmon fishing Iceland has to offer. Hvalfjördur is a long narrow bay and is the home for the only land-based whaling station in Iceland, although as mentioned earlier, its future is uncertain now that the country has agreed to curtail whaling operations. There is also an iron ore refinery to be found here.

**Borgarnes** is one of the few coastal towns which does not rely on fishing for its economy. It is the commercial and trading centre for the region and has a hotel, sports stadium, golf course, and swimming pool. The campsite is beside the road leading into the town. There is now a new bridge just outside Borgarnes which crosses Borgarfjördur and greatly reduces the journey to Reykjavík and the south. This district is one of the most fertile agricultural regions in Iceland with many large farms and ranches. There is also a park in the town where Skallagrímur, the original settler of the district, is said to be buried. With his son Egil, a famous Viking and poet, he is supposed to have farmed at Borg, a few minutes' drive from the town, but nothing remains of this today.

From Borgarnes you can head inland on highway 50, about 17km (10 miles) north of town on the ringroad for Húsafell, an area of lush vegetation lying between lava and glaciers. It is an area noted for its summer sunshine, a good place to camp and a great base for exploring the hinterland.

**Snaefellsnes** is a long mountainous peninsula separating the two largest bays in Iceland, Faxaflói and Breidafjördur which means 'Broad Firth'. A road follows the line of the bay and another runs out into the peninsula. The area is predominantly occupied with fishing and farming, although other industries are now taking a more important role. The area is domi-

THE WEST COAST AND
WESTERN FJORDS

nated by Snaefellsjökull, an extinct volcano on the tip of the Snaefellsnes peninsula, which can even be seen from Reykjavík on fine days. The long since dead volcano is now tipped with a glacier.

The mountains in the area are mainly of basalt although they contain many other interesting minerals such as rhyolite, tuff and breccia. There are many lakes, and the rivers tend to be short because of the mountainous nature of the countryside. There are a number of routes across the mountains to allow the traveller to journey from south to north, and the best crossing points are at Fródárheidi (361m, 1,184ft), and Kerlingarskard (311m, 1,020ft).

Between Búdir and Ólafsvík, towards the western tip of the peninsula, the promontory is less than 20km (12½ miles) wide, but it increases in breadth towards the east. In the east of the region, to the south of the central ridge of mountains, there is a grassy plain which accommodates most of the agriculture. The scenery here is varied, and there are marshes, with many interesting birds, as well as sandy beaches, lagoons and numerous small lakes.

The northern shore has little lowland, as the mountains plunge straight into the sea, and the coastline is deeply indented with fjords, such as Álftafjördur, Kolgrafafjördur and Grundarfjördur. The fjords, with their deep water, and protected by the towering mountains, make ideal anchorages and many ports and fishing villages have been established here.

There are extensive lavafields at the foot of the glacier, at Búdahraun, Drangahraun, and Neshraun, which were formed when lava flowed from Snaefellsjökull crater and others in the area long before Iceland was first settled. In many places the lava runs straight into the sea and produces a weird and wonderful landscape of strange twisted shapes, towering lava cliffs, pillars and so on. There are lighthouses at Malarrif and Öndverdarnes and another lavafield at Berserkjahraun, which flowed from craters near Bjarnarhöfn on the north coast. Carbon dioxide springs can be found in many places on Snaefellsnes, caused by the turbulent volcanic activity. The early settlers nicknamed the springs 'beer wells' because the water with its sparkle was so good to drink. It can still be drunk today and is said to be good for the health.

On the north coast of Snaefellsnes and to the east of Stykkishólmur is a low-lying, wooded shore leading to the Dalir, a region of hills, grassy valleys and clear rivers. Further up the coast to the north, there is a trading centre at **Búdardalur**, nestling in the shadow of another mountainous peninsula jutting out into the sea. At the tip of this peninsula reaching out into Breidafjördur, there are many small islands, said to be so numerous that they have never been counted. In places there are so many small islands that the sea is forced through narrow gaps, increasing its speed and creating tricky currents which make all navigation in this area dangerous.

Most of the islands are low and have grassy vegetation, although the Klakkeyjar group have strange pyramid shaped hills which can be spotted many miles away. The biggest island off the coastline is Brokey. In the past most of the islands were inhabited by farmers, but now almost all are abandoned except for Flatey in the centre of Breidafjördur, although summer cottages have been built on others for occasional use.

**Flatey** is the largest of the islands and a monastery was built here around 1100 which became the centre for Icelandic culture. During the eighteenth century it was the main trading centre along the west coast and sailing ships from many countries visited to trade for fish and seal skins. The library is the oldest in Iceland and the whole village has recently been restored.

The western coastline has a rich history, clearly chronicled in many of the Sagas. It was the first part of the country to be seriously settled by the Norsemen in the ninth and tenth centuries, and there are vivid records of these early days in the *Eyrbyggja*, *Laxdaela* and *Sturlunga* Sagas, written in the thirteenth century.

Many of the settlers to these parts came via the Hebrides or Ireland, especially those who made their homes on and around Snaefellsnes. Here, there are still strong traces of their Celtic origin, and recent medical tests have proved that the Icelanders are more closely related to the Celts than they are to the Scandinavians.

The method of creation of the Sagas is not known, although people everywhere have tried to record their early history in similar ways. Most literate people of this time can be traced to the monasteries, and it is thought the Celts played a great part in the writing of the Sagas. Today, there are still many place names which have Celtic links and many start with the Icelandic name for Irish. There is Írafell (Irish mountain), Íraklettur (Irish rock), Írskaleid (Irish route) and Írskutóftir (Irish homes)

British vessels, which traded off this western coast in the fifteenth century, are also believed to have been responsible for places being given such names as Bretahraun, Bretalaekur and Kumbaravogur although the names are probably earlier. The word 'Snaefell' of course, is of Scandinavian origin, and is also the name for the mountain on the Isle of Man, which was once itself a Viking colony.

The first settler to this coastline is thought to have been Thórólfur Mostraskegg, who arrived from Norway in 884. He landed near Stykkishólmur and named the promontory there Thórsnes, because it was where the pillars from his Thor temple were washed ashore. It was customary for the Norsemen to choose their home by casting overboard a sacred or treasured possession. If it drifted ashore they reasoned that the gods were happy and had chosen this as the site for settlement. Reykjavík was chosen in the same way, although legend has it that it took Arnarson several months to discover just where his 'sacrifices' had been washed up.

Mostraskegg established the first parliament in Iceland. The 'thing' or legislative assembly met on Thórsnes many times before the National Assembly was founded at Thingvellir to the east of Reykjavík in 930.

There were many other famous settlers in this area, according to the Sagas, including Audur the Deepminded, the widow of a Viking king of Dublin. She had adopted the Christian faith and had travelled to Iceland via the Hebrides.

The coastline has had a stormy history and it often resisted dictates from Denmark. British traders often plied here without the necessary permission from Denmark and in 1457, the local officials became so annoyed that they tried to stop trade. The British simply killed the governor and things continued without further interference. After the British, there was a long tradition of trading with the Germans but international trade with any other country than Denmark almost came to an end with the introduction of the Danish trading monopoly in the early seventeenth century.

There are many interesting things to see in this area including the glacier **Snaefellsjökull**, which is now one of the smallest ice caps in Iceland having an area of only about 11sq km (4sq miles). The glacier has a number of peaks, the highest of which is 1,446m (4,744ft), in the far north-west of the peninsula. It is possible to climb to the top, but late spring and early summer are the best times, as it can be dangerous later in the summer when crevasses appear in the ice. The peak was first climbed by two Icelanders in 1753, and then by an English team of climbers in 1789. The French author, Jules Verne, used the crater at Snaefellsjökull as the entry point in his story *Journey to the Centre of the Earth*.

The best starting point for the climb is near Arnarstapi on the southern slopes, and here the path is relatively easy to climb and easy to follow. The climb will take about 4 hours although guides are available and it is best to be accompanied by one of them, if you are not an experienced climber. There is a mountain hut on this southern side maintained by the Iceland Tourist Association.

The area is easily accessible from Reykjavík and there is a regular bus service into the region, and many organised tours, which can last anything from a few hours to several days. Naturalists will find much of

*Búdardalur*

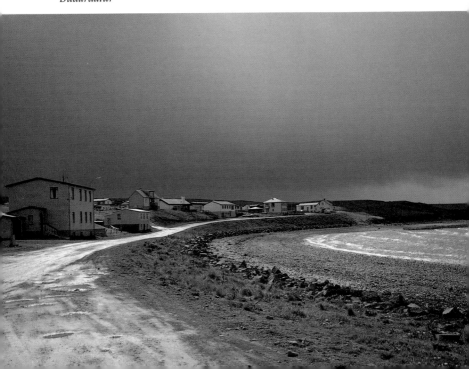

interest here. There are hotels at Stykkishólmur on the north coast of Snaefellsnes and Búdir in the south, as well as guesthouses at Ólafsvík and Grundarfjördur. Equally, it is possible to pitch a tent almost anywhere.

The southern shore of Snaefellsnes, between the salmon rivers of Hítará and Haffjardará in the east, is dominated by the **Eldborgarhraun**  lavafield. It is possible to walk for about 30 minutes from the main road to the Eldborg crater which was the site of a major eruption. Near the farm of Raudimelur, west of Haffjardará, the waters from the carbon dioxide springs, or the 'beer wells' can be sampled. The largest such springs on Snaefellsnes are to be found here. Around here there are also spectacular basalt columns.

In 1936 a French exploration ship, the *Pourquoi Pas?*, was lost here with nearly all hands, near the mouth of the river Straumfjardará, which is also famous for its salmon fishing. About half-way between here and Búdir is the parsonage of Stadastadur, where the historian Ari the Wise lived in the early twelfth century and where he wrote the *Íslendingabók*, which chronicled the early history of the country.

There are a number of other carbon dioxide springs around **Búdir**, together with a farm, Ölkelda, named after one. In Búdir there is a swimming pool built by a farmer but open to the public which utilises a hot spring. Búdir was once an important port, but is now only a hamlet with a summer hotel. It is a useful base for exploring the Búdaklettur crater and the lava, in which can be found many rare species of ferns and  wild flowers.

Also to be seen near here are the cliffs and caves at the fishing village of Arnarstapi and Hellnar, the Stapafell mountain, famous for its echoing caves, and the impressive towering Hraundrangar rocks near the light-  house at Malarrif. At the western end of Snaefellsnes is **Dritvik Cove**, which although some kilometres off the main road, is worth a visit. There are the remnants of an ancient fishing village, where the people would venture far out to sea in open rowing boats. The northern coast of Snaefellsnes is uninhabited until you arrive at Hellissandur, also called **Sandur**, which is another fishing village. It is the westernmost village of Snaefellsnes and although there is some agriculture inland, the population level has stayed virtually unchanged all this century.

There is also the fishing port of **Rif**, with its new harbour, which is now one of the busiest villages along the coast. It is not to be confused with **Ólafsvík**, farther to the east, another fishing village whose population has grown rapidly in recent years, where there is now a hotel, restaurant and community centre. A storage house built in 1841 can still be seen and is thought to be the only building of its kind left in Iceland. The building has now been converted into a small craft museum showing how the people  worked a century ago, and the sorts of tools they used. Ólafsvík is Iceland's oldest trading centre, gaining its authorisation from King Christian V of Denmark on 26 March 1687. Vessels regularly plied to Denmark, Britain and as far afield as Spain. *The Swan* is the port's most famous vessel and it traded out of Ólafsvík for 116 years until it was damaged beyond repair in an accident which beached her on the approaches to the port in 1893, the longest ever in the world.

Although Ólafsvík only had a population of 92 in 1801, this had grown to 255 in 1890 and 612 by 1901, making it the seventh largest urban area in Iceland. It now has about 1,200 inhabitants. The campsite is just outside the village, and there is a golf course and swimming pool. There is a very attractive modern architecture church consecrated in 1967 which stands on a small hill close to the town, believed to be the site of the farm of the settler Olafur Belgur. The Old Packing House dates from 1844 and is still used for trading today.

Snaefellsjökull dominates the land behind the town, and many people believe this is the most beautiful mountain in Iceland. On a good day it can even be spotted from Reykjavík. There are many good walks in and around the glacier and there is a good road leading towards it. The northern shore of Snaefellsnes is rugged and mountainous, characterised by steep cliffs and fjords with many fishing villages, nestling on the rocky inlets.

**Grundarfjördur** is a fishing village with a growing population, completely trapped by mountains and the sea. It has a hotel and is a good base for visiting one of the country's most beautiful mountains, Kirkjufell, which climbs to 463m (1,519ft). The campsite is at Kverná, about 1km (half a mile) from the village.

At Hraunfjördur the lavafield disappears into the sea. **Stykkishólmur** is the largest town on Snaefellsnes, and fishing provides the main occupation. The area also has an agricultural hinterland, so many industries connected with this can be found in the town. There is a hotel and guesthouse, restaurant, filling stations, swimming pool, tourist information centre and bus station. The campsite is by the sports field. There is an airstrip and the area around the town is very beautiful. Helgafell, a small mountain which raises to 73m (240ft) above the sea is the subject of many folk stories and legends. It is said, for example, that if someone walks up to the top for the first time, without looking back or speaking a single word, they will be allowed three wishes on reaching the top, provided they are not bad wishes, and the person making them faces the east.

The mountain is also said to have been the home of Gudrún, heroine of the *Laxdaela* Saga, and the abode of Ari the Wise, and the chieftain Snorri Godi. It was also the site of a twelfth-century Augustinian monastery which lasted for 400 years. The island's first assembly met at Thingvellir a few miles away, which is not to be confused with the site of the National Assembly to the east of Reykjavík. Nearby is the spectacular Drápuhlídar mountain, famous for its varied colours caused by the presence of rhyolite, jasper and pyrites. It is possible to arrange boat tows to Flatey.

At **Bólstadur** in Álftafjördur you can see the remains of a tenth-century farm which was excavated in the 1920s, and the whole of this district featured heavily in the *Eyrbyggja* Saga. To the east there is the parsonage

at Breidabólstadur and the Drangar rocks, where Erík the Red committed  ✳
the murders which led to him being outlawed. He fled to Greenland,
which is how the island to the west of Iceland came to be settled. It was on
the islands of Klakkeyjar, just off the coast, that he prepared for his
expedition. On Hrappsey, now owned by Iceland University, the island's
first magazine was printed in the years 1773-95.

The eastern shore of Hvammsfjördur, known as **Dalasysla**, is also rich
in historical legend and again featured heavily in the Sagas. The home of  ✳
Erík the Red is at the farm at Stóra Vatnshorn, and his son Leif Eríksson,
the discoverer of North America in 1000, is said to have been born at
Eríksstadir. Hjardarholt, at the mouth of Laxárdalur, was the birthplace
of Kjartan, hero of the *Laxdaela* Saga, and Höskuldsstadir was the home of
Höskuldur who was married to the Irish princess Melkorka, and was
father of Ólafur the Peacock. The only trading and service centre in the
Dalasysla district is Búrdardalur, which has a hotel, tourist shop, community centre and restaurant.

To the south is **Saudafell**, the home of a thirteenth-century chieftain  ✳
who went on a pilgrimage to Rome. It was in this region that the clan feuds
took place in the twelfth and thirteenth centuries which eventually led to
Iceland losing its independence to Norway in 1262. It was at Saudafell also
that the last Catholic bishop, Jón Arason, and his two sons were captured,
and then taken to Skálholt and beheaded in 1550.

The farm at **Hvammur** was the home of Audur the Deepminded and the  ✳
birthplace of the Sturlunga Clan in about 1115. On the cliffs at Krosshóla-
borg, there is a stone cross marking the spot where Audur used to pray.

The northern coast of Dalasysla, Skardsströnd, gets its name from
Skard, a farm which has been in the hands of the same family since the
eleventh century. In the fifteenth century it was the home of the local
governor Björn Thorleifsson, whose wife Ólöf the Rich avenged his mur-
der by the British at Rif by killing some British fishermen and forcing
others to work as slaves on the farm. The new church contains an altar-  ⌂
piece dating back to the fifteenth century, donated by Ólöf.

Other places of interest in the west include Reykholt, which was once  ✳
the home of Snorri Sturluson, one of Iceland's best known scholars and
author of *Heimskringla, Snorri Edda* and other works. There is a pool here
which he is believed to have used and a tunnel between the pool and
Snorri's house has been partially rebuilt. A boarding school is used as a
summer hotel. Nearby Húsafell is a large forest of birch trees and the
location for many important outdoor events. There are three large craters
with strange, eerie shapes just off the road in Borgarfjördur called
Grábrók. There is a restaurant here.

North of Svínaskard, Kastalinn, a rock formation resembling a fortress,
can be seen, which offers one of the best vantage points in the area.

*Stykkishólmur Harbour*

## The Western Fjords

The Western Fjords (Vestfirdir) form the most westerly part of Iceland, and geologically are very old. The mountains are high and the coastline indented by deep narrow fjords. There are many fishing villages along the coast and fishing and fish processing forms the major source of employment.

The most westerly point is **Látrabjarg**, which is a cliff teeming with birdlife during the summer months. This cliff is, in fact, the most westerly point in Europe and is only 278km (173 miles) from Greenland. There is spectacular scenery here in the mountains and moorland.

The whole of the Western Fjords area sticks out into the sea and the width of land connecting it to the mainland is so narrow, less than 16km (10 miles) wide, that it looks as if it might snap off at any time.

The region is one of basalt cliffs towering in places to 400m (1,312ft) high while the highest peak, Kaldabakur, is just under 1,000m high (a little over 3,000ft). The two largest fjords on the north coast are **Arnarfjördur** and **Ísafjardardjúp** and both have several smaller fjords running from them. All the fjords on this western coast tend to run from north-west to south-east. The east coast of the peninsula is known as Strandir, and the extreme north is called **Hornstrandir**, which gets its name from the word *'horn'* meaning cape. It is the most northerly point of Iceland and a very desolate area but ideal if you enjoy remote backpacking and climbing.

Although the peninsula used to support a number of small settlements and farmsteads, the rigours of the way of life had driven everyone away by the early 1950s. Apart from sometimes atrocious winter weather, the locals also had to cope with icefloes from Greenland being swept ashore with unwanted guests. Polar bears arrived uninvited several times this way, and after several days on the pack ice, they were not too friendly. The last polar bear in this area was shot in 1917.

The arctic fox is common throughout the area, and it too, is thought to have been colonised after coming in from Greenland on drifting ice more than 1,000 years ago. The whole of Hornstrandir is now deserted although the derelict buildings remain. The whole of the area was declared a nature reserve in 1974, and while it is an offence to damage the land in any way, or hunt, there are no restrictions on travel, other than the very obvious ones of actually getting into the remoter areas. As a precaution about ten huts have been situated close to the coast around the peninsula. These are open in the summer and intended really for emergency use.

It is a marvellous area to roam in. There are massive, sheer cliffs supporting huge colonies of sea birds. At the foot of the cliffs you can see seals basking in the sun, and whales are often to be seen just off shore. Driftwood, mostly from Siberia, lies piled up on the beaches. Inland, it is an area of scrubby vegetation, glacial valleys and hills, ranging from gently sloping to very steep. Breidaskardshnuker (709m, 2,325ft) is the highest point on the peninsula, due south of Horn.

The only ways in are by ferry which is the easiest, or a long trek from either Nordurfjördur on the north coast, or from Dalbaer at the end of highway 635 on the southern coast of the peninsula. The ferry makes a number of stops in inlets around the peninsula, but the usual pick up point is at Hornvík. You must allow yourself plenty of time if exploring Hornstrandir. You must be fully equipped, ready for bad weather and have extra provisions in case you get delayed by the weather. A detailed map is also essential. Recommended is the Ramblers Map of Hornstrandir 1: 100,000.

There are many routes to take in Hornstrandir. One starts from the deserted fishing village of **Hesteyri** on the south coast. This used to be a bustling place with its own fishing fleet and a whaling station further down the fjord. From Hesteyri, it is an easy hike across to Hlöduvík Bay where you can camp overnight. The path then crosses the 330m (1,082ft) Skálarkamb ridge to Hornvík Bay, then eastwards via Atlaskard pass and up into the hills, marked by a string of ancient cairns. As you near the coast again, there are impressive views of Hornvík Bay again sheltered by the towering cliffs of Hornbjarg and Haelavíkurbjarg, which climb between 300 and 500m (984 and 1,640ft) above the sea. This is a very impressive coastline and the cliffs and different inlets are all worth exploring if you have time. Látravík Bay to the south of Hornbjarg is the site of Iceland's most northerly lighthouse, and most remote districts. The only safe way in is by sea.

Because this is the oldest geological area of Iceland there has been no volcanic activity here for many years and there is little lava in evidence. There is an area of hot springs near Reykjanes at the south-eastern end of Ísafjardardjúp. Because of the steepness of the slopes, there is little vegetation, and the small amount visible is confined to the narrow coastal strips of the fjords.

There is a small glacier, Drangajökull, at 925m (3,035ft) in the north-east, but another one, Gláma, has now disappeared because of the increasing warmth of the climate. The glacier started to disappear in about 1600 and had completely disappeared by 1900.

In many ways this area has a history that closely resembles that of the Scottish Highlands. There were many powerful chieftains in this area from the thirteenth to sixteenth centuries, and their families were often feuding. The history of this period can be read in the Sagas of *Gísli*, *Hávardur* and *Fóstbroedur*, all of which are concerned with the Vestfirdir. It was in this region that Jón Sigurdsson was born in 1811. He was later to become the champion of Iceland's independence movement.

Again, as with the whole western coast, there are many names here to recall the Celtic influence on the region. There is Patreksfjördur, in the southern part of the Western Fjords, which was named after Bishop Patrick from the Hebrides. There is also Brjánslaekur, which means Brian's Brook, and other Irish-derived names.

This part of the country has often played host to foreigners. In the past,

*Ísafjördur*

*Flateyri*

*Fishermen's Museum at Bolungarvík*

*Unexpected roadworks at Hestfjardarheidi*

the ports and trading centres were often visited by German and British traders, and more recently fishermen from several nations have used the harbours to shelter from the severe storms that sweep the area. Although there are still rich fishing grounds off the west coast of Iceland and in the Denmark Strait between Greenland and Iceland, the new fishing limits now exclude most foreign vessels, and the British deep sea fleet is so reduced that its vessels look for catches nearer to home.

Because the district is so close to the Arctic, its climate is somewhat colder than the rest of Iceland, but in the summer it can still be quite warm in the shelter of the fjords, and there is the additional bonus of many weeks of perpetual daylight which allows exploration of the countryside at leisure.

Although the idea of the continual daylight for several weeks seems strange to us, it is something which is easy to become accustomed to and can quickly be taken advantage of. For climbers and walkers there is no longer such urgency, late in the day, to look for a suitable campsite. If tiredness sets in, it is easy simply to stop, cook a meal and then sleep for 2 or 3 hours at a time when necessary. It is a very secure feeling to know that if you are driving over a mountain road, the sun is not suddenly going to set, leaving you literally in the dark, and this corner of Iceland, because of its position, tends to have longer periods of permanent daylight than the rest of the country.

For a naturalist it is interesting to see how the birds adapt to these conditions. There is no longer the frantic feeding rush that birds further south have to follow in order to keep their nestlings satisfied from dawn to dusk. Here in this mountainous corner you may see the magnificent white tailed eagle. There are a few pairs still breeding here, but there are no clear signs of just how endangered the species is. In the summer there are thousands of nesting birds all along the coast, especially puffins, arctic tern and eider.

Sheepfarming is now the major form of agriculture and most other forms of cultivation have ceased, with many of the farms in the north now abandoned. Many of the people have moved to the fishing villages where processing industries have sprung up to handle the rich catches available off the coast. In times gone by there were a number of whaling stations along this coastline, set up by the Norwegians at Flateyri, Hesteyri and Tálknafjördur. The centre for the country's shark fishing industry was also here. Neither of these occupations are now pursued here.

The best base for touring the area is **Ísafjördur**, the principal town and main trading centre for the region. It is on Skutulsfjördur, surrounded by mountains on three sides and the sea on the other. It has been the capital of the Western Fjords for at least 200 years, since the King of Denmark lifted Iceland's trade monopoly. Then it was chosen to be one of six commercial and industrial centres in Iceland. A few houses dating from the eighteenth and nineteenth centuries can still be seen. The town is still predominantly a fishing centre, especially for shrimps, and it has an excellent natural harbour. There are, however, many other industries in and around the town including a flourishing boatworks. There is an airstrip with daily flights to Reykjavík as well as trips to other airfields in the area such as Thingeyri, Flateyri and Patreksfjördur. The town has hotels, restaurants, a folk museum, art gallery, swimming pool, tourist information centre and campsite in Tungudalur, 4km (2½ miles) from the town, although there is a bus link. There is also a hospital, community centre and cinema. The town makes a good base for summer walking trips, or winter skiing, and there are a number of popular boat trips to Hornstrandir and Jökulfirdir.

Because of the mountainous nature of the countryside, travel used to be very difficult, and was almost impossible during the winter months. Now, the building of airstrips at Ísafjördur and a number of other villages has overcome many of these problems.

The area is also popular in the winter with skiers, and there is a ski lodge a short distance from Ísafjördur (about 3km, 1.8 miles) which is open from February until May, depending on the snow. The lodge is at an altitude of 200m (656ft) and has both rooms and dormitories for people with their own sleeping bags. The best skiing is to be had between March and April and there are some very good runs. The lodge is open during the summer as a base for hikers and climbers.

There are many organised tours from Ísafjördur which can be arranged locally or in Reykjavík. If you have time, certainly the best way of seeing the spectacular countryside is by boat. There is a daily tour in the summer from Ísafjördur on the local ferry boat which takes several hours and visits all the interesting places en route, including the islands of Aedaey and Vigur. Food is served on board, and it is possible to take this day trip from Reykjavík because the scheduled air services have been worked out to coincide with it. It is a long day, but well worth it if time is limited. If more time is available, a much more rewarding visit is achieved by staying for a day or two.

There are taxis which are willing to take passengers to other points of interest, and if the taxi is shared, there is no reason why it should be an expensive outing. Equally, there are bus services to places such as Thingeyri, but check the timetable because they do not always run every day, and it could be a long way to walk back.

It is possible to travel by ferry from Ísafjördur across the fjord to Kaldalón and then to the Drangajökull glacier which reaches almost to the sea. During the summer, there are regular Sunday sailings around the uninhabited islands and remote fjords in northern Ísafjördur. The next fjord, Álftafjördur, can also be reached, either by car or by a limited bus service. Here there are some magnificent views and one can visit the old whaling station at Langeyri.

The northern tip of the Western Fjords is desolate and uninhabited, and access to it is difficult, but it is the perfect place for a backpacking trip provided everything necessary for the trip is carried in the pack. There are

*Esja, easily seen to the north of Reykjavík*

*One of the fast-flowing streams running down the south side of Esja to the sea*

no facilities at all, no shops and no medical treatment. So, if a trip in this area is planned, it is essential to go with someone experienced, and preferably as part of a large group; and please tell someone in advance where you are going, and how long you expect to be away. This is one of Iceland's most unexplored regions and very few tourists brave a trip here, which is a pity because it is an unspoilt, beautiful countryside where it is possible to get away from it all. It is possible to take a boat from Ísafjördur on a sightseeing trip along the coast.

**Vatnsfjördur**, due south, is most famous for being the place where the country received its name. It was here that Flóki Valgerdarson saw ice-floes drifting on the sea, and gave the country the name Iceland. It could have been given a very different name had he landed in the summer, because the fertile land surrounding the valley is lush with green vegetation, and the fjord has one of the warmest climates in Iceland.

**Patreksfjördur**, is the town on the fjord of the same name; most of its people are engaged in fishing or associated industries. There is a hospital, community centre, restaurant and cinema. There is also an airfield with regular flights to Reykjavík. **Talknafjördur** is another fishing village named after the fjord on which it stands. **Bíldudalur** is a prosperous fishing village on the southern side of Arnafjördur. Many of the country's finest shrimps are caught in the fjord and there is a processing plant in the town.

The oldest trading centre in the area is **Thingeyri**, which has a hotel,

*Breidabolsstadur near Stykkishólmur, be prepared for the dusty roads!*

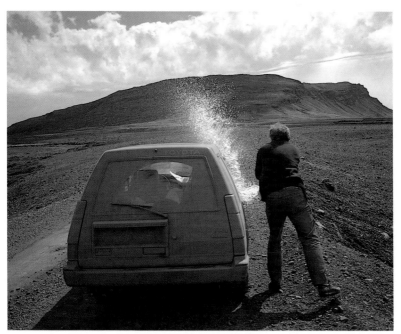

open all year. **Flateyri** is a town by Önundarfjördur which relies on fishing and agriculture for its livelihood.

**Sudureyri** is a fishing port which can be reached by driving over the 518m (1,700ft) high Botnsheidi Pass. Coastal vessels regularly stop here, and there is an airstrip, cinema, community centre and restaurant.

One of the oldest yet still active fishing ports in the country is **Bolungarvík**. The first motor-driven fishing boats in Iceland were operated from this port. The town has a hotel, airstrip, infirmary, community centre and heated swimming pool. Look out for the small Fishermen's  Museum down on the waters edge. It is unmanned and open 24 hours a day. **Hólmavík** is a fishing village which became a trading centre towards the end of the last century. It is now also the centre for the flourishing agricultural hinterland. It has an infirmary and hotel.

## Driving along the West Coast and the Western Fjords

Although most of the roads in the region are made from gravel, it is possible to cover quite long distances in comparatively short spaces of time. Hopefully, if you are driving the ring road anti-clockwise, you should have enough confidence by now to drive at the fastest possible safe speed along these roads. There are stretches of quite stunning scenery, however, and many places which are worth stopping for, either to explore or photograph.

As with many other roads through Iceland you will see cairns, or piles of stones beside the road. These date back to the times when there were no roads, and these cairns were the only indication the traveller had that he was still heading in the right direction. In this region, the farms are 25km (15 or so miles) or more apart, and a century or so ago that must have been a daunting journey in bad weather.

If you are coming across from Akureyri, it is a good idea to leave the ring road and take Route 59 across Laxardalsheidi, a rocky and imposing landscape to **Búdardalur**. In Búdardalur you can drive down to the beach and the smell of seaweed is very strong here. After the town you then have a choice of routes. You can either head south on Route 60 through the mountains to link up with the ring road at Dalsmynni, and then down to Borgarnes, via Bifröst, or you can take Route 57 and head west to explore Snaefellsnes peninsula and the settlements along its north coast.

**Bifröst** standing on the ringroad, is a good centre for exploring this area. Due south is the Glanni waterfall on the river Nordurá. It is a 15 minute walk and you can spot salmon trying to shoot the rapids. Laxfoss on the Nordurá is an hour's walk away and you can return along the banks of the River Hrauná, which flows through the lava fields. Other walks include Vikravatn by Mount Vikrafell (2 hours), the old volcano Grábrók, around the lake Hredavatn, the mountain Hraunsnefsöxl, and the more strenuous climb up Baula (900m, 2,952ft).

There are a lot of ranches in the area and horses on the road can be a hazard, so be on the alert for them. It is quite a common sight to see a string of horses being driven by a team of riders along the road, and it is safest to pull in and let them pass. If they are in ahead of you, they will usually pull off the road at a suitable point and let you pass — but do so slowly.

Route 57 follows the southern shore of Hvammsfjördur, and the grass soon gives way to rocks and mosses. The rivers have carved mini-canyons in the rocks as they have forced their way to the sea. You have to take Route 58 to divert off to Stykkishólmur, but it is worth the visit. There is a new church being built and a very good baker's shop. Then, you have the choice again of continuing westwards or cutting across the peninsula and heading south.

The road west, on Route 57 takes you to Grundarfjördur, Ólafsvík, Rif and Hellissandur before it turns south following the headland round. The road changes its number several times as you drive east along the southern shores of the peninsula — first the 574, then the 572, and finally the 54 which will take you back to Borgarnes.

The road round the peninsula is passable in either a two- or four-wheel drive vehicle but great care should be exercised when taking roads through the mountains. There are two such routes — 54 and 56 — and these can be very muddy, wet and slippery if there has been rain. Snow lies in pockets in the mountains right through the year.

Because of the damage caused to the roads by the winter weather it is not uncommon to suddenly come across a works gang with bulldozers and cranes filling in holes in the road and reinforcing the sides of the road. Often, the only thing you can do is switch off the car engine and enjoy the view until it is safe to go on and you are waved through. The new bridge at Borgarnes has cut many miles off the trip to Reykjavík, and the road improves considerably, most of it being metalled.

There are hundreds of horses kept on ranches here, and the farms follow the coast all the way down to Reykjavík, hugging the shores and dominated by Esja (914m, 2,997ft) whose slopes roll down to the narrow coastal plain.

As you round the headland at Saurbaer, with its Lutheran church, you catch your first glimpse of Reykjavík in the distance across the waters. The church is dedicated to Hallgrímur Pétersson, one of Iceland's finest poets, who was pastor to the parish 300 years ago and who died of leprosy, once rife on the island. He wrote many hymns and his greatest work *Passíusálmar*, a glorification of the Passion of Christ, has been translated into more languages than any other Icelandic work.

It is a fascinating journey. You have horses, cattle and sheep for company beside the road, and thousands of ducks, especially the splendid eider, hugging the coastline. Things worth stopping for along the way are the whaling stations at Hvítanes (and the oil tanks, a permanent eye-sore and reminder of World War II) and Borgarnes, and Glymur, at 200m (656ft) high, the country's highest waterfall.

# Additional Information

## Places to Visit

**Arnarfjördur**
*Hrafnseyri Memorial Museum and Chapel*
Open: 16 June to 15 September daily.
☎ (94) 8260

**Borgarnes**
*Borgarfjördur Museum*
Open: Monday to Friday 2-6pm.
☎ (93) 71279

**Hellissandur/Rif**
*Maritime Museum*
Open: June to August daily 1-6pm.
☎ (93) 66652

*Natural History Museum*
Open: June to August 1-6pm.
☎ (93) 66644

*Egill Olafsson Folk Museum*
En route to Látrabjarg cliffs
Open: 1 June to 15 September daily
10am-7pm.
☎ (94) 1590

**Hjardalur**
*Maritime Museum*
Open: on request.
☎ (94) 7773

**Hnjótur**
In Örlygströfn
*Regional Museum*
Open: 1 June to 15 September, daily
10am-7pm.
☎ (94) 1590

**Hvanneyri**
*Agricultural Museum*
Open: on request.
☎ (93) 70000

**Isafjördur**
*Marine Museum*
Nedstakaupstad
Open: 1 June to 15 September 1-5pm.
☎ (94) 4418

*West Fjords Regional Museum*
Austurvegur
Open: Tuesday to Saturday during
summer 1-3pm.
☎ (94) 3293

**Laugar**
*Dalamanna Folk Museum*
Open: daily 10 June to 31 August.
☎ (993) 41328

**Ólafsvík**
*Maritime Museum*
Open: daily during summer.
☎ (93) 61153

**Stykkishólmur**
Open: daily during the summer.
☎ (93) 81640

## Useful Information

### Emergency Numbers
*Police*
Borgarnes ☎ (93) 71166
Ólafsvík ☎ (93) 61219
Stykkishólmur ☎ (93) 81008
Búdardalur ☎ (93) 41405
Patreksfjördur ☎ (94) 1277
Bolungarvík ☎ (94) 7310
Ísafjördur ☎ (94) 4222

### Hospitals
**Borgarnes**
Borgarbraut 65
☎ (93) 71400

**Ólafsvík**
Engihlíd
☎ (93) 61225

**Stykkishólmur**
☎ (93) 81128

**Bolungarvík**
Midstraeti
☎ (94) 7147

**Ísafjördur**
☎ (94) 4500

## Motoring

*Information on road conditions*
Borgarnes ☎ (93) 71320
Ólafsvík ☎ (93) 61460
Búdardalur ☎ (93) 41134
Patreksfjördur ☎ (94) 1533
Ísafjördur ☎ (94) 3911

## Accommodation

*Hotels and Guesthouses*
**Bardaströnd**
Birkimelur
☎ (94) 2069

**Bifröst**
Hotel Bifröst
☎ (93) 50000

**Bjarnarfjördur**
Hotel Laugarholl
☎ (95) 13380

**Borgarfjördur**
Hvanneyri
(sleeping bag accommodation)
☎ (93) 70000

Húsafell Tourist Centre (chalets)
☎ (93) 51260

Varmaland
(sleeping bag accommodation)
☎ (93) 51301

**Flókalundur**
Hotel Flókalundur
☎ (94) 2011

**Flatey**
Veitingastofan Vogur
(sleeping bag accommodation)
☎ (93) 81413

**Helgafellssveit**
Bjarnarhöfn
(sleeping bag accommodation)
☎ (93) 81581

Near **Hólmavík**
Fjallhüs
☎ (95) 13136

**Hvalfjördur**
Hladir

(sleeping bag accommodation)
☎ (93) 38979

Close to **Stykkishólmur**
Sljöldur Community Centre
☎ (93) 81528

**Ísafjördur**
Guesthouse Austurvegur
☎ (94) 3868

**Ísafjördur**
Hotel Ísafjördur
☎ (94) 41111

**Kolbeinsstadahreppur**
Lindartunga Community Centre
(seeping bag accommodation)
☎ (93) 56633

**Látrabjarg Cliff**
Briedavík Youth Hostel
☎ (94) 1575

**Laugar**
Hotel Edda
☎ (93) 41265

**Patreksfjördur**
Guesthouse Erlu
☎ (94) 1227

**Reykhólasveit**
Hotel Bjarkalundur
☎ (93) 47762

**Reykholt**
Hotel Edda
☎ (93) 51260

**Reykhólasveit**
Baer
☎ (93) 47757

**Reykjanes**
Hotel Edda
☎ (94) 4842

**Stadarsveit**
Lysuhóll Community Centre
(sleeping bag accommodation)
☎ (93) 56730

**Snaefellsnes**
Hotel Búdir
☎ (93) 56700

**Strandir**
Hotel Djúpavik
☎ (95) 14037

Broddanes
(sleeping bag accommodation)
☎ (95) 13347

**Stykkishólmur**
Hotel Stykkishólmur
☎ (93) 81330

Egilshus
☎ (93) 814590

**Trkyllisvík**
On Strandir
☎ (95) 14031

*Camping*
**Snaefellsnes**
Búdir
Arnarstapi

**Húsafell**
Open: 1 June to 10 October.

**Stykkishólmur**
Adalgötu

**Flatey**
☎ (93) 81451

**Recreation**
*Swimming*
**Hellissandur**
(indoor pool)
Open: Monday, Wednesday, Friday 7-9am, 2-6pm and 8-9.40pm. Tuesday and Thursday 7-11am, 2-5pm.

**Ólafsvík**
(indoor pool/hot pot)
Open: weekdays 8-11am and 4-8pm.
Saturday 1-4pm.
☎ (93) 61199

*Horse Riding*
**Borgarfjördur**
Jafnaskard
(5km, 3 miles from Bifröst)
☎ (93) 50028

*Golf*
**Borgarnes**
Halmarsvöllur
☎ (93) 12711

**Ólafsvík**
Fródárvöllur

**Stykkishólmur**
Víkurvöllur
☎ (93) 81330

*Skiing*
**Ólafsvík**
Fródárheidi

**Styykishólmur**
Kerlingarskard
Grundarfjördur

**Tourist Information Centres**

**Borgarnes**
Hyrnan Service Centre (by the bridge)
☎ (93) 71200

**Ísafjördur**
Town Hall
Nordic Information Centre
☎ (94) 3722

**Stykkishólmur**
Egilshús, Adalgata
☎ (93) 81450

# 7

# GREENLAND

G reenland is the world's largest island, and just a hop across the water from Iceland, so if you have time, or can make it, a visit is well worthwhile. The island covers 2,175,600sq km, of which almost 80 per cent is covered by ice. If ever there was a case for two islands swapping their name, this was it.

## The Country

### History

Although the Norsemen started to colonise the island from the end of the eleventh century, it had been discovered and settled thousands of years earlier by the Inuit, the Eskimoes of North America. The Inuit are almost certainly descended from Siberian tribes which crossed into America when there was still a land bridge across what is now the Bering Straits, and they are first thought to have visited Greenland about 5,000 years ago. A small Stone Age settlement was established with the people surviving by hunting. Excavations show that about 2,500 years ago there was a sudden change in the climate. As it got colder the settlements were abandoned and these early Greenlanders, classified by archaeologists as Independence I, retreated to the west. They were replaced by a new breed of settlers, known as Independence II, who were more skilled in every respect. They carved weapons and ornaments from ivory and bone. They used sleds, built boats and had discovered how to burn whale and seal oil and blubber for light, heat and cooking.

The Inuits continued to expand in Greenland, and after the 'discovery' by the Norwegians, there was colonisation by the Norsemen. In the twelfth and thirteenth centuries, it is thought that as many as 5,000 people had settled in Greenland. In 1261 Greenland was annexed by Norway and a trade monopoly imposed. Norway agreed to send ships with supplies to Greenland in return for furs and oil, but as the weather turned colder, the seas became more treacherous because of ice, and the ships did not

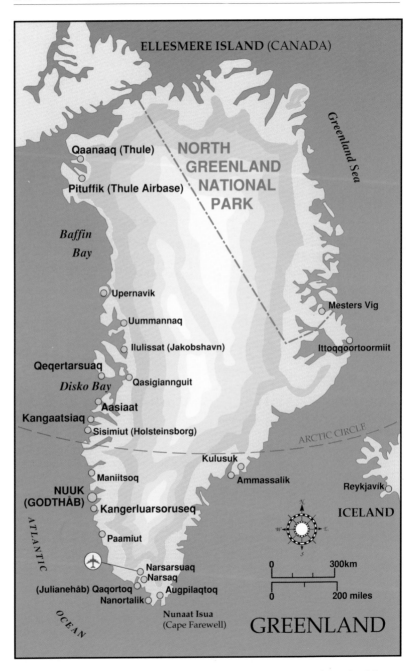

arrive with the much needed supplies. What happened to the Norse Greenlanders is not known, but whatever the reason, the settlements perished and the people vanished. They may simply have died off because of hunger and disease but there are stories handed down by folklore of battles between the Inuit and Norsemen and of raiding parties carrying the islanders off as slaves.

By the end of the sixteenth century, however, ships had started to sail to Greenland again, and re-established contact with the Inuit villages. As the search for the North West passage hotted up, more and more explorers visited Greenland on their way west. In 1605 the Danish King Christian IV sent an expedition to Greenland which claimed it for the Danish Crown, although no attempt was made to settle the island.

Henry Hudson explored the coastline of Greenland in 1607, two years before going on to discover the bay that bears his name, even though he thought he had found the North West Passage and had sailed into the Pacific Ocean. It was not until 1721 that another attempt at settlement was made when Hans Egede was granted permission to establish a trading post and Lutheran mission. He established the mission near Nuuk (Good

*Narsaq*

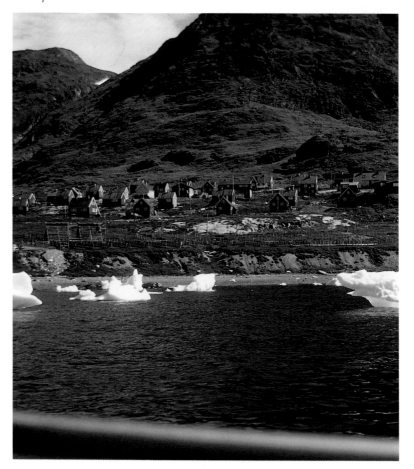

Hope), now Nuuk, on the western coast of Greenland. In 1733 another mission was set up, also at Nuuk and both were successful, so much so, that in 1176 the Danish Government imposed a trading monopoly which lasted until 1950. Under the monopoly, Greenland was not allowed to trade with anyone other than the Danish.

Denmark's sovereignty over Greenland was challenged in the 1920s by Norway, and the matter was taken to the International Court in the Hague, which decided in 1932 in favour of Denmark. During World War II, Denmark was invaded by Germany in 1940, and a year later, on entering the conflict, the United States moved in to Greenland and established two bases, at Søndre Strømfjord and Narsarsuaq.

The first was a 'weather station', and the second was used as a hospital base in both World War II and the Korean War. The authorities took the decision that it would not have done morale in the US any good to ship the most horribly injured casualties home, so they were sent to Greenland instead. It is said that no injured US service men sent to the base ever returned home.

In 1953 Greenland became a Danish county. On 1 May 1971 the county council was replaced by a parliament able to elect its own government. Despite all the dramatic political and cultural changes over the centuries, life on Greenland has not changed fundamentally although modern technology has certainly made it bearable.

The traditional occupation of sealing has now been replaced by agriculture and other methods of fishing. Sheep and reindeer are the main livestock. There are minerals on the island but a cryolite mine, important during World War II, is now worked out, and a coal mine which opened in 1924 was closed in 1972 because it was no longer profitable. There is also lead and zinc at the Marmorilik mine, but this too is no longer profitable to extract. A massive 2 billion tons of iron ore has been located north of Nuuk, and there are deposits of molybdenum, copper and scheelite on the east coast. None of these has yet been exploited, but uranium deposits near Narsaq may be tapped.

Greenland has most of what Iceland has to offer but it is bigger! It has the world's largest glacier, massive icebergs, a wealth of wildlife including reindeer, musk ox, polar bear, fox and polar hare and many rare birds, such as the snowy owl and sea eagle.

Flights from Reykjavík normally land at either Narsarsuaq, in the far south, or on the island of Kulusuk, in the entrance of Angmagssalik Fjord. There are a number of operators who offer flights to Greenland. Once you have arrived, it is possible to fly on with Greenlandair, who operate the world's largest fleet of helicopters. Reservations are essential on almost all of these internal flights.

Valid passports are required and special permits are needed if you want to travel near any of the military zones, around Søndre Strømfjord, with its US airforce base, or Thule. Permits can be obtained from Danish embassies.

There are hotels in all the main settlements, although standards vary and can be spartan. In smaller communities, there are often dormitories, rooms with four or more beds to a room. Standard cuisine varies from high in the better hotels to interesting. Local lamb, salmon and shrimps are all recommended, and you may like to try whale or seal meat.

Tipping is not obligatory but it is customary to add 10 per cent to taxi and restaurant bills. All alcohol is subject to a rationing system, and visitors can get their quota on presentation of their passport.

Souvenirs include sealskin goods, walrus ivory carvings and semi-precious stones and you can buy furs, but keep the receipt for Customs.

## Geography and Geology

Greenland is the largest island in the world, located in the northern Atlantic where the Atlantic meets the Arctic Ocean, and closer to the North Pole than any other country.

The island is surrounded by mainly cold ocean streams which have a constant cooling effect on the coastal areas. This, coupled with the very cold air coming off the inland icecaps gives Greenland its arctic climate. The ice-free area covers 350,000sq km, an area the size of the British Isles and eight times the area of Denmark.

The icecap covers an area of 1,833,900sq km — 85 per cent of the total land mass of Greenland. It stretches 2,500km (1,550 miles) north to south, and up to 1,000km (620 miles) east to west. In the centre of Greenland the icecap is up to 3km (2 miles) thick. The terrain of Greenland was formed by Ice Age glaciers, although there is considerable evidence of more recent geological pressures such as earthquakes and volcanic activity, as well as upheavals caused by mountain formation. The ocean depth in the south is not great while in the north, the water is covered by ice, and to date, no surface vessel has managed to sail round the north of Greenland.

Rocks form the subsoil over most of Greenland and these have been built up over many geological periods. Most common are the rocks from the Pre-Cambrian period, mostly granite and gneiss. Around Nuuk some of the world's oldest rocks can be found, dating back around 3,700 million years. Chains of mountains were formed in East and North Greenland during the Palaeozic period (300-400 million years ago), while the layers of sedimentary rock found in East and West Greenland and offshore on the continental shelf are very much younger. About 50 million years ago, when Greenland separated from Canada and Europe there was also considerable volcanic activity in both West and East Greenland. The Greenland icecap, however, is a relatively new formation, in geological terms, having been formed only a few million years ago.

## Midnight Sun and Northern Lights

The Midnight Sun is seen at its best north of the Arctic Circle — from the Disko Bay area northwards. Further south it can only be seen from the hills as the sun hovers just above the horizon. During the winter it is only dark

round the clock in the far north. Around Disko Bay there is twilight during the day, and as most of the population lives south of the Arctic Circle, they enjoy a few hours light during the day. The return of the sun after the polar night is a cause of great celebration in many communities in Greenland.

The aurora borealis can be experienced throughout the autumn and winter months. In most years, even in the south of Greenland you can see the northern lights from the end of August. This phenomenon is caused as fields of electrically charged particles from the sun enter the Earth's atmosphere at an altitude of about 100km (62 miles). According to Inuit mythology, the northern lights occur as the souls of the dead play ball with a walrus skull, thus their name for the northern lights is *arsarnerit* which means 'ballgame'. There is also a legend that if you whistle at the northern lights you will attract them, and they will come closer. If you do not stop whistling in time, they will reach down and carry you away. Equally, legend has it, that if you bark like a dog, you frighten the lights and they will move away from you.

### Climate

Because of Greenland's size, there can be huge variations in the weather. As a general rule, the best weather is enjoyed around Disko Bay and at the most inland points of the longest fjords.

*(Opposite) Camping in Greenland should only be attempted by the experienced*

*Try your hand at dog sledding on an organised trip*

Greenland has an arctic climate which means that even in the warmest months, the temperature rarely exceeds 10°C (50°F). This explains why Greenland has no trees. There can be massive climatic fluctuations between north and south, although as a general rule, it becomes colder, dryer and less stormy the further north one travels.

Most of the rain falls around the coastline and inland, the summers are usually dry although this, too, can vary enormously from year to year. As the air in Greenland is normally very dry, temperatures often feel warmer than they actually are, and if the sun is shining, one can tan very quickly so take care.

The Arctic Circle crosses through Greenland near the town of Sisimiut. In Nuuk snow lays on the ground for about seven months of the year, and building work is usually planned so that the main structure is built during the summer, and the interior can be finished during the winter. In Nuuk, temperatures can range from -9°C (16°F) in January to 6.8°C (44°F) in July. The annual average temperature is -2.5°C (27°F). In Pituffik February temperatures can be -27°C (-16°F) or lower rising to 6.2°C (43°F) in July. The warmest places are likely to be Kangerlussuaq and Narsarsuaq with July temperatures of 12°C (53°F) and 11.5°C (52°F) respectively.

**Flora and Fauna**

There are eight land-based animals on Greenland, the most common of which are polar bear, Arctic fox, Arctic hare, musk ox, lemming and Peary Caribou. Sheep and reindeer are reared and bred in the south. There are about sixty species of breeding bird and a further ninety or so visiting species. The seas are rich with fish and marine mammals, especially whales. Whale species include beluga (white), the tusked narwhal, fin, pilot, blue and the orca (killer). Walrus, sealions and many species of seal are found, including the harp seal, whose Latin name *Pagophilus groenlandicus*, means 'ice lover from Greenland'. The harp is the most hunted by the Inuit. Fish are abundant both in the sea and in the lakes and rivers with trout, salmon and Arctic char all common.

Insects, especially the biting kind, can be a plague during the summer months, and you must be well prepared to combat them. The only other insects seen are the occasional butterfly.

The Arctic weather and winds do not allow trees to grow although there are stands of dwarf birch, alder and willow in some well-sheltered areas, particularly around Qaqortoq and Narsarsuaq. Despite the climate, Greenland can, at certain times of year, be bedecked with flowers. The national flower is the willow herb which flowers in late summer carpeting the ground, and other bloomers include chamomile, buttercup, gentian, dandelion and saxifrage. On the tundra, there is both boggy and dry vegetation depending on the conditions, miniature plants, lichens and grasses as well as a number of ground hugging, fruit yielding, plants such as cranberry, crowberry and huckleberry.

## Tourism

Organised trips and excursions are available in almost every town and you can sign up at both Narsarsuaq and Kangerlussuaq airports. Trips range from short guided walks round town to helicopter rides over the surrounding countryside, and from mountain hikes to dog sledding. Local tourist offices and hotels will provide details of all excursions and take your bookings.

Hiking, backpacking and mountain walking in Greenland is not for the inexperienced. There are no marked paths away from the settlements, and outdoor enthusiasts must be skilled map readers and proficient at using a compass. There are a number of mountain huts which have been built in the last few years, most of them on the sheep farms in the south. These huts are usually open from mid-June to early September but can be very popular, so walkers are recommended to carry tents just in case. Most of the mountain huts are to be found on the Narsaq and Qaqortoq peninsulas, and around Vatnahverfi. There are also huts on the route between Sisimiut and Kangerlussuaq which are used by people booked on dog sled trips, but space may be available for backpackers.

In the south of Greenland in particular, there are many hikes and longer walks organised with guides, and these are strongly recommended in view of the conditions and terrain which can be experienced. Weather can turn very severe very quickly, and only the experienced should set out without a guide. The usual common sense rules apply — always walk with a friend or group, always tell someone where you are going and your expected time of arrival, and always tell someone once you have arrived. If you are competent and have the right equipment, however, it is possible to hike from Narsarsuaq over the mountains to the Kiattuut Sermiat Glacier. Ice from this glacier is exported as cubes around the world.

Even dog sledding is tailored to the tourists' demands. There are short trips to let you get the feel of it, longer trips but overnight accommodation in hotels for those who enjoy their comfort, and real expeditioning for those who want to experience the real thing. Expeditions are usually accommodated in hunting huts or tents. The dog sled season usually runs from February to May. Two points to remember: dog sled teams always have the right of way and as they can move very quietly, you must always be looking out for them, and the dogs used for sledding are not family pets. They are kept tied up because they are not tame, so beware.

While Greenlanders can hunt and fish by right, visitors must apply for a licence, obtainable from the police, at most large hotels and tourist offices. If you are caught hunting or fishing without a licence you can face heavy fines, and confiscation of your gear. Also take care, because protected species vary from area to area, so seek advice before setting off on a hunting or fishing trip. You are not allowed to hunt polar bear or musk ox, or shoot or trap eagles, falcons and snowy owls. For people who want a more gentle pursuit, the museums of Greenland are a major attraction.

Every Greenland town boasts its own museum, and these are usually housed in protected buildings of historic interest. The museums give a fascinating insight into both the country and the different localities. For instance the museums in South Greenland have many exhibits relating to the Norse colonisation of the area; in Ilulissat the museum is housed in the home where the famous polar explorer Knud Rasmussen was born, and now features exhibits about his life and travels. In Aasiaat, the museum concentrates on the development and importance of fishing, while in Ammassalik the very special cultural traditions of East Greenland are portrayed.

The National Museum of Greenland is in Nuuk, and exhibits include the famous fifteenth-century mummies from Qilakitsoq, near Uummammaq, and discovered by two brothers out hunting in 1972. There are also very interesting permanent exhibitions on the geology, culture and arts and crafts of Greenland. It is also encouraging that many of the country's most prized treasures which had over the years been taken to Denmark as private collections, have now been returned and are on permanent display either in Nuuk or in other museums around the country.

*(Opposite) Colourful national costumes of Greenland*

*Boats in Greenland have to be sturdy in order to navigate through ice*

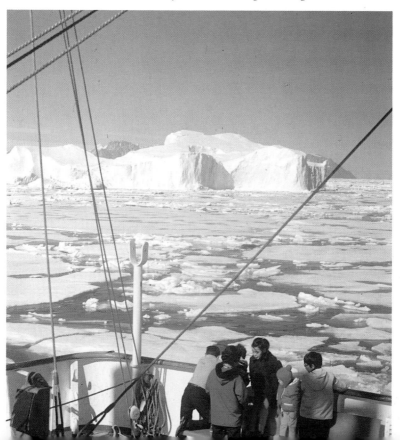

Local museums can also give you details about all historical monuments in the area. These are protected and sites must not be damaged in any way, or objects removed from them. If you do discover something which you think might be old, you should report it to the nearest museum. Do not remove the object and try not to disturb the site further.

## People

Greenland is inhabited today by a mixture of Europeans and Eskimos, or 'Inuit', as the aboriginal peoples of the Arctic prefer to be called. The island population is now around 56,000 — about 45,000 were born in Greenland and almost all the others are Danes working there. Virtually the entire population lives either in the ice-free coastal region or on the islands off the coast, with 90 per cent living in West Greenland.

The largest settlement is the capital city of Nuuk with a population of around 13,000. There are about 70 populated areas in Greenland and most settlements have a population of between 1,000 and 5,000. Settlements do not normally have doctors or police but there is always a school. In the most remote parts of the country there are meteorological and scientific stations.

It is remarkable that Greenland's housing stock has all been built since 1950, and most homes have been built in the last twenty-five years. The state builds all the homes, and owns all the building sites. The Greenland Government has a policy of doing everything possible to maintain the seventy settlements to try to ensure that the area of uninhabited land does not increase any further. Considerable resources have been allocated for this, but it is unlikely that all the current settlements can survive. Lack of pollution both on land and in the coastal waters means the water is safe to drink anywhere on Greenland.

## Language

Greenlandic is the official language. It is the Eskimo language and very complex with composite words built up around a stem. A single Eskimo word can have the same meaning as a sentence, or even several sentences in other languages. It has existed as a written language for more than 100 years, but it is not related to the Inuit languages in Canada, the USA and Russia. All Greenlanders are also obliged to learn Danish, and many, especially the younger people speak English.

## Government

On 1 May 1979 Greenland was granted home rule although it is still part of the kingdom of Denmark. The Provincial Council was dissolved and replaced by a Parliament (Landstinget) and Government (Landsstyret) of six executive 'ministers' and a Prime Minister. The executive have responsibility for most of the island's affairs and legislation — economy, trade and industry, social affairs, housing and science, health and environment, culture, education, labour and religious affairs. The Danish Government, however, retains control over foreign policy, defence, the justice system and financial matters. Greenland's natural resources are under the joint control of both governments.

The Greenland Home Rule Parliament has twenty-seven members, and meets two to four times a year in Nuuk. There are five political parties and general elections are held every four years. Greenland also elects two members to serve in the Danish Folketing (Parliament). There are eighteen municipalities in Greenland, each of which has a local authority. All settlements are represented on the local councils, which meet four times a year.

## Economy

Hunting is still the main occupation and income earner for about 2,500 islanders. Seal, walrus and whales are the main quarries. Seals are the most important catch and most of the sealskins are processed at the Great Greenland tannery, which also processes sealskin furs for both the home and export market. Hunting is particularly important in East and North Greenland, as are the traditional arts and crafts.

The main reason for hunting is meat so the skins are a by-product, albeit a useful and profitable one. Only fully grown animals are hunted.

The main industry in Greenland, like Iceland, is fishing and fish and fish products account for 85 per cent of the island's total exports. The most important markets are Europe and Japan. In South Greenland, crop and sheep farming provides a living for about 100 families.

There is little industry although Nuuk has a mineral water bottling plant which meets the requirements of the whole country, as well as a beer bottling plant. There is comparatively little mining in Greenland although some mines have been worked since the mid-nineteenth century. Minerals mined include zinc, lead, coal, graphite and cryolite, which has been the most profitable. Exploration for precious and rare minerals such as gold, niobium, chromium and molybdenum has gathered momentum in recent years, and although discoveries have been made, they have not been in commercial quantities. There has been considerable on and off-shore exploration for oil and hydrocarbons.

Greenland Trade (KNI) is the largest trading company in Greenland. It is owned by the Home Rule Authority and supplies goods and produce throughout the island through its own shops. It charges the same prices everywhere. Tourism is becoming increasingly popular and Greenland has much to offer visitors whether it be spectacular natural beauty, fascinating culture and traditions, and a huge range of outdoor activities in some of the most exciting scenery on earth. Great effort has gone into boosting Greenland as a tourist destination in the past few years, and this is reflected in the range of accommodation and activities now offered.

*Disko Bay*

# The Regions

### North and West Greenland

The north is the land of the Midnight Sun and the polar night. An area of ice and glaciers and iceberg strewn fjords. If you are visiting North Greenland, a dog sled trip is a must, and worth considering, depending on your budget, are the incredible helicopter trips over the glaciers, or one of the boat trips along the ice fjords. Aasiaat, at the junction where the northern and southern passenger ship routes meet, is on an island, which, like its neighbours in the archipelago, is best explored by kayak provided you stick to the sheltered waters. Disko Bay and the archaeological excavations near Qasigiannguit are also worth visiting if you have time. Some of the finds made there have caused a radical rethink about how Greenland came to be settled. The museum houses many of the finds, and there are organised tours of the area.

 Disko Island, with its towering basalt mountains, has three natural science research stations, and at altitude it is possible to dog sled and ski all year round. Huge icebergs, many more than 100m (328ft) high, are often trapped for long periods in the shallow waters off Ilulissat before drifting out into the bay. Close to the town is Sermermiut, likely to be your first port of call if you have flown into North Greenland. Sermermiut is the birthplace of Knud Rasmussen. It is an easy walk from the town.

From Uummannaq, north of Nuussuaq peninsula, you can arrange sled rides to the seven settlements in the area during the spring, or take a boat during the summer. A boat trip has the added excitement of whale spotting, and several species can usually be seen in the fjord. It was at Qilakitsoq, near Uummannaq that the fifteenth-century mummies were found.

Upernavik and the many settlements in this area north of Melville Bay rely heavily on hunting, especially for seal and whales, and despite its northern location, visitors are constantly surprised by the area's rich and varied vegetation. Qaanaaq is the most northerly town in Greenland and depends solely on hunting.

In west Greenland the towns of Nuuk, Maniitsoq and Sisimiut all enjoy ice free coastal waters year round because of the 'warming' ocean currents. The main effect is that the fishing fleets can operate all year which explains why fishing, for shrimp, cod, wolffish and halibut, and fish processing is the mainstay of all three settlements.

Nuuk is the bustling capital city, and the administrative and educational centre for the country. It has a bus service around town, but only a few minutes drive or boat ride out of Nuuk and you are in spectacular, desolate countryside. Maniitsoq, 'the uneven place', is dominated by mountains, and one of its great attractions is to leave the island by boat and within a short time, be skiing on the Apussiot glacier — even in the summer. The glacier covers 350sq km and offers both downhill and cross country skiing and every degree of difficulty. If you are flying in to the  region you will land at Kangerlussuaq airport, built as a US base more than 50 years ago. You can hire cars, and even bicycles, to explore the region which has a reasonably well-constructed road system.

Another way in, of course, is by foot or dog sled from Sisimiut, several days exciting travel away. This does mean that you can plan trips starting or finishing at Kangerlussuaq with its international airport.

**Nuuk** (Danish name Godthåb), is the island's largest town and the administration centre. People have lived on the site for as long as the island has been inhabited, and there are still the remains of early Norse and Eskimo settlements. The present town was founded in 1728 by the missionary Hans Egede, and his house survives today. The old town has changed little since those days, and the area around the harbour is charming and interesting. The newer buildings lack any real charm. There are hotels, restaurants, banks, shops, hospital, teachers training college, national library and national museum which occupies a number of build-  ings in Koloniehavn. Its most famous exhibits are the fifteenth-century mummies found near Uummannaq, and discovered in 1972. There are also outfitters where you can hire clothing, camping gear and fishing equipment and guides for trips.

**Sisimiut** (Danish name Holsteinsborg) is the island's second largest town. It is built on hilly terrain near the Polar Circle in a region which is free of ice nearly all the year. In 1756 a colony was founded just north of the town at Sydbay, and within eight years had spread to take in the present site. It was a centre for the whale industry, and today is still heavily involved with fishing, and has one of Greenland's most modern fleets. It has a fine old town area and a very interesting museum, housed  in even more interesting buildings, dating back to the 1750s.

The first church, built in 1773 is still standing and well preserved, as are  a number of the town's original buildings, including the Old House dating from 1756, and the Governor's House built in 1846. The town has the island's only high school, and a large shipbuilding yard. There is a hotel and hostel, a number of restaurants, and during the summer there is also accommodation in the high school.

Tours from here can be arranged to the ghost towns of Avssakk'utak and Ikerasak. The first is about an hour's sailing away and contains many well preserved houses dating back to 1730, while Ikerasak is on the site of an ancient burial ground. The Sisimiut to Kangerdlusuaq trail is one of the most popular long distance walks in Greenland. It covers 150km (93 miles) but you should allow anything between 10 to 14 days for it. Local guides are available if you want expert company.

**Ulkebugten** is also only an hour away, a waterfall on the Ulkebugten, where in June you can find the yellow snow anemone, one of only two places it grows on the island, the other being Evighedisfjord.

**Ilulissat** (Danish name Jakobshavn), means the Ice Mountains, and the

*Sisimiut is Greenland's second largest town*

town is situated north of the famous Ice Fjord, from which some of the world's greatest icebergs are launched. It is a centre for the shrimp industry in the summer and halibut in the winter. Founded in 1741 by a trader Jakob Severen, it is being groomed as a tourist destination. There are several helicopter flights each week. There are two hotels, both with restaurants and discos, and many well-preserved old buildings. Ilulissat was one of the first places settled by the Inuit, perhaps 4,000 years ago. The village of Sermermiut, now abandoned, is at least 3,500 years old. The Knud Rasmussen Museum, formerly the vicarage, is dedicated to both the life and exploits of the great Greenland explorer after whom it is named, and the history of the district. The museum is open between 2-4pm Monday to Friday during the summer. If you are visiting the town the Kangerdliag (Ice Fjord) is a must. There is a lot of good walking in this area, the most popular is around the abandoned settlement of Sermermiut.

**Maniitsoq** has two fine churches, one old and one new and both worth visiting. The museum on the outskirts of the town shows that the first settlers lived in the area more than 3,000 years ago.

**Disko Bay** and **Aasiaat** is an area worth visiting for its walking and the activities off shore. The bay is famous for spawning gigantic icebergs during the summer months. There are many old buildings in Aasiaat, and across the river there is a traditional hunter's village. There is a small museum tracing the history of the region.

**Uummannaq** in north-west Greenland, is on an island and has a fine sod church, lots of old buildings, a museum, which was formerly a hospital, and plenty of things to see and do. It is a good place to try out your sea-kayak skills, or whether you can handle a dog sled and team.

*Turfed roofs on buildings in Greenland are a good form of insulation*

## South Greenland

This region stretches from the **Nunaat Isua** area (Cape Farewell) to Paamiut, and enjoys a very varied landscape. There are high mountains around Nanortalik, which offer exciting climbing, long fjord valleys and green highlands for backpacking, and the fjords themselves for boating, kayaking and fishing. During the spring and summer you can enjoy the marvellous spectacle of 'field ice' drifting round the coast. These colossal ice floes are formed when sea water freezes high in the Arctic Ocean. The floes drift southwards down the east coast of Greenland, round Cape Farewell and then away to the west. The ice can be so thick that even the ships cannot get through, but the floes often carry seals and polar bears which are then hunted.

The south is also the only region which supports agriculture, although this is largely confined to sheep farming and growing animal fodder. The sheep farms are strung out at intervals along the shores of the fjord, and most are connected by a network of tracks and paths. It is a very popular area for backpacking, and overnight facilities are generally provided by the sheep farmers in huts and hostels. If you want to camp, ask the farmer where you can pitch your tent.

This region is also rich with historical monuments and was the first to be colonised by the Norsemen more than 1,000 years ago. It was where Erík the Red established a settlement having been exiled from Iceland. Places worth visiting are the bishop's residence at *Gadar* (now called Igaliku), Brattahlid (Qassiarsuk) where Erík the Red is first thought to have settled, and the ruins of the church at Hvalsey. According to records, a wedding took place at the church in 1408, and that is the last written evidence of the Norsemen's presence in Greenland.

ㄇ **Narsarsuaq**, is in the southern part of Greenland on the Tunungdliarfik Fjiord, named after Erík the Red. There are also the remains of an Eskimo settlement which is thought to date back to the seventeenth century. The town is 69km (43 miles) from the main coastline. During the last war a US airbase, Blue West One was established there and it is now a weather and radio station. The town has two hotels, restaurants and, just outside, a geophysical observatory and satellite station.

There is a monument opposite the airport terminal to Naomi Vemura, the Japanese arctic explorer who travelled solo to the North Pole crossing Greenland's inland ice. There is also a picturesque walk up the hill to the radio tower. There are great views from the summit of the 240m (787ft) hill.

**Qagssiarssuk**, a sheepbreeding village about half an hour's sailing away, and the site of Erík the Red's farm. Ruins of the farm can still be seen as well as traces of the first Christian church in Greenland built by his wife, Tjodhild, in about 1000. It was discovered during excavations which started in 1961.

ㄇ After a 90-minute boat trip, passengers have to walk several kilometres to **Igaliko** village where there are the ruins of St Nicolai, the Norsemen's first cathedral and a bishop's tomb. If you are lucky they will lay on a tractor to take you back to the ship. **Qoroq Fjord** is at the end of an active glacier which throughout the summer feeds icebergs into the water. Inland Ice is a trip for good walkers who have to hike about 12km (7 miles). The guided round trip takes between six and eight hours.

**Narsaq**, in the south-west corner of Greenland, is a small town surrounded by deep fjords. Fishing is the main industry, especially cod and shrimps, which are frozen or tinned and sent all over the world. The rest of the economy comes from farming and the local abattoir, furs and semiprecious stones. There was a settlement here as far back as AD986. Today there are hotels, restaurants and shops, specialising in Eskimo crafts, precious stones and silver. The Narsaq Harbour Museum is based in one of the old trading stations built around 1883. If it is not open, ask at the tourist office for someone to show you around. There is also a small museum in memory of Henrik Lund, the poet and priest who wrote *Nunarput*, which became Greenland's national anthem.

Things to do in the area include the ascent of Qaqaarsuaq (685m, 2,247ft) which stands behind the town. There are great views from the top. About 3km (2 miles) north of the town there are the ruins of a Norse church, and you can pop in on your way to Kvanefjeld, about 8km (5 miles) north of Narsaq. It is about an hour's walk to the small Eskimo village of **Cape Dan**, one of the most isolated settlements on earth. It was discovered by Europeans in 1844 and the community was still 'living in the Stone Age'. The houses are still small and made of wood, and the cemetery, which you pass on the way into the village, consists of piles of stones. The ground is too hard to dig, so the coffins are laid on the ground and then covered with rocks. There are still less than 500 people in the village, mostly dependent on fishing and seal hunting, but bone carvings and bead ornaments are now being produced to sell to the tourists. After taking off and before heading back for Reykjavík, the plane normally circles over the village so you can see just how cut off it is.

**Qaqortoq** (Danish name Julianehåb) is the largest town in southern Greenland. Its main industries are fishing, sheep farming and canning. It was founded in 1775 by merchant Anders Olsen, and the town still has a number of well-preserved houses from this town, and nearby there are remains of earlier Norse settlements, including the Hvalsey church, probably the best preserved ruin from this period. In the town's market place is the Memorial Well, Greenland's only fountain. There is a hotel, hostel, restaurants and the Julianehab Museum, the largest local museum on the island, situated in an old smithy, showing how the Greenlanders used to live. It is open 2-4pm weekdays from June to September. The prefabricated church was a gift from the Danish Missionary Society.

**Nanortalik** (Bear country), is the southernmost town in Greenland, and was founded in 1797 although the original settlement was a short way away at Sigssaritoq. It moved to its present site in 1830. The old harbour is very quaint and is surrounded by many old buildings dating from the

*(Opposite) Outdoor activities can take on a whole new meaning in
Greenland*

early nineteenth century. The local museum is housed in a number of old 🏠
buildings, the oldest of which was built in 1820, the blubber house dates
from 1852, the oil boiling house from 1839 and the stables from 1840. This
is another excellent base for a hiking holiday and there are many good
walks to keep you busy, ranging from a few hours to several days. You can 🎿
visit the hot springs on the island of Unartoq or explore the beautiful
Tesermiut fjord — known as the Italy of Greenland — or Lictenau fjord,
famous for its Viking remains and Greenland's largest waterfall. Consult
the tourist office for details and up to date conditions.

## East Greenland

This is Greenland's outback. Even the Inuit call it 'Tanu', meaning 'the
back of the country'. Because of its remoteness, the people even speak a
different dialect here, and their cultures and traditions have marked
differences in many instances, than in other areas of Greenland.
Ammassalik is the main town, and hunting is the main occupation, but
because of its closeness to Iceland, in particular, the region has some of the
best organised tourist facilities in Greenland. The only other town in the
region is **Ittoqqoortoormiit**, which is close to the world's largest national
park. The town has no accommodation and has something of a 'wild west'
reputation. Covering 972,000sq km (602,640sq miles) the park is larger 🎿
than Britain and France put together, and it is a rich haven for animal and
birdlife. There is limited access to the park and prior permission is required.

The tourist office has a comprehensive list of walks in the area, the most 🚶
impressive of which is the six day hike from Qaqortoq to Igaliko.
**Ammassalik**, is just across the fjord from Kulusuk and is an Eskimo
settlement. It was discovered by a Danish naval expedition in 1884 led by
Gustav Holm, which was making its way along the east coast in rowing
boats made from skins stretched over wooden frames. There were 413
inhabitants, but when a second expedition returned eight years later the
number had fallen to 294, the lack of seals having led to chronic starvation.
Today it is East Greenland's largest town with about 1,000 inhabitants,
while a further 1,500 make their living from fishing and sea hunting, in the
seven surrounding villages of Ikateq (Murky Waters), Isortoq, Querner-
tuarssuitt (Black Mountains), Kungmuit (River Dwellers), Tiniteqilaq
(Dry Sound), Sermiligaq (Beautiful Glacier Fjord), and Kulusuk.

The settlement is 30km (18 miles) from Kulusuk airport, and there are
regular helicopter flights between the two. Tours here normally include
a guided helicopter tour of the area. You can also fly over the ice cap, and
there are a number of walking tours. From March to May there are a
limited number of dog sled and ski tours. All special equipment is provided together with a hunter guide and cooking staff. The tours are based

at Hotel Angmagssalik, the town's only hotel. There are good walks in the area, and the hotel offers hiking, boating trips and even helicopter tours if your budget can run to it.

## Additional Information

### *Tourist Information Centres*

**Aasiaat**
☎ 42088

**Ammassalik**
☎ 18176

**Ilulissat**
☎ 43079

**Maniitsoq**
☎ 13277

**Nanortalik**
☎ 33398

**Narsaq**
☎ 31325

**Nuuk**
☎ 22700

**Qaqortoq**
☎ 38444

**Sisimiut**
☎ 14848

The town halls in **Uummannaq**, **Upernavik**, **Kangaatsiaq** and **Qasigiannguit** also carry tourist information.

### *Accommodation*

**NORTH AND WEST GREENLAND**
**Aasiaat**
Seamen's Hostel
PO Box 216
☎ 42175

**Ilulissat**
Hotel Arctic
PO Box 501
☎ 44153

Hotel Hvide Falk
PO Box 20
☎ 43343

Hotel Naleraq
PO Box 320
☎ 444040

**Kangerlussuaq**
Lufthavnshotellet (airport hotel)
PO Box 1006
☎ 11180

**Maniitsoq**
Hotel Maniitsoq
PO Box 272
☎ 13035

Seamen's Hostel
PO Box 35
☎ 13535

**Nuuk**
Lufthavnshotellet (airport hotel)
PO Box 1006
☎ 11180

Hotel Hans Egede
PO Box 289
☎ 24222

Seamen's Hostel
PO Box 1021
☎ 21029

**Qaanaaq**
Hotel Qaanaaq
PO Box 88
☎ 50234

**Qasigiannguit**
Hotel Iglo
PO Box 160
☎ 45081

**Qeqertarsuaq**
Hotel Puisi
PO Box 34
☎ 47310

**Sisimiut**
Hotel Sisimiut
PO Box 70
☎ 14840

Seamen's Hostel
PO Box 1015
☎ 14150

**SOUTH GREENLAND**
**Inuili**
Hotel Perlen
PO Box 123
☎ 31313

**Nanortalik**
Hotel Kap Farvel
PO Box 159
☎ 33294

Hotel Tupilak
PO Box 4
☎ 33379

**Narsarsuaq**
Hotel Arctic
☎ 35253

**Paamiut**
Petersens Hotel
PO Box 67
☎ 17299

**Qaqortoq**
Hotel Qaqortoq
PO Box 509
☎ 38282
Seamen's Hostel
PO Box 330
☎ 38239

**EAST GREENLAND**
**Ammassalik**
Hotel Angmagssalik
PO Box 3
☎ 18293

# FACT FILE: ICELAND

## Accommodation

### Camping
There are about seventy campsites around the country, and most population centres have camping facilities, either free or for a small charge. Facilities available can vary and when provided, may not always be on site. If the site is manned, you are required to sign in and pay all fees in advance. Motor vehicles are banned from campsites between 11pm-8am and motor cycles must be wheeled, not driven, on the site.

Camping in the interior is not restricted unless you are in a protected area or nature reserve, in which case it is forbidden. Tents and camping equipment can be rented from Sportleigan (☎ 91-19800), which is in front of the BSI Bus Terminal in Reykjavík.

### Farmhouse
The Icelandic Farm Holiday Service can arrange accommodation on farms. It is either in the farmhouse, or cottages. Most farms also offer a wide range of activities including horse riding, hiking, swimming, fishing, hunting and even sheep gathering. Travellers can usually choose between bed and breakfast and sleeping bag accommodation. Cottages can be rented for longer periods. For more information contact:
Baendahöllin
Hagatorg
Reykjavík
☎ (91) 623640

### Hotels
There are hotels and guesthouses to suit all tastes and budgets. Children's discounts are widely available. The Icelandic Hotel and Restaurant Association publish an annual brochure with a list of all major hotels and guesthouses. It is available from:
Gardastraeti 42
Reykjavík
☎ (91) 27410

Iceland Tourist Offices can also supply details and help make arrangements. Many travel agencies and airlines offer special accommodation packages which amount to a substantial discount on published prices. Hotel prices are fixed according to facilities offered.

## Summer Hotels

Many of these are boarding schools which operate as good value hotels while the pupils are away on summer holidays. Many have licensed restaurants and bars and offer reasonable comfort.

## Youth Hostels

The Iceland Youth Hostel Association (BIF) is a member of the International Youth Hostel Federation (IYHF) and offers full facilities to hostellers from all Federation member countries. Youth hostels provide a cheap form of accommodation for individuals, groups and families. There are 22 youth hostels, with more than 700 beds available during the summer. All hostels have members' kitchen, hot and cold water, showers and central heating, and most have family rooms. Youth Hostels are listed at the end of each chapter in this guide book. BIF does arrange organised tours and combined bus/hostel voucher packages if you want to travel around.

Fore more details write to BIF headquarters at:

Sundlaugarvegur Youth Hostel
Sundlaugavegi 34
PO Box 1045
121 Reykjavík
Iceland
☎ (91) 38110

## Huts

The Touring Club of Iceland have about twenty-five huts in some of the remotest areas of Iceland. They are all marked on the Tourist Map 1:750,000. The huts are very popular in the summer and reservations should be made well in advance. Some of the huts are locked during the summer and you have to collect the key before setting out. For further details contact:

Ferdafélag Islands
(Touring Club of Iceland)
Mörkinni 6
Reykjavík
☎ (91) 682533

## Edda Hotels

There are sixteen tourist class Edda Hotels in Iceland offering both bed and breakfast or sleeping accommodation. Hotels offering sleeping bag accommodation are listed at the end of each chapter in this guide book. The following is a list of Edda and other hotels accepting the 'open Edda vouchers' on the same conditions as Edda Hotels.

EDDA Hotels

1. Laugarvatn, Hotel EDDA ML ☎ (98) 61118
2. Laugarvatn, Hotel EDDA HSL ☎ (98) 61154
3. Akranes, Hotel Ósk, Vogabraut 5 ☎ (93) 13314
4. Reykholt, Hotel EDDA ☎ (93) 51260
5. Snaefellsnes, Hotel Búdir ☎ (93) 56700
6. Snaefellsnes, Langaholt Guesthouse ☎ (93) 56789
7. Ólafsvík, Höfdi Guesthouse ☎ (93) 61650
8. Grundarfjördur, Ásakaffi Guesthouse ☎ (93) 86988
9. Stykkish, Hotel Eyjaferdir-Guesthouse Egilshús ☎ (93) 81450
10. Saelingsdalur, Hotel EDDA, Laugar ☎ (93) 41265
11. Hotel Bjarkarlundur ☎ (93) 47762
12. Vatnsfjördur, Hotel Flókalundur ☎ (94) 2011
13. Ísafjördur, Hotel Ísafjördur ☎ (94) 4111
14. Reykjanes, Hotel EDDA ☎ (94) 4844
15. Hrútafjördur, Hotel EDDA, Reykir ☎ (95) 10004
16. Midfjördur, Hotel EDDA, Laugabakki ☎ (95) 12904
17. Blönduós, Hotel Blönduós ☎ (95) 21426
18. Húnavellir, Hotel EDDA ☎ (95) 24370
19. Saudárkrókur, Hotel Áning ☎ (95) 36717
20. Ólafsfjördur, Hotel Ólafsfjördur ☎ (96) 62400
21. Dalvík, Hotel Saeluhúsid ☎ (96) 61661
22. Akureyri, Hotel EDDA ☎ (96) 24055
23. Nr Akureyri, Hotel EDDA, Thelamörk ☎ (96) 21772
24. Ljósavatnsskard, Hotel EDDA, Stóru Tjarnir ☎ (96) 43221
25. Lake Myvatn, Hotel Reykjahlíd ☎ (96) 44142
26. Bárdardalur, Hotel Kidagil ☎ (96) 43290
27. Vopnafjördur, Hotel Tangi ☎ (97) 31224
28. Eidar, Hotel EDDA ☎ (97) 13803
29. Hallormsstadur, Hotel EDDA ☎ (97) 11705
30. Fáskrúdsfjödur, Hotel Skálavík ☎ (97) 51298
31. Breiddalsvík, Hotel Bláfell ☎ (97) 56770
32. Djúpivogur, Hotel Framtidin ☎ (97) 88887

33. Höfn, Hotel EDDA, Nesjaskóla ☎ (97) 81470
34. Nr Skaftafell, Hotel Freysnes ☎ (97) 81845
35. Kirkjubaejarklaustur, Hotel EDDA ☎ (98) 74799
36. Skógar, Hotel EDDA ☎ (98) 78870
37. Vestmannaeyjar, Braedraborg Guesthouse ☎ (98) 11515
38. Hotel Hvolsvöllur ☎ (98) 78187
39. Hotel Flúdir ☎ (98) 66630
40. Hafnarfjördur, Hotel Berg, Baejarhraun 4 ☎ (91) 652220
41. Reykjavík, Hotel ÍSÍ, Laugardalur ☎ (91) 813377
42. Reykjavík, Baldursbrá Guesthouse, Laufásvegur 41 ☎ (91) 26646
43. Reykjavík, Guesthouse, Brautarholt 4 ☎ (91) 16239
44. Reykjavík, Jörd Guesthouse, Skólavördustígur 13a ☎ (91) 621739
45. Reykjavík, Guesthouse, Laugavegur 101 ☎ (91) 626101
46. Reykjavík, Guesthouse, Miklabraut 1 ☎ (91) 622144

## Alcohol

Alcohol is sold in hotels, bars, pubs and restaurants and through State Monopoly Shops. Light beers can be bought in supermarkets. You can buy alcohol from the duty free shop at Keflavík airport on arrival. You may bring into Iceland 1 litre of spirits and 2 litres of wine or 6 litres of imported beer or 8 litres of domestic beer.

## Arrival and Customs

A valid passport is necessary for visitors to Iceland, except those from Denmark, Finland, Norway and Sweden. A visa is not required for stays of less than three months.

## Banks

Banking hours are 9.15am-4pm and some branches open later on Thursday between 5-6pm. Most banks are closed over the weekends. The Landsbanki branch at Hotel Loftleidir, Reykjavík, is open weekdays 8.15am-4pm and 5-7pm, Saturday 2.15am-7.15pm and Sunday 15 May to 15 September 12noon-5pm. The Tourist Information Centre at Búnadarbanki, Reykjavík, is open at weekends to exchange foreign currency 1 June to 15 September weekdays 4.30-6pm and Saturday 9am-1pm.

## Chemists

Chemists are normally open 9am-6pm and in larger towns there is a rota for evenings and weekends usually posted in the window.

## Climate

Iceland has a variable climate and you should be ready for anything.

Thanks to the Gulf Stream, winters are surprisingly mild while summers are cool. The afternoon temperature in mid-summer is usually between 12 and 15°C at low altitudes. January is the coldest month. However, it can be very hot during the summer one minute and bitterly cold the next.

Maximum and minimum daily temperatures

Average monthly rainfall

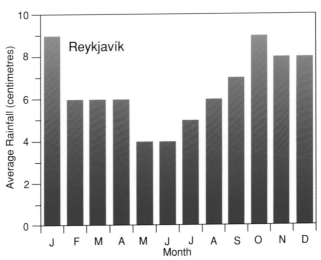

## Clothing

Stout footwear and warm, waterproof, windproof clothes are essential. Work on the layer principle so that you can add something if you feel cold, or strip something off if you are too warm.

## Currency and Credit Cards

The *króna* is the unit of Icelandic currency with 100 *aurar* = 1 *króna*. Coins come in 5, 10, and 50 *aurar* and 1, 5, 10 and 50 *Króna*. All major credit cards are accepted in Iceland. The following have offices in Reykjavík:
American Express, Alfabakki 16 ☎ (91) 682050
Diners Club International, Engjateigur 9 ☎ (91) 686111
Mastercard/Eurocard, Armúla 28 ☎ (91) 685499
Visa-Island, Hófdabakka 9 ☎ (91) 671700

## Eating Out

Dining out in Iceland can be expensive, especially if you are on a limited budget. Buffet breakfasts offered by many of the hotels are an excellent way of eating relatively cheaply.

The Icelandic Hotel and Restaurant Association offers a special tourist menu each summer with emphasis on 'good food at cheap prices'. Normally soup, a meat or fish course, and coffee is served at either lunch or dinner. Children up to five eat free, and those between 5 and 12 get a 50 per cent discount. For further information contact:
The Icelandic Hotel and Restaurant Association
Gardastraeti 21
Reykjavík
☎ (91) 27410

## Electricity

The voltage is 220, 50HZ AC. Check to make sure your plugs fit correctly, if not you will damage your appliances.

## Embassies and Consulates

The main embassies and consulates in Iceland are:
*Embassies*

**UK**
Laufásvegur 49
Reykjavík
☎ (91) 15883

**USA**
Laufásvegur 21
Reykjavík
☎ (91) 29100

**Canada**
Skúlagata 20
☎ (91) 25355

**Ireland**
Thverholt 17
☎ (91) 26300

Other Icelandic embassies
are:
**UK**
1 Eaton Terrace
London
SW1 8EY
☎ (071) 730 5131

**USA**
2022 Connecticut Avenue
N.W Washington DC
20008
☎ 202 265 6653

## Facilities for the Disabled

Many hotels and youth hostels have rooms specially designed for the disabled, and larger stores tend to be accessible to wheelchair users. All airlines are equipped to accommodate wheelchair users, and a few buses are equipped for wheelchair users but it is advisable to check in advance. Further information can be obtained from:
Icelandic Association of the Disabled
Hátún 10
Reykjavík
☎ (91) 12512/26700

## Health Insurance and Medical Treatment

Citizens of Scandinavia and the UK are covedred by reciprocal national health insurance agreements. Travellers from other countries should ensure they have adequate health insurance.

There are health centres and hospitals in all the major population areas, but you may still be a long way from one if you have an accident. If travelling in remote areas, have an adequate first aid kit, and know how to use it.

## Language

A Guide to Icelandic Pronunciation
*Vowels*
a (a) as in English, father.
á (au) as in English, now.
e (e) when short (ie before two consonants) as in English, get. When long as in English, air.
é (jé) represents the sound of English, yes, occasionally also written je.
i (I) as in English, bid.
í (i) as in English, green.

ö (o) as in English (not American) not.
ó (ou) as in English, slow.
u (Y) is not found in English, but represents a sound like ü in *Küste*.
ú (u) as in English, school.
y (and y) are pronounced like i and í respectively.
æ (ai) as in English, high.
au (öy) represents a sound not found in English (ie it is not the sound
represented by au in other languages), but closely approximated by
the French *feuille*. It is composed of Icelandic ö and í.
ei and ey (ei) similar to English, hate, or Dutch ij in fijn.

*Consonants*
Icelandic has two letters of its own which resemble 'p' and 'd' but must
not be confused with them. The crossed 'ð' letter is pronounced like
a hard 'th' as in 'them', while the hooked 'Þ' is pronounced like a soft
'th' as in 'thing'. They have been printed as 'th' in the following text.
j (j) like English y in yes.
v (v) is pronounced as in English
r (r) is trilled, as in Scotch, Spanish, etc.
ll is pronounced (dl) eg Hella (hedla), fjall (fjadl).
f before l or n is pronounced like b, eg Keflavík (kehblavik), Höfn
(höbn).
rn is pronounced dn, eg barn, (badn).
rl is pronounced like Icelandic ll (dl), eg karl (man) (kadl).
p, t, and k when doubled or when followed by l or n are preceded by
a breath of air known as 'pre-aspiration': eg epli (apple) is pronounced
(ehpll), hætta (to stop) (haihta), takk (thank you) (tahk).
Otherwise, most Icelandic consonants are pronounced like their English or German counterparts.

**Useful Words and Phrases**
N.B. The 'd' in nearly all these words transcribes 'ð', pronounced 'th'
as in 'them'.
English — *Icelandic*
I — *ég*
she — *hún*
you — *thid*
you — *thú*
it — *thad*
they — *their/thær/thau*
he — *hann*
we — *vid*
What is your name? — *Hvad heitir pú?*
My name is … — *Ég heiti …*
Where are you from? — *Hvadan ert pú?*
I am from England — *Ég er frá Englandi*
Where do you live here? — *Hvar byrd thú hér?*
I live at Hotel Saga — *Ég by á Hótel Sögu*
Do you speak English? — *Talar thú ensku?*

Who is this? — *Hver er thetta?*
This is my — *thetta er*
brother — *bródir minn*
sister — *systir mín*
mother — *módir mín*
father — *fadir minn*
wife — *konan mín*
husband — *madurinn minn*
daughter — *dóttir mín*
son — *sonur minn*
friend — *vinur minn*
Can you tell me the way to Hotel Saga? — *Getur pú sagt mér hvar Hótel Sögu er?*
How far is it? — *Hvad er langt thangad?*
Where does this bus go? — *Hvert fer thessi vagn?*
How much does it cost? — *Hvad kostar thad?*
Can you help me please? — *Getur thú hjálpad mér?*
Waiter! — *thjónn!*
What can I do for you? — *Hvad get ég gert fyrir thig*
I'd like some — *Ég ætla ad fá*
tea —*te*
coffee — *kaffi*
milk — *mjólk*
soda — *gosdrykk*
whisky — *whisky*
beef — *nautakjöt*
fish — *fisk*
lamb — *lambakjöt*
veal — *kálfakjöt*
pork — *svínakjöt*
a sandwich — *samloku*
an egg — *egg*
Thank you — *Takk fyrir*
Can I help you? — *Get ég adstodad?*
Yes, thank you — *Já, takk*
I'll have a kilo of apples — *Ég ætla ad fá kiló af eplum*
half a kilo of eggs — *Ég ætla ad fá hálft kiló af eggjum*
500 grams of oranges — *Ég ætla ad fá 500 grömm af appelsínum*
I'd like to look at some sweaters — *Get ég fengid ad lita á theysur?*
What colour? — *Hvada lit?*
blue-*bláan*  green-*grænan*  red-*raudan*  yellow-*gulan*  black-*svartan*
white-*hvítan*  grey-*gráan*  brown-*brúnann*  violet-*jólu-bláan*
   pink-*bleikan*
Which size? — *Hvada stærd?*
How much for a postcard/letter to England? — *Hvad kostar undir póstkort/bréf til Englands?*
20/30/40/50/60/70/80/90kr. — *tuttugu/thrjátíu/fjörutíu/ fimmtíu/sextíu/sjötíul/áttatíu/nítíu kr.*

Where can I phone? — *Hvar get ég hringt?*
The number is 1-2-3-4-5-6-7-8-9-10-11-12 — *Númerid er einn-tveir-thrír-fjórir-fimm-sex-sjö-átta-níu-tíu-ellefu-tólf*
Your passport please — *Vegabréfid takk*
Fill in this form please — *Vildir thú fylla út eydubladid takk?*
Sign here please — *Skrifid undir hér*
Where is the next hotel/youth hostel/camping place? — *Hvar er næsta hótel/farfuglaheimili/tjaldstædi?*
Is there a hotel/youth hostel/camping place near here? — *Er hótel/farfuglaheimili/tjaldstædi hér nærri?*
Do you have two single rooms? — *Áttu tvö einstaklings herbergi?*
a double room? — *Áttu tveggja manna herbergi?*
For how many persons? — *Fyrir hve marga?*
How long will you stay? — *Hve lengi ætlid thid ad vera?*
Where is the toilet please? — *Hvar er badherbergid?*
dining room? — *matsalurinn?*
What is the matter? — *Hvad er ad?*
Where do you feel pain? — *Hvar finnur thú til?*
In my arm — *Í handleggnum*
leg — *fætinum*
stomach — *maganum*
neck — *hálsinum*
head — *höfdinu*
back — *bakinu*
heart — *hjartanu*
I've got a toothache — *Ég er med tannpínu*
headache — *höfudverk*
stomach ache — *magaverk*

## Maps

Good maps are essential if you are travelling into the interior. For general 'sightseeing' and motoring, the Landmaelingar Islands Road Map 1:500,000 is fine. For information on detailed maps, contact:
Iceland Geodetic Survey
Laugavegi 178
105 Reykjavík
☎ (91) 681611

## News

The news is broadcast in English on the radio at 7.30am every morning between 1 June and 30 September. Tune in to FM 93.5 or 92.4.

## Post Offices

There are post offices in every town and almost every village. They are generally open between 8.30am-4.30pm Monday to Friday. It is possible to make international calls from Post Offices.

## Public Holidays

New Year's Day: 1 January
Easter: Maunday Thursday, Good Friday, Easter Sunday, Easter
    Monday
First day of summer: third week of April
Labour Day: 1 May
Ascension Day: third or fourth week of May
Whit Sunday and Monday
Independence Day: 17 June
August Bank Holiday: first Monday in August
Christmas Eve, Christmas Day and Boxing Day: 24 to 26 December
New Year's Eve: 31 December

## Shopping

Shops are open weekdays between 9am-6pm and usually from 10am to either 2 or 4pm on Saturdays although many shut throughout the weekend during the summer. Supermarkets stay open later on Friday evenings. Shops outside Reykjavík in service centres or garages are often open from 9am-11.30pm seven days a week.

**Tax Free Shopping**
Visitors are entitled to receive a refund of most of the 24.5 per cent VAT paid on purchases if claimed within thirty days. Individual purchase receipts must not exceed 5,000IK, and apart from woollen goods, all items must be packed in sealed bags or containers. Tax Free Shops are identified by the prominently displayed red and blue stickers.

## Sports and Pastimes

**Birdwatching**
Iceland is a bird watcher's paradise. Látrabjarg in the western fjords are the world's largest bird cliffs. Almost anywhere around the coast can be rewarding, and Myvatn is a must.

**Canoeing**
There are opportunities for very experienced canoeists only. River rafting tours are arranged by B.G. River Rafting and Guiding ☎ (91) 72852.

## Cycling

Cycling in Iceland offers enormous scope for the experienced, fit cyclist with the right machine and equipment. Although it is claimed that 60 per cent of the ring road is asphalted, the surface deteriorates quickly, and huge sections together with thousands of kilometres of other roads and mountain tracks are bumpy, pot holed and grit strewn. Cyclists heading off the beaten track must have good maps, and know how to ford rivers. Mountain bikes with wide rims and tyres are essential. Tools and spares must also be carried. Goggles are also a good idea as passing vehicles can throw up gravel, grit and sand. Road surfaces make travelling uncomfortable over long distances and you should be adept at mending punctures.

The Icelandic Mountainbike Club (IFHK) can provide specialist information for cyclists, and they organise regular events and week-end trips during the summer. Further details as well as information about IFHK, can be obtained from the Reykjavík Youth Hostel which organises cycle tours to the interior. For more casual cycling, it is possible to rent bikes in a number of areas, and it is a good way of getting around. Useful addresses are:

BSI Travel
Bus Terminal
Reykjavík
☎ (91) 22300

Icelandic Highland Travel
Bankastraeti 2
Reykjavík
☎ (91) 22225

Rent a Bike
Hverfisgötu 50
Reykjavík
☎ (91) 15653

Samvinn Travel
Austurstraeti 12
Reykjavík
☎ (91) 691070

For information about organised tours contact:
Utivist Touring Club
Grófin 1
Reykjavík
☎ (91) 14606

## Fishing

Iceland is famous for its salmon and trout fishing, and deep sea fishing is becoming more popular. The main salmon season is 20 June to mid-September. The trout season varies from lake to lake and river to river, but the normal season is April/May to late September/October. During the winter there are opportunities for ice fishing. For salmon fishing a permit is required, and it is advisable to reserve these well in advance. Trout fishing permits can often be acquired on the day they are required. The top ten salmon rivers are: Laxá (Adaldalur), Ellidaár, Laxá (Dalir), Thverá-Kjarrá, Laxá (Leira), Midfjardará, Grimsá, Vididalsá, Laxá (Kjós), and Nordurá.

For further information contact:
The National Angling Association
Bolholt 6
Reykjavík
☎ (91) 31510

The Icelandic Farm Holidays service also publishes an information brochure on fishing with details about a number of lakes. Fishing rods can be rented.

## Golf
Iceland boasts a number of very good courses and hosts The Arctic Open at the end of June every year in Akureyri. Tee off is just before midnight. All courses are open to visitors and green fees are reasonable. Further information from:
The Golf Union of Iceland
PO Box 1076
Reykjavík
☎ (91) 686686

## Hiking
There are so many good opportunities for hiking that you would have to keep returning year after year to exhaust just a handful. You must be fit, well prepared, adequately equipped with good maps and know how to use them.
Further information from:Touring Club of Iceland (Ferdafélag Island)
Oldugata
Reykjavík
☎ (91) 1953

Utivist Touring Club
Grófin 1
Reykjavík
☎ (91) 14606

## Horse Riding
There are a growing number of farms offering horse riding. Treks can vary from an hour or so, to ten-day explorations of the interior. Little experience is required as the horses are so well trained, they tell you what to do. For further information contact:

**Eld-Hestar**
Laugarskardi
Hveragerdi
☎ (98) 34884
Daily from 8 June to 31 August, tours lasting from one hour to one day.

**Hestasport**
Varmahlid
☎ (95) 38021

**Hekla Horses**
Hella
☎ (98) 76598

**Volcano Horses**
Hveragerdi
☎ (98) 34884

**Icelandic Riding Tours**
Baerjarhraun 2

Hafnarfjördur
☎ (91) 653044
Daily treks ranging from 1-4 hours, plus 6, 8 and 10-day treks.

**Laxnes Pony Farm**
Varmá
☎ (91) 666179
Treks daily 10am-2pm March to September.

**Polar Horses**
Akureyri
☎ (96) 33179

**Saga Horses**
Hvolsvöllur
☎ (98) 78138

**Njála Tours**
Hvolsvöllur
☎ (98) 78133

## Mountaineering

Rock, snow and ice climbing in Iceland are all sports for the very experienced. If you want to learn, go with a guide. The rock in Iceland tends to be loose and is not generally suitable for climbing. Falling rocks and landslips are common. Crevices on the glacier may be covered and prove a constant hazard. It is essential to be properly equipped and ready to meet all eventualities. The weather can deteriorate very quickly and you may have to stay put longer than planned.

If you are planning to spend some time in the interior, make sure someone has your itinerary, and any contingency plans if you have to vary your route or are delayed. Make sure to report back on your return. Further information from:

**The Iceland Touring Club**
Oldugata 4
Reykjavík
☎ (91) 19533

**Utivist Touring Club**
Grófin 1
Reykjavík
☎ (91) 14606

**Iceland Alpine Club**
PO Box 1054
Reykjavík
☎ (91) 53410

## Skiing

There are lots of opportunities for winter skiing in many parts of the country, and summer skiing is possible at Kerlingarfjöll. A ski school operates there from the end of June to the end of August. A ski lift on the Myrdalsjökull glacier is also open during the summer with skimobiles taking you even higher for the 6km (4 miles) run back down the glacier.

## Swimming

There are swimming pools throughout Iceland, both indoor and outdoor. Most are naturally heated from hot water pumped up from deep underground. Many pools also have hot tubs and saunas. Bathers are required to shower before entering the pool.

## Taxis

Taxis are available round the clock and are numerous. Fares are not expensive and you do not have to tip. The only problem time is when the clubs and pubs turn out at the weekend, around 3am and then taxis are very busy.

## Telephones

Direct calls can be made from public phone boxes to all parts of Iceland, and phone boxes are readily available at garages, stores, cafés and so on. Each area has a two-digit number, followed by a four (West Fjords) or five or six digit number.

Many Icelanders use mobile phones and when calling one, dial 985 only before the personal number, no area code is necessary.

The code from abroad to Iceland is 354, then the area code omitting the 9, plus the number you wish to call (eg dial 91 for Reykavík when dialling from Akureyri, but only 1 if dialling from outside the country).

Direct long distance calls can be made from Iceland to Europe and the USA by dialling 90 followed by the country code, the area code and the telephone code. If assistance is required, dial 08 for information, and 09 to place a call with the operator.

Coin and card operated public phones are available at post offices and telephone exchanges around the country, and operators can place a call for you and monitor the duration so that you can settle up afterwards. Phone call charges in Iceland vary. It is cheaper to ring in the evening and at weekends, and many hotels charge higher rates, plus a charge for connecting long distance calls. International codes for calls made in Iceland are: Ireland 90353, UK 9044, USA and Canada 901.

Telex and Telefax services are available at most hotels and post offices. The telex code into Iceland is 0501, and the telefax code is 354 plus area code and telefax number.

## Time

Iceland is on Greenwich Mean Time throughout the year. When it is noon in Reykjavík in the summer, it is 8am in New York, 1pm in London, 2pm in Paris, and 9pm in Tokyo.

## Tipping

Tips are not expected in Iceland. Restaurants usually add a service charge although you may wish to leave a little extra. You may tip the coach driver after an excursion.

# Tour Operators

**Airtours**
Vesturgata 12
Reykjavík
☎ (91) 620066

**Austurlands Travel**
DraghÁls 6
Reykjavík
☎ (91) 678545

**BSI Travel**
BSI Bus Terminal
Vatnsmyrarveg 10
Reykjavík
☎ (91) 22300

**Iceland Tourist Bureau**
Skógarhlíd
Reykjavík
☎ (91) 623300

**Iceland Highland Travel**
Bankstraeti 2
Reykjavík
☎ (91) 22225

**Reykjavík Excursions**
Hotel Loftleidir
Reykjavík
☎ (91) 621011

**Westfjords Travel Service**
Adalsstraeti 11
Isafjördur
☎ (94) 3557

**Utivist Tours**
Hallveigarstíg 1
PO Box 236
Reykjavík
☎ (91) 14606

## Travel

### By Sea

In June, July and August the car and passenger ferry *Norröna* sails weekly from Hansolm in Denmark and Bergen in Norway, via the Faroe Islands and Shetland to Seydisfjördur on the east coast of Iceland. There are connecting ferries from Lerwick in the Shetlands to either Bergen or Tórshavn in the Faroe Islands.

Eimskip of Iceland operates a year round weekly cargo service with cabins for 12 passengers to Reykjavík from Immingham, UK, Hamburg, Antwerp and Rotterdam.

Further details from:

**Smyril Line**
PO Box 370
FR-110 Torshavn
Faroe Islands
☎ (298) 15900

**Norröna Travel**
Fjardargata 8
710 Seydisfjördur
☎ (97) 21111

**Norröne Travel**
Laugavegur 3
Reykjavík
☎ (91) 626363

**Smyril Line Shetland**
Scottish Ferries
Holmsgarth Terminal
Lerwick, Shetland
☎ (05) 95 4848

**Eimskip**
Urval-Utsyn Travel Bureau
Pósthússtraeti 13
Reykjavík
☎ (91) 26900

**By Air**
Icelandair has regular scheduled services to Iceland from London,
Glasgow, Copenhagen, Stockholm, Gothenberg, Oslo, Helsinki, Faroe
Islands, Frankfurt, Salzburg, Luxembourg, Paris, Amsterdam, Hamburg,
Milan, Zurich, Narssarssuaq, New York, Baltimore and
Orlando. Scandinavian Airlines SAS fly between Reykjavík and Copenhagen,
and Lufthansa operates between Keflavík and Frankfurt.
Odin Air services the link between Keflavík and Kulusuk in Greenland,
and Greenland Air operate scheduled services to Iceland from
Nuuk, Kulusuk and Narsarsuaq.
International flights fly in and out of Keflavík Airport and there is
a connecting bus service to the Hotel Loftleidir in Reykjavík. The
journey takes between 40-50 minutes depending on traffic. Taxis are
also available. Buses to Keflavík Airport leave Hotel Loftleidir two
hours before the scheduled departure of international flights.
Icelandair offices are:

**Reykjavík**
Laekjargata 2
☎ (91) 690100
Domestic service
☎ (91) 690200
24 hour information
☎ (91) 690595/(92) 50200

**Faroe Islands**
N. Winthersgöta 3
100 Thporshavn
☎ 10024

**UK (Tourist Office)**
172 Tottenham Court Road
London W1P 9LG
☎ (071) 388 5599

Heathrow Airport
Terminal 1
☎ (081) 745 7051

Glasgow Airport
☎ (041) 889 1001

**USA (Tourist Office)**
610 B Fifth Avenue
Rockerfeller Centre
New York NY 10020
☎ (212) 967 8888
Toll free 800 223 3031

# Motoring in Iceland

**Bringing Your Own Car**
When bringing a car into the country one must produce the driver's
passport and driving licence, the car's registration certificate (log
book) and a green card. The car is examined and a temporary importation
permit issued. Maximum dimensions are: Width = 2.5m, length
= 13m. Vehicles which take fifteen or more passengers may not have

trailers. Coach crew and passengers must leave the country with their vehicle.

Fuel may only be imported in the vehicle's fuel tanks (maximum 200 litres). Fishing equipment which has been used abroad will be sterilized at customs unless a valid sterilization certificate is produced. The import of weapons and drugs is not permitted.

Most of the road surfaces are unmade and drivers should watch out for loose gravel at the road side. Gas containers should neither be stored under nor outside the vehicle. Mud flaps are compulsory, to minimise the chances of stones being thrown up in the path of oncoming vehicles. In dry weather dust from the roads can impair visibility and in some parts of the country sandstorms can hold up traffic for hours. There are free facilities for washing your car at filling stations.

### Driving in Iceland

Drive on the right-hand side of the road. Most country roads are unmade and not suitable for fast driving. Speed limits are 50km/h (31mph) in built-up areas and 80/90km/h (50-56mph) on highways. Drive carefully and show consideration for other road users. Use headlights day and night — dust often impairs visibility. Decelerate and keep well to your side of the road when meeting oncoming traffic. Blind spots at the top of hills are common and not always marked. They are, however, usually marked with a 'danger ahead' sign (an exclamation mark within a triangle) and the word BLINDHÆD below.

Bridges usually only allow one lane of traffic. Many unbridged rivers appear quite safe at first sight but can prove extremely difficult once the crossing has been embarked on. Check carefully before fording the river, especially if there are no accompanying vehicles.

Get the latest information on mountain roads and tracks. They can be impassable long into the summer. Pay close attention to all road signs, especially on routes new to you. The use of seat belts in front seats is compulsory in Iceland, and the use of seat belts in rear seats is encouraged. Drinking and driving is forbidden by law in Iceland.

### The Interior

Once away from the main roads the traveller will find himself in uninhabited country, mostly highland, where more primitive conditions prevail, with nature delicately balanced and hardly any tourist services. There are no shops and no filling stations.

There are some travellers' lodges in the interior but members of the touring clubs which own them take preference for accommodation, so one should book in advance at the touring club office. Bring an accurate map with you and plan your route in advance. Make enquiries about the situations you are likely to encounter and write an itinerary. Remember that roads in the interior are slower than the highways so don't reckon a day's journey on the basis of kilometres.

In early summer when the frozen earth is thawing, many unmade roads can become waterlogged and one can expect some highways to be closed for a time or for axle weight restrictions to be imposed (down to max. 5 tons axle weight). Roads in the interior are only passable by 4-wheel drive vehicles and are closed to all traffic until the first week in July. Some roads in the interior are not opened until mid July, e.g. Landmannalaugar-Eldgjá, Gæsavatnaleid, Kverkfjöll, Snæfell and Fjallabaksleid sydri. There are many unbridged rivers to be crossed in the interior and they should be treated with extreme caution.

Find out when the roads in the interior are open (radio broadcasts in English) and take account of this when planning your route. It is an offence not to keep to the road when driving (a measure taken when it was realized how quickly erosion took hold and spread where car tracks on soft ground and moss had left deep scars). The police monitor traffic, sometimes from the air, and impose fines.

### Driving in the Interior
It is essential to plan your route, collect information about it and find out how the roads are before commencing your journey. Enquire about weather and road conditions on the route you plan to travel. Take warm clothes and rainwear and all necessary equipment and spares for the car. When planning your route, take into account the fact that the roads in the interior are slower than the highways.

Check unbridged rivers by wading across them before attempting to drive over. Don't travel alone in the interior in winter, nor in the summer if the weather outlook is poor. If your vehicle gets stuck or breaks down, wait for help in the vehicle (it provides shelter). If the engine starts then don't waste fuel. Preserve heat and electricity. Put on warm clothing before you feel cold. Ration food and water.

Don't leave your vehicle unless you have given the matter considerable thought and never on your own. If the decision is taken to leave the vehicle, a note should always be left stating number of passengers, their names and ages, the time of departure from the vehicle and the intended destination.

Be on the lookout for search parties and remember that you will be more visible if you are wearing bright-coloured clothing.

### Unbridged Rivers
When planning a trip in the interior it is necessary to find out if there are any unbridged rivers on the route and where the fords are. Accurate maps are available in the bookshops and at certain places in the interior there are wardens who know the condition of the rivers at any given time. Rivers often change course and an apparently harmless river can become a raging torrent almost without warning. Never take risks. If there is a lot of water in the river, wait until it subsides. Never attempt to cross a river unless another vehicle is waiting to assist if you get into difficulties.

Wade across the ford before attempting to drive over, and check the condition of the river bed. Look out for quicksand. The person who wades across the ford should wear a life jacket and be attached to a life line. The cold water in Icelandic rivers can cause cramp in those who fall in and even death. It is often difficult to see the river bed of glacial rivers as the water can be muddy. Check the strength of the current and its course. The best point to ford the river is not necessarily the narrowest. The one who wades the river should carry a pole to test the river bed and for support in strong currents. Face upstream in deep water and don't let the current hit you behind the knees.

Never assume that wheel marks leading into a river indicate that the river can be forded at that point. Never try to cross a river in a small low-powered car with an ill-protected ignition system. (The ignition system can be protected for a short while by covering the leads and distributor with loose wool or other material.) Make sure the air intake is not submerged and switch off the lights when driving into cold water. Remember that brakes often do not work for a short while after driving in water.

## Spares and Safety Equipment

When you travel into the interior it is as well to keep in mind the fact that there are no shops and no repair services there. It is essential to carry both spares for the car and some safety equipment in case of mishap.

*Spares*

Distributor cap, rotor arm, condensor, fan belt, spare plugs (4-8), fuel pipe, jubilee clips (various sizes), insulated wire, spare bulbs, lubricating oil for a complete all-round oil change, sealing compound for radiator and fuel tank, waterproofing spray for ignition system, penetrating oil, brake fluid, extra fuel, cotton waste or rags.

*Safety Equipment*

Tow rope, spade, crow bar, general purpose tool set, common bolts, nuts and screws, twine, jack, wheel brace, wheel nuts, good torch, batteries and bulbs, a good map of the area you are travelling in, waders, emergency rations, distress flares, extinguisher for general use, emergency radio transmitter or two-way radio.

## Car Hire

Drivers must have held a valid driving licence for at least one year, be at least 20 years old, and 23 in most cases, if wishing to rent a four wheel drive. Reservations in the summer, especially of four wheel drive vehicles is advisable.

Major car hire companies are:

**Icelandair/Hertz**
Reykjavík Airport
☎ (91) 690500
Also at Keflavík, Akureyri, Egilsstadir, Höfn and Vestmannaeyjar airports.

**Arnarflug**
Reykjavík Airport
☎ (91) 614400

AKA
Vagnhöfdi 25
Reykjavík
☎ (91) 674455

Avis
Sigtún 5
Reykjavík
☎ (91) 624433

InterRent/Europcar
Skeifan 9
Reykjavík
☎ (91) 686915

Budget
Dalvegur 20
Kópavogur
☎ (91) 641296

Fuel
Filling stations are usually open between 7.30am and 8pm Monday to Saturday, and between 9am-8pm on Sundays during the summer. After regular hours, self service is available at pumps marked 'Sjálfsafgreidsla', which take 100 or 1,000 *Króna* notes.

Traffic Regulations
Speed limits are usually 50km (31 miles) in urban areas, and 70km (43 miles) elsewhere unless otherwise posted. Drivers and passengers must wear seat belts, and headlights must always be on.

## Public Transport

Air
Domestic flights operate from the terminal on the west side of Reykjavík Airport: ☎ (91)-690100. Domestic flight information is available on ☎ (91) 690200. Three regional airlines operate serving the north, east, and western parts of Iceland respectively.

Norlandair (Flugfélag Nordurlands) is based in Akureyri and operates schedules between Akureyri, Egilsstada, Grímseyjar, Húsatíkur, Isafjardur, Keflavíkur, Kópaskers, Raufarhafnar, Reykjavíkur, Vopnafjardar and Thórshafnar. For further information ☎ (96) 12100.

Flugfélag Austurlands is based in Egilsstadir ☎ (97) 11122. It operates flights to Borgarfjördur, Breiddalsvik, Höfn, Neskaupstadur, Reykjavík and Flugfélagid Ernir is based at Isafjördur ☎ (94) 4200. It operates flights between Reykjavík and Isafjördur, and between Isafjördur and Holt, Thingeyri, Bíldudalur, Patreksfjördur and Ingjaldssandur. Mýfkug, based in Myvatn, flies daily between Myvatn and Reykjavík during the summer ☎ (96) 44107.

Bus and Coach Services
There is a very efficient bus network covering Iceland centred on the BSI Terminal in Reykjavík. Most long-distance coaches leave the terminal between 8-9am each day, while the returning vehicle usually arrives in Reykjavík between 6-8pm. You can buy your tickets in advance or from the driver.

The terminal is open June to August, Monday to Friday 7.30am-7pm, Saturday 7.30am-2pm, Sunday 7.30am-2pm and 5-7pm. During the winter it is open Monday to Friday 9am-5pm. The baggage storage office is open Monday to Friday 7.30am-10.30am, Saturday 7.30am-2.30pm, and Sunday in the summer only from 5-8pm. The BSI terminal restaurant is open between 7am-12midnight daily.

Travellers wishing to see as much of the country as possible are recommended to buy either:

1) The Full Circle Passport which allows you to travel right round the country and is valid between May and September. You can stop off along the route as often as you wish, provided you always continue your journey in the same direction.

2) The Omnibus Passport is a special discount bus ticket, offering unlimited travel on any routes in any direction, within your chosen time limit of one, two, three or four weeks. It also allows you discount fares on many of the special tours organised by BSI. The passports are valid on all scheduled services except city buses in the major towns, and entitle you to a number of discounts — 10 per cent off normal Edda sleeping bag accommodation rate, 10 per cent off campsite charges and some ferries, and up to 50 per cent off some bike rentals.

There are also air bus tickets which allow you to fly one way and travel the other by bus. For further information contact:

BSI Travel
Umferdarmidstödin/Vatns-
myrarvegi 10
Reykjavík
☎ (91) 22300/623320

**Internal Travel by Bus and Plane**

**Akureyri**
Bus daily.
Planes daily (6-7 flights).

**Akranes**
Buses daily.
Boat daily (3-5 sailings).

**Blönduós**
Buses daily.
Planes Tue, Wed, Thur, Fri, Sun.

**Borgarnes**
Buses daily.

**Búdir (Snæfellsnes)**
Buses daily.

**Egilsstadir**
Buses from Akureyri, daily.
Buses from Höfn daily.
Planes from Reykjavík daily (2-3 flights).

**Fagurhhólsmyri**
Buses Tue, Thur, Sat, in June, daily in July and August.

**Gullfoss** and **Geysir**
Buses daily.
Conducted tours during season.

**Hredavatn** (Borgarfjördur)
Buses daily.

**Husavík**
Buses from Akureyri daily July-Sept.
Planes daily.

**Hvalfjördur**
Buses daily.

**Hveragerdi**
Buses daily.

**Hvolsvöllur**
Buses daily.

**Höfn** (Hornafjördur)
Buses Tue, Thur, Sat in June,
daily July and August.
Planes daily except Sat.

**Ísafjördur**
Buses Tue, Thur, July and August.
Planes daily (2-3 flights).

**Keflavík**
Buses daily.

**Kirkjubaejarklaustur**
Buses Tue, Thur, Sat in June,
daily July and August.

**Laugarvatn**
Buses daily in June, July and
August.

**Lake Myvatn**
Buses daily from Akureyri.
Buses daily from Húsavík,
June-August.

**Patreksfjördur**
Buses Mon, Thur.
Planes Mon, Wed, Thur, Fri.

**Reykholt** (Borgarfjördur)
Buses daily.

**Saudárkrókur**
Planes daily except Sat, Sunday.

**Selfoss**
Buses daily.

**Seydisfjördur**
Buses from Akureyri Wed.
Buses from Höfn Wed.

Buses from Egilsstadir daily
except Sat, Sun.

**Siglufjördur**
Buses from Varmahlíd, Tues,
Wed, Fri.
Planes from Reykjavík daily.

**Skaftafell**
Buses Tue, Thur, Sat in June,
daily July and August.

**Stykkishólmur**
Buses daily.
Planes daily except Sat.

**Thingvellir**
Buses daily.

**Thorlákshöfn**
Buses daily.

**Varmahlíd**
Buses daily.

**Vík (Myrdalur)**
Buses Tue, Thur, Sat in June,
daily July and August.

**Vestmannaeyjar** (Westman
Islands)
Planes daily (4 flights).
Boat daily from Thorlákshöfn.

**Vopnafjördur**
Buses from Húsavík Mon,
Wed.
Planes from Akureyri daily
except Sat, Sun.
Planes from Egilsstadir Mon,
Wed, Fri.

**Ferries**
*Reykjavík-Akranes* (55 minutes)
Sails daily from Reykjavík Monday to Saturday 9.30am, 12.30pm,
3.30pm, 6.30pm, Sunday 12.30pm 3.30pm, 6.30pm. From Akranes
Monday to Saturday 8am, 11am, 2pm, 5pm, Sunday 11am, 2pm, 5pm.
There are additional late night sailings on Friday and Sunday during
the summer. Further information from:
Skallagrímur
Akursbraut 13
Akranes
☎ (93) 12275
or Reykjavík ☎ (91) 16050

*Stykkishólmur-Brjánslaekur* (3 hours)
Sailings daily during the summer.
For further information contact:
Flóabáturinn Baldur
340 Stykkishólmur
☎ (93) 81120

*Thorlakshöfn-Westman Islands* (3 hours)
The ferry Herjólfur sails daily between the Westman Islands and
Thorlákshöfn, and, if traffic permits, twice daily. There is a connecting
bus service between the ferry terminal and Reykjavík.
For further information contact:
Herjólfur
PO Box 320
Vestmannaeyjar Island
☎ (98) 12800

*Isafjördur-Isafjardardjúp-Hornstrandir*
Summer schedule from Isafjördur:
Isafjardardjúp Tuesday and Friday at 8am (all year).
Jökulfirdir Friday 2pm (26 June to 14 August).
Hornstrandir Monday and Thursday 8am (26 June to 14 August).
Reykjafjördur/Furufjördur (☎ 94-31555 for specific information).

*Arskógssandur-Hrísey* (15 minutes)
From Arskógssandur 1 May to 15 September daily between 7.30am
and 11.30pm.
From Hrísey 1 May to 15 September daily between 7am-11pm.
Further information from ☎ (985) 22211

*Akureyri-Hrísey-Grímsey*
From Akureyri Monday and Thursday 9am.
From Hrísey Monday and Thursday 12noon.
From Grímsey Monday and Thursday 6.30pm.
For further information: Nonni Travel, Akureyri (96) 11841

# FACT FILE: GREENLAND

## Accommodation

All the larger towns have hotels and standards have improved considerably in recent years. The hotels are usually small to medium size, offering good standards of service with telephone and TV in rooms and en suite bathrooms. The standard of hotels in the smaller towns varies enormously. There are also five seamen's hostels in Greenland which offer accommodation. There is often great demand for hotel rooms and it is advisable to reserve well in advance. Do not simply arrive in Greenland in the hope of finding a room. For a list of accommodation see Additional Information page 216 and 217.

### Youth Hostels
There are Youth Hostels at Narsarsuaq, Narsaq, Qaqortoq, Nanortalik and Sisimiut. There are also slightly more expensive Nuna-Tek hostels in many towns and settlements. Sleeping bag accommodation is available in most towns and settlements in hostels, schools and community centres. The local tourist office will provide details of what is available.

Mountain huts do offer accommodation, and local tourist offices have details, but you cannot always guarantee finding a bed. It is advisable always to carry a tent and all-season sleeping bag with you just in case.

### Camping
There are no campgrounds in Greenland, but almost all towns and settlements have an area where tents can be pitched. Ask at the hotel or tourist office. Away from populated areas there are only two restrictions on camping — you cannot camp in an area of protected ruins, and in the south, camping is not allowed on cultivated land.

## Banks and Currency

There are two Greenland banks, Gronlandsbanken A/S and Nuna Bank A/S. Both have headquarters in Nuuk and have strong business links with Danish banks. KNI stores in all towns and settlements provide basic banking services.

### Currency
Danish currency is legal tender in Greenland and there are no restrictions on the import or export of money. Cheques drawn on Danish banks or Eurocheques are honoured in banks, and bureau de change facilities are available in all large towns. Credit cards are generally

only accepted in large towns and hotels. Notes come in denominations of 20, 50, 100, 500 and 1000 *króna*. Coins in use include 5, 10, and 25 *øre* and 1, 5 and 10 *króna*.

## Clothing

You will need lots of warm, windproof, waterproof clothing and sturdy shoes or boots. Rubber boots (wellingtons) are also a good idea, as well as warm headwear and gloves. If taking boat trips you will always need to wrap up well as the water temperature is rarely much above freezing. Even when the weather is cold, the intensity of the sun and the purity of the air makes sun lotion and sun glasses essential. Insect repellant is also a must. Winter travellers must be prepared for violent fluctuations in temperature which can drop to -40°C (-6°F). Extra warm clothing is also essential if you are taking a dog sled ride. If you still feel the cold with all your warmest clothes on, you can usually hire fur clothing from some hotels and tourist information offices.

## Customs Regulations

Greenland is a non-EEC country but for European and North American citizens a valid passport allows entry for up to three months. There are restrictions on the amount of alcohol and tobacco that can be imported. All live animals are banned. Some sporting guns are allowed but permission in advance is required and special arrangements will have to be made with the airline you are travelling on. *Exports.* Some countries ban the import of goods made from sealskin or whale ivory, others may require a certificate stating that the materials did not originate from a threatened species. Certificates can be provided by shops and tourist information centres.

## Festivals

The return of the sun after the polar night is celebrated throughout Greenland, but especially in the north when the population gathers on hills to greet the sun as it comes up over the horizon. In Ilulissat this occurs around 13 January. Several North Greenland settlements hold dog sled races over the Easter holiday. Every summer in South Greenland there is a sheep farmers' show, one of the highlights of which is a sheep shearing contest.

## Health

There are dentists, doctors and a small hospital in every town. Every settlement has a nurse or a specially trained health worker. Health insurance is essential because although medical treatment is usually provided free of charge, transport costs are not, and if you are taken ill on an expedition and have to be flown out it can be very expensive. Also, if you require special medication bring your own, as it might not be readily available.

## Maps

The entire coastal area of Greenland is available on 1:25,000 scale maps, and there are detailed maps of all inhabited areas. For further information contact: Nordisk Korthandel/Scanmaps, Studiestraede 26, 1455 Copenhagen K, Denmark. Tourist offices and shops sell maps but it is worth getting maps in advance so you can plan your trip thoroughly.

## Photography

A UV or skylight filter should always be used together with a lens hood because of the intensity of the light. Film is available on Greenland but it is expensive, and it is advisable to bring your own, especially if you use a special film.

## Post and Telephone Services

There are post offices (Kalaallit Allakkeriviat), international telephone and telegraph facilities in all towns, and faxes can be sent and received at post offices. Reverse-charge calls are not accepted, however. The larger coastal ferries (*Disko* and *Kununguak*) offer radio telephone services.

Greenland's country code is (299). If you want to call out of Greenland, you must first dial (009) for international access, then the desired number. In the settlements, phone calls can be made from the local KNI office, although this is most often via ship to shore radio. They are normally open Monday to Friday 9am-12noon and 1-3pm.

To receive mail, have correspondence addressed to you care of Poste Restante in the main village of the area you will be visiting. For south Greenland, it is probably best to use DK 3920 Qaqortoq and, for the south-west, use DK-3900 Nuuk. For west central use DK-3952 Ilulissat and, for the east, DK-3913 Ammassalik. Write 'Greenland via Denmark' in addition to the postal code for a faster service.

## Public Holidays

1 January: New Year's Day
6 January: Epiphany
Easter: Maunday Thursday, Good Friday, Easter Sunday and Easter
    Monday
1 May: Labour Day

May: Ascension Day
June: Whitsunday
21 June: Midsummer's Day
1 November: All Saints' Day
24 December: Christmas Eve
25 December: Christmas Day
31 December: New Year's Eve

*National Day*
June 21 is Greenland's National Day or 'Ullortuneq' in Eskimo, which means 'longest day'. It is celebrated everywhere with speeches, entertainment and outdoor banquets. It is also Greenland's official flag day, as it was on 21 June 1985 that the flag of Greenland was first flown. The colours of the flag are red and white — the red semicircle symbolising the Midnight Sun, and the white symbolising ice.

## Religion

The national Protestant church of Greenland is part of the Lutheran Danish National Church, but services are usually held in Eskimo rather than Danish. There are churches in all towns with chapels in the settlements and services are held regularly. Other denominations are also represented in Greenland. There is a small Catholic church in Nuuk. The churches are worth visiting and if one is locked, the local tourist office can normally arrange for it to be opened so that you can look around. You are not allowed to photograph in churches or chapels during services or other religious activities.

## Restaurants and Food

Most hotels also have restaurants which serve typical Danish cuisine as well as local specialities. Prices because of subsidies are generally cheaper than those in Iceland, but are still expensive when compared with North America and Europe, except the Scandinavian countries. All drinks, both soft and alcoholic are expensive. Good value meals, however, particularly breakfasts can be had in the cafés and seamen's hostels, and most cafés and restaurants offer good-value fixed menu lunches and dinner. Prices normally include the tip, and it is illegal to serve alcoholic drinks in Greenland before noon.

Most frequent items on restaurant and café menus are fish, mutton and beef. Traditional dishes include fresh or frozen seal meat, whale steaks and blubber. Food for free includes a wide range of berries and fungi, the former generally available from late August to mid-September, and the latter ready for picking throughout August. Fishing can also provide tasty meals and eke out expenses for those on a limited budget, but make sure you have a licence.

You can buy food from the supermarkets, generally run by the state-owned KNI or the cooperative Brug Brugsen. Fresh bread is readily available in most towns and large settlements.

## Shopping

Food on the whole tends to be expensive although supermarket prices do not vary. Small shops and kiosks, however, which often stay open longer, charge more.

Souvenirs, especially arts and crafts, are widely available and best value are carvings in bone, antler and soapstone, jewellery, beadwork, and leather or fur products. If buying leather, make sure it is tanned, because it will not last long in other climates. Inuit music is very attractive, and tapes of local artists also make an interesting and memorable souvenir.

## Tourist Information Centres

For information on Greenland abroad contact the Danish Tourist Board in:

| UK | Canada | USA |
|---|---|---|
| Sceptre House | PO Box 115 | 655 Third Avenue |
| 169 Regent | Station N | 18th Floor |
| Street | Toronto | New York NY 10017 |
| London W1 | Ontario | |

## Travel

### Getting There
From Iceland: Greenland Air flies between Nuuk and Reykjavík, and between Ittoqqoortoormiit and Reykjavík. Both Greenland Air and Icelandair fly between Reykjavík and Narsarsuaq. During the winter Odin Air flies to Kulusuk in East Greenland with year round connections to Ammassalik, and Icelandair also has this route during the summer.

From Denmark: There are year round flights by SAS and Greenland Air between Denmark and Greenland with departures several times a week. Flights are direct from Copenhagen to Kangerlussuaq or Narsarsuaq where connecting flights to other towns in Greenland are usually available.

From Canada: Greenland Air and First Air fly between Nuuk and Iqaluit in Canada, where there are normally connecting flights to Montreal and the USA.

### Travel within Greenland
Greenland Air flies to all towns on the west coast of Greenland from Nanortalik in the south to Upernavik in the north. It also flies to

Kulusuk/Ammassalik and Ittoqqoortoormiit on the east coast. Flights are either by DASH-7 aircraft or S-61 helicopters. Frequency of flight depends on how popular the route is and weather conditions. All seats are bookable and it is recommended you book before you leave for Greenland. Any extra expenses incurred in accommodation, meals and so on, because of cancelled flights due to bad weather have to be met by the traveller. Light aircraft and helicopters are available for hire for sightseeing trips and longer expedition requirements.

Almost all goods are transported to and between towns and settlements by ships that ply all the sea lanes that are not blocked by ice. Small craft are usually available for charter.

**Airline**
Greenland Air
(Grónlandsfly)
Nuuk
☎ 24488

**Ferries**
KNI Trafikkontoret
Aqqusinersuaq 4
PO Box 608
Nuuk
☎ 25211

**Tour operators in Greenland**
(for individual and group trips)
Grønlands Rejsebureau A/S
PO Box 330
G-100 Nuuk
☎ 24455

Grønlands Rejsebureau A/S
PO Box 1001
G-200 Ilulissat
☎ 43246

Polar Rejser
PO Box 329
G-110 Sisimiut
☎ 15747

Internal transport is almost exclusively by plane, helicopter, ship or on foot. If you want to climb mountains or glaciers, cross the inland icecap or visit the National Park, you must apply for permission well ahead of your proposed visit to Dansk Polarcenter, Hausergade 3, 1128 Copenhagen K. Denmark. If the authorities think the purpose of your visit is unjustified, it can ban it. You must also get permission from the centre if you want to carry out any scientific studies in Greenland, even if these do not constitute an expedition.

Detailed guidelines for expeditions have been published in English by the Kommissionen for Videnskabelige Undersogelser (Commission for Scientific Studies), and these are available from the Dansk Polarcenter.

For further information on Greenland:
The Greenland Home Rule Authority Information Service
Tusagassivik
PO Box 1015
G-100 Nuuk

Greenland Tourism
PO Box 1552
G-100 Nuuk

## Useful Words

Hello — *Kutaa*
Thankyou — *Qujanaq*
Yes — *Aap*
No — *Naaga*
Very good — *Nuuenn*
Where is? — *Qanoq?*
When? — *Qaqugu?*
Ticket — *Billettit*
Ship — *Umiarsuaq*
Plane — *Timmisaatit*
Helicopter — *Helikopterit*
Dog sled — *Qimussit*
Weather — *Silalu*
Rain — *Sialuk*
Sun — *Seqineq*
Snow — *Aput*
Ice — *Siko*
Wind — *Anoreq*
Today — *Ullumi*
Tomorrow — *Aqagu*
Water — *Imeq*
House — *Iglu*

Tent — *Tupersuaq*
Museum — *Katersugaasivik*
Post Office — *Allakkeriviat*

**Animals**
Bear — *Nanoq*
Caribou — *Tugtu*
Dog — *Qimmeq*
Mosquito — *Ippernaq*
Seal — *Puisi*
Sheep — *Sava*
Whale — *Arfeq*

**Geography**
Fjord — *Kangerdluq*
Hot spring — *Puilassoq*
Ice berg — *Ilulissat*
Island — *Qeqertaq*
Mountain — *Qaqaaq*
River — *Kuuk*
Sea — *Imiaq*
Valley — *Qooroq*

---

## A Note to the Reader

Thank you for buying this book. We hope it has helped you to enjoy your visit. We have worked hard to produce a guidebook which is as accurate as possible. With this in mind, any comments, suggestions or useful information you may have would be appreciated.

Please send your letters to:
The Editor
Moorland Publishing Co Ltd
Moor Farm Road West
Ashbourne
Derbyshire
DE6 1HD

*The Travel Specialists*

# Index

# Visitor's Guides
## *Tour & Explore with MPC Visitor's Guides*

Austria
Austria: Tyrol &
   Vorarlberg

*Britain:*
Cornwall & Isles of
   Scilly
Cotswolds
Devon
East Anglia
Guernsey, Alderney
   and Sark
Hampshire & Isle of
   Wight
Jersey
Kent
Lake District
Scotland: Lowlands
Somerset, Dorset &
   Wiltshire
North Wales and
   Snowdonia
North York Moors,
   York & Coast
Northumbria
Northern Ireland
Peak District
Sussex
Yorkshire Dales &
   North Pennines

Crete
Cyprus
Denmark
Egypt
Florida

*France:*
Alps & Jura
Corsica
Dordogne
Loire
Massif Central
Normandy Landing
   Beaches
Provence & Côte
   d'Azur

*Germany:*
Bavaria
Black Forest
Rhine & Mosel
Southern Germany
Northern Germany

Iceland

*Italy:*
Florence & Tuscany
Italian Lakes
Northern Italy

Mauritius, Rodrigues
   & Reunion
Peru

*Spain:*
Costa Brava to Costa
   Blanca
Mallorca, Menorca,
   Ibiza &
   Formentera
Northern & Central
   Spain
Southern Spain &
   Costa del Sol

Sweden
Switzerland
Tenerife
Turkey

**World Traveller**
*The new larger format*
*Visitor's Guides*

Czechoslovakia
France
Holland
Norway
Portugal
USA

# WE ARE THE BUS PEOPLE
## COME AND EXPLORE ICELAND WITH US

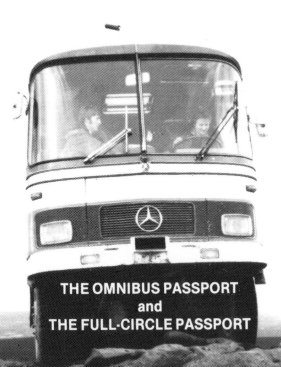

**THE OMNIBUS PASSPORT**
**and**
**THE FULL-CIRCLE PASSPORT**

is your key to a successful and inexpensive holiday in Iceland.

As an extra bonus your buspass entitles you to many favourable discounts on various travel services in Iceland.

Ask your travel agent for details or contact:

**BSI - TRAVEL,**
**BSI - BUS terminal, Umferðamiðstöðinni**
**Reykjavík, Iceland, Tel. 91-22300, Telex 3082**